THE LA

An Orphaned Child Fights to Survive the Killing Fields of Cambodia

Marin R. Yann

outskirtspress
DENVER, COLORADO

Outskirts Press, Inc.
http://www.outskirtspress.com

ISBN: 978-1-4787-1282-4

Library of Congress Control Number: 2013903307

Outskirts Press and the "OP" logo are trademarks belonging to Outskirts Press, Inc.

PRINTED IN THE UNITED STATES OF AMERICA

*This book is dedicated to my family, all of whom I lost:
Pa, Mak, my older sister Vanny, and my young brother Roth.*

*This book is also especially dedicated to the millions of
Cambodian people who were killed during the Khmer Rouge
regime from April 1975 to January 1979; in particular,
the over 200,000 children who were orphaned.*

Table of Contents

Part I

Our Evacuation

Part II

My Desperate Survival

Part III

Year Three of the Khmer Rouge Regime

Acknowledgements

I have immense gratitude to many people. First, I would like to thank Sophal, a young Khmer Rouge comrade who saved my life by picking me up beside a small water canal and took me to his home. Without Sophal and his mother, I would not have survived and been able to write this book.

Second, I would like to thank my adopted families for generously accepting me to be a part of their families: Chhon Um and her husband, and Sarin Chhim for adopting me and bringing me to the United States. I would also like to acknowledge Mr. Luke for sponsoring my adopted family and me to the United States. Without him, I would not have been able to come to America.

Third, I am indebted to Pu Ti and his wife Sross, and to Mrs. Phim and her family, for adopting me and providing me food and shelter. Without them, I would have been stealing and begging for food on the streets.

In addition, I especially wish to recognize and thank Mr. Long Sedtha, the founder and director of an organization called "Building Your Future Today Center" (BFT), which helps orphans and impoverished children in the province of Siem Reap, Cambodia. His inexhaustible energy in helping children who are living in hardship inspired me and many others to be a part of the BFT team.

I wish to express appreciation to Mr. Chhang Youk, Director of the Document Center of Cambodia, for his endless work of collecting and preserving documents as evidence in order to bring the Khmer Rouge leaders to trial. I thank him for the correct spellings of the phonetic Khmer language terms that the Khmer Rouge used.

I also gratefully thank all of the people who believed in me and encouraged me to complete my education and this memoir, especially Professor Susan Needham at California State University of Dominguez Hills, Karen Quintiliani at California State University of Long Beach, and Mr. Sombo Manara, Director of Pannasastra University of Cambodia.

I also extend gratitude to my friends and coworkers who have provided encouragement: Justin Sok and Sophay Nan, Charles and Teresa Maury-Darensbourg, Penh Keo, Mr. Junji Suzuki, Hayato Dobasha, Tatsuya Noda, Makoto Oikawa, Gentaro Matsubara, Sophorn Em, Samon Yann, Sopheak Tuon, John Weeks, Sompia Paigne, Sovann Tith, Matthew Chheng, Ted Shred, Chhem Sip, Ponlork Den, Mr. Long Sedtha and family, Mr. Po Walter, Mr. Thoeung Son and Tony Son, Mr. Jim Chhun, Mrs. Dena Thong, and Tom Chic.

Likewise, I thank The Long Beach Meetup members, a Long Beach writing group: Neil V. Young, Brennan Harvey, Dava White, Joe Marie Johnson, Tamara Ocean, George Snyder, Terry How, Patrice Hickey, Tom Riordan, and Petricia, for being patient and understanding the challenges of my writing. Their guidance and critiques of my writing style made it possible for me to finish this memoir.

Finally, I express my sincerest appreciation to Ms. Denise A. Scott for allowing me to use her art studio and materials to draw artwork for this book. She not only pushed me to complete this book, she also helped to critique and edit the manuscript.

I am also very grateful and indebted to many other people who spent time and energy helping me to edit this work: Brian Delas

Armas, Araceli Rios, Jeanne Shimatsu, and Kristine Delgado, who spent countless hours reading my drafts and gave me positive comments. Most especially, I thank my friend Mr. Tom Tor who allowed me to use his painting "Khmer 1975" and designed an exceptional book cover. I am also very grateful to my final copyeditor Charol Messenger for her amazing editing work in enhancing the clarity while keeping the original voice of the story. In addition, she helped to steer me in the right direction working with a publisher.

Lastly, I humbly acknowledge Timothy E. Smith for his stimulating questions, which helped me to dig deeper into my thoughts and feelings during my experiences under the Khmer Rouge regime, which are the true strength of this memory—for it is a very potent recollection that totally altered my life, both then and now.

Historical Context

According to history books and newspaper accounts, the Communist Khmer Rouge captured Phnom Penh, the capital city of Cambodia, in April 1975. They ruled the country until January 1979. I have no recollection of those dates and times. All I remember are the daily events that I survived as a child.

During the Khmer Rouge reign, nearly two million Cambodians died from disease, starvation, and execution. Tens of thousands were made widows and orphans. The Khmer Rouge attempted to transform the whole of Cambodia into a classless, rural society. They evacuated people from the cities to the countryside and forced them to work in the rice fields and at building water canals. They abolished money, markets, schools, private properties, religions, and the traditional Cambodian culture. They separated children from their families. Anyone who opposed or was suspected of opposing their ideologies or looked educated or Westernized would be killed, including teachers, doctors, singers, and engineers, even people simply wearing eyeglasses.

To learn more about the atrocities in Cambodia, go to the Document Center of Cambodia at https://www.dccam.org.

FAMILY CHART

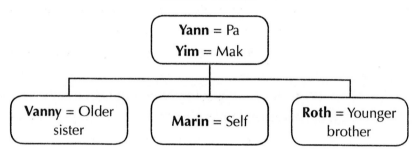

Preface

Personally, I don't want to write about my story. I just want to forget and hope that all the horrific memories will disappear. However, the more I try to forget, the more the memories haunt me.

Whenever I meet new people and we engage in conversation, usually these questions come up: "What country are you from? Are your parents living with you in the States or in Cambodia?"

My response is, "I live here by myself."

As we continue to chitchat, another question always pops up: "How often do you go to visit your relatives in your country?"

I answer, "I don't have any family members in Cambodia."

By now, the persons assumes, "Oh. All your family members must live in the States with you?"

I answer, "I don't have a family member over here. And I don't have a family member over there, either."

"What do you mean? You don't have family members?"

"No, I don't. I am the only person to survive in my entire family. I was orphaned when I was six years old."

The person raises his eyebrows, drops his face, and says, "Oh. I feel sorry for you. It must be hard for you."

Then he asks another set of questions. "How did you live? How did you survive?"

These are the two most challenging questions for me to answer. How I lived and how I survived are very complicated and cannot be explained in one sentence. It cannot be explained in five sentences or fifty sentences. Writing this book is a way to share with people how I lived and how I survived.

PART I
Our Evacuation

1
The Jungle

I was barely five years old. My parents hadn't enrolled me in school. I was home with my younger brother, Roth. Mak (mom) stayed home to watch the two of us. Every morning, Pa (daddy) dressed up and went to work. My older sister, Vanny, put on her school uniform, a white blouse, dark-blue skirt and shiny black slippers, and went to school.

One morning, my parents were acting a bit strange. Mak closed all the doors and windows of the house and told everybody to stay inside. Pa didn't go to work. Vanny didn't go to school. Mak and Pa appeared to be restless. They walked back and forth inside the house as if they were thinking and preparing for something. Pa opened the front door and stood on the patio. I followed him. His face looked grim and his eyes were fixated on the empty street. Pa had his mind set on something. I had my mind set on ice cream.

That midmorning, I noticed that the sky was clear blue. The hot summer heat suppressed the wind from blowing. The trees near my house didn't sway to send old leaves to the ground. I continued to stand by the front patio of my house and wait for the cart-pushing ice-cream vendor to sell his ice-cream sticks. But he never came.

Then I heard the sound of rockets flying over my head. They exploded near my house. The sound of explosions shook everything around me. I was frightened. My heart was beating faster than it ever had.

Mak and Pa shouted and screamed at each other to gather all the children to safety. They grabbed whatever they could and got away from the house. Mak carried my younger brother, Roth, in front of her and ran out of the house. Pa picked me up and held me to his chest, with one hand wrapped around my back to protect me from falling. With his other hand, he held onto Vanny's hand.

My parents rushed out of the house and approached the main road to escape the explosions. The bombing intensified. Some landed just a few hundred meters behind us and sent thick black smoke into the air. My parents ran faster, seeking safety in a bunker under a stilt house. We cramped together with a few other families. Pa and another man stood up, listening to the sound where the bomb should have landed. The explosions were intense in every direction, but we didn't get hit.

After the explosions stopped, my parents ran back home to grab whatever they could to take back to the bunker under the stilt house.

I never saw my home again. We evacuated our hometown, Ta Khmao, and walked along the main paved road with hundreds of other frightened evacuees. After we walked about one kilometer, we saw a small civilian pickup truck coming from behind us. Pa stood in the middle of the road and waved, signaling the truck to stop. He negotiated with the truck driver to take us to Phnom Penh, the capital city of Cambodia. Pa put Roth, Vanny, Mak, and me in the back of the pickup truck, which was already crammed with other people. My exhausted father stood at the back edge of the truck, his legs spread to guard us from falling. He held onto the top frame of the truck.

As we approached the capital city, I didn't see a single person walking on the sidewalks or on the road. The city was completely empty. It was like a ghost town. It appeared to me that were no people living in the houses or in the buildings. There were no cats or dogs running, only trash and debris flying around.

The driver drove toward the Independence Monument, a tower structure that looked like a giant closed-bud lotus flower. The monument stood in the center of the traffic circle, with its tip pointed straight up to the sky. The truck driver drove around the circle a few times, looking for a safe place to drop us off.

Finally, he exited the traffic circle and dropped us off by the mouth of the Mekong River. I stood at the river bank and noticed that the Independence Monument was less than one kilometer away. All the roads and parks that led to the Royal Palace were blocked by barbed-wire fences. Behind the fences were several small groups of soldiers in black uniforms. They were holding rifles and told us to stay within the area. We were warned not to touch the fences.

My parents had no other options of getting around. We decided to stay along the mouth of the river with the thousands of other evacuees. My parents set our belongings on the ground, and I stood and watched the murky Mekong River below.

Then I turned and looked toward the Independence Monument. All the roads on my left were closed. The park extending from the monument to the river behind me was filled with refugees. Several meters from me, a lady was carrying a crying baby on her hip, while balancing a large bag on her head. I was amazed that she could carry that bag without holding it. As I looked farther in the distance, I saw people walking around as if they were looking for a place to settle. No one was walking with any free hands.

We were confined between barbed wire on my left and right. Perhaps my family and the people who took refuge in the park were the last wave of refugees in Phnom Penh. I didn't see any newcomers.

Mak set a *kontael*, a Cambodian floor mat, on the ground for us to sit. Pa looked for sticks or posts to stand up *kontaels* as a shelter to protect us from the scorching sun. My parents complained about not having food or clean water. Mak and Pa cooked whatever they could find for our lunch and dinner.

The next morning, Pa went to the Buddhist temple three-hundred meters from our shelter to get a small amount of rice. Mak scooped three handfuls of rice from a piece of cloth sack and placed it into the cooking pot. Then she cooked the rice to feed us all.

After two nights of staying at the mouth of the river, I saw many big military trucks come into the city. They stopped along the road just a few hundred meters from where we were. Several soldiers with black uniforms jumped off the back of each truck, with their rifles drawn. At the time, I didn't know they were Khmer Rouge. They ordered all of us to get into the backs of the military trucks. The moment we did, we were driven out of Phnom Penh.

The truck was covered, so we couldn't see what was in front of the road or on the sides. We could only see out the back. Inside the truck, it was hot and crowded. Babies were crying and gasping for air. People deep in the truck had difficulty breathing. Some people got car sick and vomited.

My family sat all the way at the outside end of the truck where we could catch fresh air and see the views behind the vehicle. I saw many military trucks following one another. I saw brown rice fields and bushes along the side of the road and green forests in the distance. I saw dogs running along the street, cows eating grass in the rice fields, and birds flying in the sky. The animals roamed freely on the ground. The birds were flying freely as if they had no fear. Then I began to realize that these animals had more freedom than my family.

As the truck drove further out of the city, it swerved left to right and right to left to avoid potholes. When the truck hit potholes, it shook violently and threw people side to side, causing them to bump onto each other's heads. Pa stood with his legs slightly spread, with one hand holding a string attached to a metal bar over his head to prevent him from falling. Mak sat and leaned back against Pa's legs. She held Roth in her skirt pouch, like a kangaroo carrying its baby.

Vanny and I sat next to her and held tightly onto Pa's feet.

After long hours in the truck, the soldiers dropped us off for a lunch break. Quickly, women rushed straight into the rice fields with their *kromas,* a typical Cambodian scarf. They wrapped their *kromas* around their waists, pulled down their pants, squatted, and urinated near some bushes. They had been holding their pee. Pa and I stood on the shoulder of the road and urinated in the bushes.

There were hardly any trees around. I looked in all directions. All I saw were rice fields with dead and brown rice straw. Pa set up a small makeshift shelter in the rice field to protect us from the scorching sun. Then he went with a few other people into the fields to search for water.

Pa fetched just enough water, from a distance, for cooking and cleaning ourselves. To conserve water, Mak bathed Roth and me at the same time. She poured a small amount of water on our heads, and washed our faces and bodies to remove the sticky sweat. After a short afternoon rest, we got back onto the truck and continued on to our unknown destination.

The road got much better, the truck didn't shake as much, and Vanny and I played a knowledge game. She asked me general questions and I answered them.

"What part of this body called?" she asked and pointed.

"Knee," I responded.

"What part of this body called?"

"Chin."

"How many fingers in my hand?" She raised her hand and showed me fingers.

"Five."

"How many fingers do I have now?" She raised both hands and folded one thumb.

I counted and thought for a moment. "Nine."

"You are a very smart boy," said Pa.

"What do you call those animals eating in the field?" Vanny asked.

"They are cows."

"What are those black animals?" she asked and pointed.

"They are baby elephants."

Mak and Vanny laughed at my answer. "No, they are not baby elephants," Mak said with a big smile on her face. "They are water buffalos. Son, buffalos have horns. They have no long nose hanging to the ground like elephants do."

At home in Ta Khmao, I had seen a huge black elephant walking in front my house with a man riding on its neck. The man had commanded it to use its long trunk to suck water from a bucket and to spray it into the air. It was fascinating and I had enjoyed watching it. I had never seen a water buffalo before. That was why I said, "baby elephant."

The long afternoon ride made me exhausted and I fell into a deep sleep. When I woke up, I saw my parents situated in the middle of the jungle among several other families. My parents made a temporary shelter the size of an office cubicle; using leaves, small tree branches, and wild bamboo. The shelter was supported by four small wooden posts, and thin blue plastic wrapped around the posts to serve as walls. Then Pa bounded big leaves together to make a roof.

There was no food or water. There were no farms or rice fields. Pa had to collect water from far away. Days later, he was sick and tired of his daily long walk just to collect water. He decided to borrow people's tools to dig a water well near our shelter. He and Mak worked hard digging the well, removing dirt from the ground until they reached water. Vanny, Roth, and I couldn't help. All we could do was play with the freshly piled dirt and watch sweat pour out of their bodies.

While my parents temporarily solved our water-shortage problem, they had not yet solved our food-shortage problem. We especially missed rice, our main source of sustenance. The soldiers were distributing a small amount of rice to feed families for several days. However, each time Pa went to get rice from the communal center, they gave him less and less.

The amount of rice the soldiers gave us was impossible to live on, so Mak and Pa fetched whatever was available in the jungle to feed us: wild leaves, wild cabbage, mushrooms, toads, frogs, and rats. Mak cooked conservatively. Sometimes, she cooked a small amount of rice mixed with wild vegetables and roots or wild yams.

After many days of starving in the jungle, Roth became ill. He was always hungry and demanded food. But when Mak tried to feed him, he couldn't eat. Pa crushed a half pill of medicine in a spoon and mixed it with water to feed Roth almost daily, but he didn't seem to get any better.

One evening, Roth cried very loudly. Mak cooked rice porridge to feed him, but he couldn't eat. She sat Roth on her thigh and soothed him until he fell asleep.

One morning, while Mak prepared food outside the shelter and Pa chopped firewood under a big shade tree, Mak told Vanny and I to watch over Roth while he was asleep. Vanny and I sat next to each other and took turns cooling Roth by fanning him with a piece of cloth. After the food was cooked, Mak brought a plate into the tent, set it in the corner, and prepared to feed him. In her sitting position, she bent over and spoke softly into Roth's ear.

"Roth, my son, wake up. Wake up, son. I have delicious food for you. Wake up, my son!" Then she spoke louder and louder, calling his name, and shook his body gently. But he didn't wake up.

Mak rushed outside to call Pa, and they hurried into the shelter. Pa used his fingers to feel Roth's arms, chest, and forehead. With his other hand, he shook Roth slightly to wake him up. "Roth, my son, wake up. Wake up, son! Wake up, my son!"

Pa lowered his head and rested his ear on Roth's chest. He tried to listen for a heartbeat or feel a pulse. Minutes later, Pa raised his head slowly, with tears falling.

Mak began to cry out loud. She picked up Roth and held him to her chest. "Don't die, my son. I have food for you! I love you, my son. Wake up, son! Wake up! Wake up!" she cried, holding Roth tightly to her chest.

When I saw Mak cry, I felt my chest tighten and a sudden emptiness in my heart. I felt sad. I felt shocked. I cried and touched Roth's motionless fingers, hands, legs, and face. Vanny also cried, hugging Roth in Mak's arm. Pa leaned against the thin blue plastic wall, hopeless with grief.

In the afternoon, Mak dressed Roth's body up with all of his clothes. Pa cut some portions of *kontael* to wrap him from head to toe until his head, arms, and legs were no longer exposed. Then he crafted many small sticks to wrap him tightly, like a woven cocoon. Pa carried the body on his shoulders and walked deeper into the jungle to bury Roth. Mak, Vanny, and I walked behind Pa, crying. My parents chose a burial site under a sizeable tree with lots of shade, and Pa began to dig a grave.

After hours of digging and pulling dirt out of the grave, Pa tossed the shovel to the side. In the grave, he leaned back against the dirt wall, took deep breaths, wiped sweat off his grim face a few times, and talked to Mak with a broken voice.

Then he stood up straight, tilted his head up, and looked at Mak with both hands raised, signaling her to pass Roth's body to him. She began to cry again, holding and kissing Roth, and refused to give Roth's body over to Pa.

Pa took Roth out of Mak's hands, and gently lowered him down to his place of rest. Pa moved out of the grave, with sweat and dirt clumped on his body. He stood before Roth's grave, holding Mak. Vanny and I stood, watching with silent tears.

Pa let Mak go from his hands and began to bury Roth. He scooped the dirt and poured it slowly into the grave. Mak continued to scream for Roth until the body was no longer visible. At that moment, I felt a weightlessness and emptiness in my heart, and realized I didn't have a brother to talk to or play with.

After Roth's body was completely buried, my parents picked several tiny sticks from the forest to use as incense sticks. They burned the tips of the sticks so they would slowly burn down. While the sticks were burning and producing strands of smoke, Mak and Pa prayed to Buddha and Tevada, an angel who dwells in Heaven, to take care of Roth's soul. They stood the burning sticks on the grave. A strand of smoke ascended slowly and dissolved into the air as if it carried Roth's soul to Heaven.

That night, my family couldn't sleep. I couldn't sleep either. We missed Roth. I missed his smile, his laugh, and the sound of his crying. I wished he could wake up from the grave and walk home to play with me.

Mak heard the sound of wild dogs and wolves howling in the distance and got nervous. "Is our son okay?" she asked Pa. "Is the burial deep enough to protect my son from the wild creatures?"

"Just calm down. It should be okay," he said softly.

Mak began to pray to Tevada. "Tevada, please help chase all the wild dogs and wolves away from my son's grave."

In the morning, we walked to Roth's burial site to see if it was safe from the wild creatures. The burial site was untouched. Pa used a machete to cut tree branches and lay them over the grave to prevent creatures from digging. Then he and Mak burned a few more small sticks and prayed again to Buddha and Tevada to protect my brother.

Several days after Roth's death, I began to play outside our tent. One late morning, I saw two soldiers forcing a man who lived less than fifty meters away to get out of his freshly built tent. They pointed their rifles at the man's chest and escorted him into the jungle.

"I didn't do anything wrong. I was a cock-fighter," he said to the soldiers.

His wife ran after him. "Please don't take my husband away. He is a nice guy. He was not a soldier. He was a cock-fighter."

"Go back to your tent or I will kill you in front of your children!" the soldiers shouted at her.

Her husband shouted to her, "Just go back to the hut! Don't run after me! Go back to take care of the children!"

The panicked conversation between the wife and husband tested the soldiers' patience. "Go back to your hut!" shouted a soldier to her. "Or I will shoot your husband right now!"

The other soldier aimed his rifle at her. "If you don't go back to your hut right now, I will kill your whole family."

She walked backward to the hut, crying. I heard her entire family crying inside their hut, shouting for their dad. The soldiers pushed the man in the back with their rifles and forced him to walk into the jungle.

Pa pulled my hand and drew me closer to him. He held my head against his thigh as if to prevent me from seeing the situation. With a pale face, he took me into our tent. Mak and Vanny peeked from inside and whispered to each other in fear. I couldn't hear their whispering, but I could sense they were whispering about the man being taken by the Khmer Rouge.

Not too long after the soldiers forced the man into the forest, I heard two gunshots. The sound of the gunshots echoed throughout the forest. My parents' faces looked pale. Hundreds of panicked birds flew out of the jungle and into sky, shouting and calling in the air. The sound of the gunshots, the sound of the panicking birds, and the fainted faces of my parents sent fear into my heart. My heart pounded loud and fast, and I rushed to hug Pa for comfort.

2
The Village

Many days after Roth's death, the Khmer Rouge moved people from the jungle to the village. They assigned my family to live in an old thatched house that faced the sunrise. The house sat on nine rounds of crooked wooden posts just a bit taller than my dad. The roof and walls of the house were made of combed palm leaves.

While my parents were talking with soldiers under the house, Vanny and I climbed up the stairs to explore what was inside. When we got inside the house, there was nothing in it. The house didn't have a bedroom, bathroom, or kitchen. The floor was made of small shredded bamboos nailed together to wooden frame studs and, when I walked, I heard a squelching noise under my feet.

"This house is too small," I said. "It is smaller than our house in Ta Khmao."

Vanny put a hand on my shoulder. "Yes. It is small. But it is bigger than the shelter we stayed at in the jungle."

My parents walked up the stairs and placed our belongings inside the house. Pa opened the shutter to let the light and air in.

Vanny stood by the stairs. "Pa, the door of this house is missing."

We all turned and realized there was no external door.

Mak got herself situated. She unrolled the *kontael* and set our belongings by the wall. Then she lay down and rested.

While Mak was resting, Pa was looking for materials to make a door. He gathered bamboo and wood, and put them under the stilt house. Then he took off his shirt, dusted off his short wavy hair, and got to work. I wanted to help him, but I couldn't because it looked complicated and dangerous. All I could do was watch. He cut, shredded, trimmed, and bound the bamboo. While he was working, I watched sweat drip down on his body. He finished the door installation right after sunset. Now, the house seemed to be complete. It kept us warm and secure.

A few days after my family settled in the house, I saw Pa cutting wood and shredding bamboo under the house. I approached him. "What are you making, Pa?"

He paused and looked at me. "I'm making a kitchen. When the kitchen is finished, your mother can cook food in it."

While he was working, I saw several soldiers walking with ten unarmed female soldiers. They were confiscating people's belongings. Both the soldiers and the females had *kromas* tied to their necks, which were hanging down in front of their bellies like giant neckties.

About fifty meters before they approached our house, the soldiers distanced themselves with watchful eyes over my dad and me. The female soldiers continued walking toward our house. Pa stopped what he was doing and called Mak to come down. Pa took a few steps toward me and pulled me against his thigh. I lifted my chin to look up at his face and saw that his eyes were fixated on the female soldiers. Then he pushed my head slightly and said, "Go inside the house, son." I ignored what he told me, because I wanted to know what these soldiers were going to do.

By the time my mother and sister got halfway down the stairs, the female soldiers had arrived. They ordered Mak to bring all the cooking utensils from inside the house and put them on the ground. "We were ordered by Angkar Luer to confiscate cooking utensils, rice scoopers, wok, kettle pot, thermo pot, and cooking pots," said one of the females.

At first, Mak refused. "Who is Angkar Luer? If Angkar Luer takes my pots and pans, how am I going to cook for my family?"

I could sense that Mak was mad, but she controlled herself and talked to them calmly.

I thought the same thing, *Who or what is Angkar Luer? What does it look like?*

(Months after, I learned that the word *Angkar* means organization or institution. *Luer* means over the top or above. Soldiers and leaders of the Khmer Rouge referred to *Angkar Luer* as the highest communist organization, or the governing body of the Khmer Rouge regime. Angkar Luer was also used interchangeably with the more commonly known phrase Khmer Rouge.)

The soldiers looked at Mak and said, "Nobody can disobey Angkar Luer. Whatever Angkar Luer tells you to do, just do it. Stop asking questions. Bring everything out."

Mak turned around and walked into the house to grab a cooking pot. She set it on the ground in front of them. "That's all I have," she said.

Then two of the Khmer Rouge soldiers went inside the house and took our kettle pot, thermo pot, spatula, spoons, rice scoopers, dishes, and bowls. Mak grabbed the kettle pot and the thermo pot back from their hands and got into a brief argument with them. Pa was stunned and speechless. I was nervous and ran to Mak. I looked at the soldiers with hatred.

"You don't need these pots and pans, because Angkar will provide you food at the communal cafeteria," said one of the female Khmer Rouge. "You don't need to cook anything. Angkar will make life easier for everyone. Angkar will cook for you at the communal cafeteria."

"I want the kettle and thermo pot back," Mak said firmly. "I need a kettle to boil water. And the boiled water is to be put into the thermo pot. We need to drink boiled water in case our families get sick. How could we possibly cook food in a kettle?"

She talked to them until they gave up and left. They took our cooking pot, spatula, rice scoop, plates, and spoons. Since we had four people in our family, the Khmer Rouge left us four plates, four spoons, one bowl, the kettle and the thermo pot. They took the rest.

That evening the Khmer Rouge ordered people to a meeting in the field in front our house. I was feeling lazy and tired. I sat on the stairs and watched my parents and sister crossing the oxcart road to the meeting. I was about fifty meters away. I could see and hear the Khmer Rouge preaching to the people. There were several female Khmer Rouge standing near two soldiers. A female Khmer Rouge, in her late twenties, ordered the people to sit in front of her. She took a few steps forward and began to speak. She said many things, but I could only understand and remember a few phrases.

"Anyone who picks watermelon leaves for food or steals watermelon will be punished. Fruits and vegetables in the garden around your house belong to Angkar. All domestic animals such as chicken, pigs, cows, and buffalos also belong to Angkar Luer. Angkar will cook for you and distribute food equally to everyone."

A few days after our pots and pans were confiscated, Mak, Vanny, and I were sitting inside the house. We had the door and shutters open to let the light and fresh air in. Pa wasn't home; the Khmer Rouge had assigned him a job: clearing bushes in the field.

Mak was leaning her back against the door frame. Mak had similar features to Vanny: a light-yellow complexion, round face, and full cheeks.

"Vanny, come sit over here," said Mak. "Let me groom your hair." Vanny sat down and positioned her back to Mak. I lay down next to them.

Then two female Khmer Rouge stopped in front of our house, I looked at their round faces. I wanted to punch them in the mouth. Before they even started talking, I thought, *They must be coming to confiscate the last of our possessions: spoons, plates, kettle, and thermo pot.*

But my thinking was wrong. The Khmer Rouge ladies wanted to separate Vanny from us. They talked to Mak about sending Vanny to the *Kang-Komarey*, a female children's group. According to the Khmer Rouge, Vanny was old enough to be separated from her parents and live with the girl group ages eight to twelve.

They said, "Angkar Luer already talked to you in the meeting. You must send your daughter to the *Kang-Komarey* center. This is the order from Angkar Luer."

"Yes, I want to send my daughter to live with the *Kang-Komarey* group, but I want to learn more about the center," Mak said. "Will Angkar allow my daughter come home to visit me?"

I knew Mak was lying to them. She never wanted Vanny to live in the center.

"There is nothing you should worry about. Angkar will give your daughter a place to stay and food to eat. Angkar is not stupid. Angkar will schedule study time, work time, and play time for your child. We even have time for your daughter to visit you at home. If we don't see your daughter in the next three days, we will come to drag your daughter out of the house."

After the Khmer Rouge left, Mak continued to groom Vanny's hair. Mak looked sad. Her mind appeared to be somewhere else. But her hand continued to run the comb slowly through Vanny's straight hair.

"Mak, are you going to send me to the *Kang-Komarey* center?" asked Vanny.

Mak had her eyes fixed on the wall and didn't answer. She moved her head slowly and kissed Vanny on the head.

Two days later, Mak sent Vanny to the *Kang-Komarey* center. Mak prepared several pair of clothes and wrapped them in a *kroma*. She cut Vanny's hair to shoulder length and bathed her. She dressed Vanny and walked her out of the house. Vanny came to hug me, and advised me to stay home and obey Mak.

Mak pushed Vanny's back slightly and encouraged her to walk along the oxcart road to the center. Vanny looked down, holding her tears, and walked north to the girl group. Mak and I stood silently and watched Vanny walking past the field and bushes along the way. We stood and watched her until she was out of sight.

The next day, Mak went to work. I had no idea what kind of work she did. She left me home alone inside the house.

Now, I was lonely and bored. My interaction with Pa and Mak was limited. Most of the time, they came home from work late in the evening. I would meet them only at lunch and dinnertime at the communal cafeteria.

Every day, when the bell rang for lunch or dinner, I rushed to get bowls and spoons. I ran toward the communal cafeteria to get food. Once I got there, I stood in line with the rest of the children my age. My parents stood in another line with the adult group less than ten meters away. They looked at me as if they wanted to hug me with affection. While I was moving in line, I looked at my parents and wanted to hug them, but I was too hungry and not willing to lose my spot in line. The line continued to move forward. I could smell food from the communal kitchen. Its scents made me even hungrier. I felt like I wanted to eat everything in the cooking pots.

When it was my turn, the communal chefs dipped the scoop into a big cooking pan, scooped plain rice porridge, and poured it into my bowl. A few steps further, another female chef dipped a spatula in a huge wok and gave me a little bit of stirred fried vegetables, putting it over the rice porridge. The rice porridge turned from a milky to a brownish color. Without any delay, I raised up the bowl and drank the porridge juice.

The plain rice porridge contained only two spoonfuls of rice. The rest was liquid. After a quick drink, I scooped solid rice from the bottom of the bowl and shoveled it into my mouth. My stomach was now full with porridge. When I walked, I heard and felt the liquid in my stomach bouncing as if it created its own tidal waves.

When people finished eating, they went home and rested. But I didn't go home. I hung around the communal cafeteria to watch the communal chefs and their families eating. I hoped they would give me the leftovers, but they never did. They had full meals to serve themselves. They had the best food, including steamed rice, meats, pork, and fish. The chefs ate the meat attached to the bones and sucked the juice out. They threw the bones to the ground.

I was like a starving puppy. I ran to pick up the bones to suck the leftover flavor. I didn't have strong jaws like a dog to crush the bones, but I used stones and bricks to crush the bones open to suck and to lick the bone marrow. Sometimes I removed the dirt before I shoveled the bones into my mouth, but sometimes I didn't.

I was the first person to pick the leftover bones, but I soon had a competitor whose belly was as hungry as mine. His name was Visoth. During the time that we lived in the jungle, Visoth was my neighbor. His father was the one I had witnessed being taken out of the tent away from his wife by the two Khmer Rouge soldiers. The memories of hearing the two gunshots in the distance echoing through the forest reminded me of the death of my younger brother, Roth.

Visoth and I had the same height and appeared to be the same age, about five years old. He had a light-yellow complexion like my younger brother. He and I became competitors. Both of us were skinny and always starving. We were like starving baby dogs watching the communal chefs chewing, slurping, and licking all the juicy bones. We drooled and swallowed our own saliva while watching them eat. We watched them scoop food into their mouths. We stared at the muscles in their jaws moving while they chewed food. We watched their hands moving the bones against their lips. And we watched which direction they would throw the bones. Visoth and I fought each other to claim the bones before they even dropped to the ground.

The Uselessness of Money

One night, I saw my parents boiling water in a kettle. Instead of using firewood for fuel, they were using money. I was confused and surprised. I thought they were stupid. There was plenty of firewood around here, why would they use money for fuel? It didn't make sense.

They took out all the money stored in our pillow cases and burned it like useless paper. I was surprised that I hadn't known the money was hidden in the pillow cases. I had rested my head on those pillows every night and had never noticed there was money in them.

Before the invasion of the Khmer Rouge, I had seen Mak and Vanny using money to buy ice-cream sticks and snacks for me. I used to see Mak pay the restaurant cashier when we finished eating. However, in this new life, I began to realize there were no markets. There was no trade. There were no ice-cream men pushing ice-cream carts along the oxcart road in front of our new house. All money ended up in the fire pit.

The Khmer Rouge Escorted Men Away

Every morning when I woke up, I didn't see my parents. I only saw a bowl of water they left for me to drink and to wash my face. After I washed my face to refresh myself in the morning, I sat on the stairs by the door, wondering what I was going to do or what I was going to eat.

Many times I stared at the bright morning sun and told it to rise faster over my head so the Khmer Rouge would ring the bell for lunch. But the sun didn't listen to me. It moved at the same pace and left me hungry most of the time.

Every few days, when the sun rose over the treetops in the

distance, I saw Khmer Rouge soldiers escorting between five to twelve men along the oxcart road in front of our house. Sometimes, I saw men with their hands tied behind their backs. One morning, I saw more than ten men with their wrists tied behind their backs. They had long bamboo sticks binding them by their elbows. They walked in a line, single file. The majority of the tied men had no shirt on; they wore only long pants or shorts. Some men wore a *kroma* around their waists. Their faces looked sad and as hard as rocks. They didn't cry or try to escape.

I had no idea what the Khmer Rouge would do to these men. I sat on the stairs and was amused by it. I was not nervous or scared, but in my head I had many questions. *Why did the Khmer Rouge soldiers tie up these men? What did these men do to the Khmer Rouge? Where did the Khmer Rouge take them?*

Vanny's First Visit

One evening when I went to the communal cafeteria for dinner, I noticed something unusual. I didn't see any adults coming from work to stand in line for dinner. While I stood in line with a group of children for food, I looked in every direction for my parents or any sign of an adult walking toward the communal cafeteria. But I didn't see anybody. I began to feel a hollowness in my chest, as if my heart was missing.

I was hungry, but my stomach stopped craving food. The Khmer Rouge scooped the porridge and placed it in a bowl, but I didn't eat it right away. I took the food out of the cafeteria and ate it while walking home. When I got home, I didn't see my parents there, either.

Horrific images began to get into my thoughts. *Maybe the Khmer Rouge tied my parents' hands to their backs and took them somewhere?*

That thought depressed me. The Khmer Rouge had separated my parents from me.

Khmer Rouge escorted men

Depression began to build up. I sat on the lower step of the staircase and waited for my parents to come home from work. I turned my head and looked down both sides of the oxcart road. But I didn't see them.

The sun was already set, but it left the light bright enough for me to see the blue sky and field in front of my house. While I was waiting, I saw Vanny walking along the oxcart road. When I first saw her, I felt my face glowing. I had a big smile on my face. All the stress and depression was replaced with excitement. I got up and jumped off the step and ran to her. I ran so fast that my feet tangled and I fell to the ground. My excitement rejected the pain. I got up and ran to hug Vanny. After I released her from my hug, I jumped up and down in front of her like a puppy teasing its friend.

Vanny's face was glowing. She smiled and laughed with me. "I missed you, Marin." She hooked a hand around my shoulder and pulled me tightly to her. With her other hand, she brushed off the dirt from my face and belly.

"I missed you, Vanny. Every day I stay home all day. I don't have anybody to talk to. I don't have anybody to play with. Sometimes, I talk to the small sticks that I play with." I talked to Vanny as if I never ran out of breath. I talked to her until we got home.

When Vanny got into the house, she asked, "Have Mak and Pa come from work yet?"

"No. I have been waiting for them for a long time, but I didn't see them. I see you, instead."

Vanny removed a *kroma* from her neck and put it near the shutter where we placed bowls, plates, and the kettle. She untied one end of her *kroma* and said, "Look what I got for Mak and Pa. This is *domloung-tian*."

I had no idea what it was. It was roots that looked like candles. They were twice the size of my big toe and the length of a pencil. They were wild yams and white from the inside out.

While Vanny was removing the yams from her *kroma* to put on a plate, Mak and Pa arrived. They were surprised. They rushed up the stairs and closed the door. Vanny got up, hugged them, and said, "I missed you, Mak. I missed you, Pa."

"I missed you too, my child," said Mak.

Pa was stunned. He stood still like a dead tree.

Mak pulled Vanny's hand from Pa's waist and told her to sit down. Mak sat facing Vanny and said in a whisper, "Don't talk too loud, my child. How did you get here? Did you ask the permission from your group leader?"

"Yes, I got permission from my group leader. Otherwise, I wouldn't be able to leave the center," said Vanny.

"My child, did they give you enough food to eat?" asked Mak.

"Yes. No. I get two small scoops of cooked rice. Sometimes the communal chefs serve rice with soup. Other times, they serve vegetable stir fry," Vanny responded to Mak in a whisper. She added, "Mak, here are candlestick yams, wild roots that I got from the forest. On my way home along the path, I saw the vine plants and dug them up. These are edible roots."

Mak picked up one root from the plate for inspection. "My child, are you sure they are safe to eat?" She looked at Vanny, then turned her head and looked at the root in her hand.

"Mak, these roots are not poison," Vanny said with confidence. "Children in my group eat them all the time. I ate the root with them, too, and I had no problem."

Mak cleaned them up, cut them into small pieces, and set them in the kettle. Pa took the kettle from Mak, filled it with water, and boiled it. When the roots were cooked, Pa took the kettle upstairs, removed the cooked roots from the kettle, and put them on a plate to cool off. Mak shut the door to prevent the Khmer Rouge from seeing us eating. She took a bite of the roots first to make sure they were safe to eat.

"Hmm, the roots taste good," Mak said. "Maybe they are edible.

It tastes like taro, but not as sweet."

Then she distributed the roots to everybody. I didn't really care. Whatever they ate, I ate too. The root filled my stomach and I went to sleep. After I finished eating, Mak was still concerned about poisonous side effects.

Vanny didn't want to go back to the *Kang-Komarey* center. I didn't want her to go back, either. I wanted her to stay home and keep me company. But Mak insisted that she must go back. "My child, you have to go back, I don't want to see Angkar or the Khmer Rouge drag you out of the house and punish you. I love you, but you have to return to your group," Mak said with tears rolling from her eyes.

Vanny grabbed her *kroma*, hung it on her neck, and walked slowly from the house.

Mak shouted to her, "Vanny, make sure you ask for permission from Angkar Luer when you plan to come home."

I stood with my back against the guardrail of the stairs and watched Vanny walking until she was out of my sight. Then I started to cry, missing her. I had no idea where she lived or how she lived with her group.

Vanny had permission from her leader to come home once in a while. Whenever she came home, she brought wild vegetables, wild mushrooms, or wild leaves. She picked them along the road on the way home. At night, Mak and Pa carefully inspected them before cooking.

Vanny always had terrifying stories to tell us. One of the stories that I remembered most was about a girl caught stealing.

"I saw the Khmer Rouge catch a girl in her group stealing something from Angkar. The Khmer Rouge punished her by tying her to a tree, leaving her there for fire ants to kill her."

My New Treasure

Starvation forced me to venture farther away from our new home. As I wandered around, I saw several Khmer Rouge leaders unloading sacks of rice from oxcarts into a warehouse. I pretended I didn't see them. After they drove their oxcarts away from the warehouse, I walked closer to investigate, looking for an opportunity to steal the rice. The rice warehouse was big, four times the size of our new thatch house. The warehouse had a wooden wall and wooden floor. It sat on wooden posts slightly taller than me.

After several days of investigating the warehouse, I had the courage to sneak under it to look for a crack or a hole or any opening. Finally, I found one small opening in the wooden floor. I looked around for a sharp object to poke the hole and make it bigger.

I found a rusted nail under the stairs of the warehouse and used it to cut out a hole. Bit by bit, with patience and determination, I made a hole in the wooden floor about the size of my index finger. I poked a sack open to make the grains of rice drop, tilted my head up, and opened my mouth wide to catch the grains. I used a tiny twig to push and to pull, to control the amount of rice, and let it flow down freely into my mouth. Once I had a mouthful, I chewed everything, including the rice husk. I sucked the rice juice and spat out the tasteless skin. Sometimes I ate everything without spitting the skin out. Sometimes, the rice husk cut my mouth and my tongue, but I continued to eat anyway.

Once I finished eating, I sealed the hole with mud or leaves. The rice warehouse was my treasure. I kept the place a secret. I didn't even tell my parents because I was afraid they might stop me from stealing from Angkar. Whenever I felt hungry, I approached the rice warehouse to feed myself.

An Unlucky Day

It was morning. The sky was partially cloudy. The village was quiet as usual. My stomach was groaning and demanding food. I walked into the field in front of my house, and scanned around the area to see if the Khmer Rouge soldiers were watching me.

Got caught stealing rice

I didn't see anyone. So, I went under the warehouse and removed the leaves from the hole. I tilted my head up and opened my mouth wide to catch the flow of rice.

I felt someone grab me by the throat, choking me. I was horrified! It was a Khmer Rouge soldier!

He lowered himself down to prevent his head from hitting the beam overhead and dragged me out to the field. He removed his hand from my neck and grabbed me by the hair. He pushed my head down and forced me to spit the rice out of my mouth.

I gasped for air and coughed with sharp pain to spit out the rice.

He pulled my head up to look at his brown wrinkled face. His eyes were wide open. His eyebrows were raised to his forehead.

I was so scared that I couldn't see the black pupils in his eyes. All I could see was the white in his eyeballs.

He clenched his teeth and shouted at me as if he wanted to eat me alive. He grabbed the back of my neck, dragged me to the small canal and pushed my head toward the water. He held my head inches above the water and ordered me to look at my own horrified reflection.

"Look at your reflection! Do you want to die like this?" he shouted.

I struggled to push my head away from the water. Tears and mucus rolled down to my chin and dropped in the water, creating small ripples that changed my clear reflection to fuzzy and wavy. I pleaded for my life, while struggling to release his hands from my neck.

"No! No! Please don't kill me. I will not do it again. Please! I don't want to die. I will stop stealing forever."

He switched his hand and choked me by the throat again. I could barely breathe. I raised my tiny hands to grab his fingers to release his grip from my throat, but I couldn't. I didn't have enough strength. All I could do was struggle to gasp for air and scream. I cried so hard, but no one could hear me.

"No! No! No! Don't hurt me. Please stop hurting me. No, I don't want to die." In pain, I pleaded with tears.

The man lowered himself to my level and stared at me in the eyes. His age and short body frame didn't seem to match his cruelness. He was in his forties, but his cruelness made him look old and ugly.

"Stop crying if you want to live!" he shouted.

I clenched my eyes and bit my teeth to stop myself from crying.

He released his hand from my throat. "If I catch you stealing again, I will kill you and your family," he said.

"I promise. I will never steal again," I said, holding my tears.

He kicked my buttocks and shouted, "Go home now!"

I ran straight home, crawled up the stairs, and sat in the corner of the house in pain and in terror. I was also furious. My head was numb and full of thoughts of taking revenge. I folded my fists and clenched my face. I wanted to fight the man. I wished angels would come from Heaven to make me as big as the man who hurt me. *Tevada, please inflate me like a balloon and give me strength. I want to fight him for what he did to me. I want to punch him in the face, kick him in the head, and break his neck.*

Sadly, all my wishes and fantasies of revenge against him would not be fulfilled. Instead, I fell asleep and got sick.

When my parents came home from work, they were concerned about my illness. Pa thought I had a throat infection. I had difficulty eating and swallowing food. I didn't tell them about the incident, because I didn't want them to know that their son was a thief, stealing things from Angkar.

Pa got a tablet of medicine that he hid in the house and crushed it with a spoon. He mixed it in water to feed it to me. I was so sick that I couldn't walk to the communal kitchen for lunch or dinner. Pa had to bring my ration of food home to feed me.

Although I got sick, my parents couldn't take a day off from work to take care of me. They left me at home alone. During my illness, I couldn't sleep much. Most of the time, I sat on the stairs by the door, facing the morning sunrise. I fantasized about how to take revenge by killing the man who had hurt me.

Many days later, I recouped from the illness, but I was still traumatized. I was afraid to get out of the house to explore the area.

New Food Sources

After I recouped from the illness, I never went back to the rice warehouse. I began to explore alternative food sources. I chased after grasshoppers in the field in front of our house.

When I first saw grasshoppers land, I snuck up from behind to try and catch them, but I couldn't. Every time I approached closer to them, they flew off and landed somewhere else. No matter how softly I walked or how slowly I crept, they flew off and escaped. I was exhausted and mad.

I ran home to pick a stick the size of my finger, less than two ·meters in lengths. I ran back to the field to find grasshoppers. Not long after, I saw a grasshopper the size of my thumb, camouflaged in a surrounding weed. I snuck up slowly behind it with a stick raised over my head. I whipped it with all my might. My stick landed on the grasshopper and its body almost broke apart. The grasshopper died instantly.

It was my first snack. I couldn't believe how accurate I was. I was excited and proud of myself. I was proud of my right hand and my stick for being accurate. I tossed the dead grasshopper into the fire pit near the communal cafeteria. When the grasshopper was on fire, its whole body turned from green to red, like cooked shrimp. Once it cooked, I took it out of the fire and ate it. It tasted like overcooked crab meat.

After my first kill, my ego was high. With the stick in my hand, I envisioned killing lizards, frogs, and toads. Any creature that moved slower than me would become my food. I even envisioned killing birds that flew within reach.

I ran back into the field to kill more grasshoppers, but I wasn't as lucky as with the first kill. It took me a while to kill a few more for snacks. While I ate grasshoppers at the fire pit, I saw grains of rice mixed with rice husk. I collected them one grain at a time to eat. I was always hungry, but not as much as before. Every day, I would have a handful of grasshoppers and a small amount of rice grains.

The Emergence of New Life

The rainy season began to move in. I sat on the upper step and watched thick, grave clouds move fast over my head, blocking the sunlight from shining into the village. Violent wind began to blow dead leaves and small tree branches onto the field. Clouds roared violently and shot streaks of light out of the sky, followed by thunder.

When the lightning and thunder intensified, I was scared. I moved from the stairs, got inside the house, and closed the door to shield myself from the violence of the rain. I sat inside the center of the house and wrapped myself with a blanket to keep my body warm and to hold myself from being too scared.

Not long after, the rain poured down with madness from the sky onto the roof. The old roof couldn't hold the force of the heavy rain and it began to leak in several places. All I could do was sit and watch water soaking the floor.

That evening, I was hungry and afraid to walk to the communal cafeteria for dinner. I began to pray. *Tevada, I'm scared and hungry. Please move the rain, the wind, and the clouds away from my house. If the rain doesn't stop, I won't be able to walk to the communal cafeteria to eat.*

Tevada didn't help me. The rain continued to pour and the wind continued to blow. I fell asleep without food.

The rain had stopped by morning. Insects and other small creatures came out of their homes underground to enjoy the cool morning. The songs of frogs, toads, and crickets echoed everywhere in the field and beyond. The sound of the frogs and toads gave me amusement. It made me forget about being lonely. I had fun making sounds repeatedly after the frogs and toads, as if I were singing along with them.

Not long after the sunrise, I saw thousands of termites flying in the field. The flying termites attracted birds. Hundreds of birds were excited and flew in a zigzag pattern, maneuvering to catch the flying termites.

That morning, I was as excited as the birds. I ran after the flying termites to catch them for food. But catching them with my bare hands wasn't easy. So, I picked small tree branches that had a lot of leaves and smacked them in mid-air. When they fell to the ground, I rushed to pick them up, pulled off their clear wings, and tossed them into my mouth. They tasted like tofu. My instinct told me that if a bird could eat them, I could too.

During the rainy season, the sky poured down rain as it pleased. Sometimes it rained during the day, sometimes it rained during the night.

One morning was a bit strange. My parents woke me early in the morning. I was barely awake and in disarray. I rubbed my eyes and saw them sitting beside me. Pa bent over, kissed my forehead, and said, "Son, today, you cannot play outside the house. There are many poisonous mushrooms in the field. I don't want you to pick them or play with them. Don't eat the mushrooms. They can make you sick and you could die."

I could hear his deep voice clearly, but I could barely see his face because it was dark in the house.

Mak adjusted the blanket on my body to keep me warm. She leaned forward and kissed me on the cheek. "I love you, son," she said softly in a whisper. Then they got up and get out of the house to work. After they left, I continued to sleep.

That morning, after I woke up, I opened the door to look at the field. I noticed the sky was clear blue, but the field in front of the house was misty. It seemed like a thin smoke rose from the ground and dissolved in the air. After the mist disappeared, I saw hundreds of wild mushrooms growing on the ground. They stood and baked in the sun, like miniature umbrellas.

The colorful mushrooms—white, yellow, red, blue, brown, black, and purple—tempted me to roam onto the field and I disobeyed part of my parents' advice. I picked up a stick and decided to walk the field to learn about the mushrooms. I walked carefully to avoid stepping on them. I entertained myself by beating the least attractive mushroom with the stick, focusing my attention on a skinny gray mushroom. I didn't touch it with my hand because I was afraid I would get sick and die. After I learned enough about the mushrooms from observation, I sat under the thatched house and waited for a bell to ring for lunchtime.

Our Family's Special Meal

One night, we were all reunited again. When I last saw Vanny, she had given us roots. That was a few months ago. She had gotten permission from her leader to visit us again, and we were excited to see each other.

Mak managed to exchange her jewelry for a cup of rice, with a corrupt Khmer Rouge chef, and that night my family celebrated silently. We talked to each other in a whisper because we were afraid the Khmer Rouge would sneak under our stilt house and listen to our conversation.

I heard Mak and Pa talk to each other in a whisper, but I couldn't hear their conversation clearly. From what I heard, they were talking about how to cook rice without a cooking pot.

My parents eventually came up with a clever way of doing it. Mak placed the rice into the thermo pot. Pa boiled water in the kettle under the stilt house. After the water boiled, Pa brought the kettle into the house. He pushed the door shut and poured the hot water into the thermo pot to cook the rice. Then he sealed the thermo pot with its cap and wrapped it tightly with clothes and a blanket to seal the heat. While we waited for the rice to cook, Mak put me to bed.

"You need to go to sleep, my son. When the rice is ready, I will wake you up," she said softly while laying me down and putting a blanket over me.

I was hungry and couldn't wait to eat. I closed my eyes, pretending I was asleep. My eyes were half closed. However, my ears were fully alert to detect any sounds surrounding me. Frequently, I saw Pa peek through the shutters of the house to make sure that no Khmer Rouge soldiers were spying on us.

After a long wait, I heard my parents scoop the rice out of the thermo pot onto the plates.

Mak whispered in my ear, "Marin, wake up. The food is ready, my son."

I quickly got up, grabbed the hot steamed rice, and shoveled it into my mouth.

"Don't eat too loud. Don't make a sound on the plate," Mak whispered.

I emptied my plate within seconds. This was the first time I had steamed rice since the Khmer Rouge evacuated us from the city.

A Quick Escape

Night had turned into day. My parents had already left home to work. Vanny and I decided to walk into the forest behind our house to collect wild edible leaves and wild mushrooms.

She walked ahead of me into the forest, moving her head side to side, looking for whatever she could find. When we got deeper and deeper into the forest, she ran back toward me. She covered my mouth with one hand. Her other hand pushed my head to the ground behind the bushes.

"Don't make noises," she whispered into my ear.

I could feel her body shake as she squeezed my head tightly toward her. Suddenly, I heard the sounds of horse footsteps running toward us.

A man shouted from a distance, "Who is it? Do you see anything? If it is people, just kill them."

Once I heard that, my heart began to pound fast. My body began to shake and sweat dripped down my forehead. I sat still and held my breath and hoped the man wouldn't find me. I moved my head up slowly and tried to see through the thick bushes. Briefly, I saw a Khmer Rouge soldier on horseback, scanning the bushes. "No, I don't see anything," he shouted to his men. "I think it was maybe an animal."

After the soldiers left, Vanny and I continued to hide silently until the sound of the horse footsteps disappeared. She took her hand away from my mouth and slowly stood up from the bushes and scanned the area. She then grabbed my hand and we ran home in fear.

"I saw Khmer Rouge soldiers kill people near the tree," she said to me, gasping for air.

When she said that, I was scared even more, realizing that I had almost been killed twice by the Khmer Rouge.

The rainy season was almost over. The scattered clouds in the sky were thinner and more scattered. The rain was replaced with drizzle. Violent wind was replaced with cold breeze.

3

Forced to Move North

Stealing for Survival

The Khmer Rouge moved my family several kilometers to the North. They ordered us to live in a new location near a huge open field that was newly plowed. Pa built a thatch house facing the pond and the sunset, near a termite mound. The pond was small, less than thirty meters across. It was filled with water, full of trees and vines, and surrounded by small trees. The branches of the trees provided shade for the house and kept it cool from the summer heat.

The Khmer Rouge transferred us to eat at a different communal cafeteria, which was far away from the rice warehouse where I had been caught stealing.

Living in this new place presented new challenges. The Khmer Rouge continued to be strict in their policies. They now confiscated our bowls and spoons. We only had left the kettle and thermo pot. Pa found me a tin can the size of a coffee mug and twice as tall. The can had a ring pattern and could hold as much as two bowls of porridge. This tin can became my survival tool. Pa didn't teach me how to use the can; starvation forced me to be creative. During meal time, I walked to the communal cafeteria, with the can hidden in my shirt under my armpits.

At the communal cafeteria, the Khmer Rouge put a spoon in each bowl and set the bowls on the ground in two long rows. From the distance, I could see that the food was still warm. Steam came out of each bowl like strands of mist. Minutes later, two female chefs carried a huge pot and scooped the soup into a larger soup bowl set between our individual porridge bowls. The soup was intended for two people to share.

While the Khmer Rouge set food on the ground, starving children pushed each other in line in attempt to devour the food. I, too, was starving, but I didn't push anyone. I stood still to control myself and I tried to study who would eat next to me.

When the food was ready to be served, the Khmer Rouge began to let the children walk past a bamboo gate. The leaders pulled the children by the hands to the designated food bowls.

The minute they sat me down, I picked up the porridge bowl next to me and poured the fluid into my tin can. I quickly shoveled the rice into my mouth and transferred any leftover fluid into my tin can. I did the same thing with the soup. Starvation forced me to be greedy, to cheat and steal the other children's food. Whoever sat next to me went home with an empty stomach.

Other parents saw me stealing their children's food, quarreled with my parents and reported me to the Khmer Rouge. The Khmer Rouge never caught me in the act, but they told my parents to discipline me.

"I cannot discipline a starving child," Pa said to them in a soft tone that was clear and firm. "He is just a child and he is hungry. He wouldn't steal food from anyone if he had enough food to eat."

On the way home from the cafeteria, Pa did not discipline me for my greedy actions. He did not tell me to steal the other children's food. Neither did he tell me to stop.

"Son, you are a smart boy," he said.

Is It a Bird or a Chicken?

One morning, the sun was still asleep on the horizon. It was still dark and silent. Mak woke me up and took me to work with her near our old home and the rice warehouse. On the way, there was an injured bird crying in the bushes.

"Kaaak...... Kaaak! Kaaaaak! Kaaaaaak! Kaaaakaaaak!"

The bird cried and shouted so loud that it would wake up the Khmer Rouge who lived in the area.

"Aah! Wake up!" I heard a lady shouting one hundred meters away. "There are people stealing chicken! You have to wake up and find out who the thief is!"

I ignored her shouting and, meanwhile, followed the sound of the crying bird. The bird struggled to get out of the thick thorny bushes. Quickly, I grabbed it by the neck and pulled it out.

"Kaaak...... Kaaak! Kaaaaak! Kaaaaaak! Kaaaakaaaak!" the bird continued to cry louder and louder, trying to escape from my hands.

Meanwhile, the lady continued to shout louder and louder. "Wake up! There are thieves stealing chicken."

I was nervous, but at the same time I felt innocent because I did not steal a chicken.

"Kill the bird! Just kill the bird!" Mak shouted at me in a whisper.

"I don't know how to kill it," I said.

She snatched the bird from my hands, said a quick prayer to the bird, then smashed its head on her machete's wooden handle a few times. The poor injured bird died instantly, and the fuzzy dark morning turned into silence.

I could read my mak's heart. She didn't have the heart of a killer. When she smashed the bird's head, her face looked full of guilt and sympathy. If she had any killer instinct, it would have taken only one smash to kill the bird, instead of a few times.

The lady continued shouting. "Is there someone checking the chicken barn!"

I thought this lady was dumb. She couldn't even tell the difference between bird cries and chicken cries. And the bird that I caught sounded more like a duck crying.

The bird was the size of a dove and had feathers like a blue jay, thick, blue and shiny. The bird couldn't fly because its wing was broken.

Mak put the dead bird in her pocket and we walked fast. She pretended like nothing had happened. With one hand, she held her machete on her shoulder; with the other, she held my hand. There was no one chasing after us, so we continued to walk until we got to the field of our old house where I used to roam for crickets and grasshoppers.

At work, the rumor spread that there was a thief stealing chickens. I knew I was innocent. I had killed a bird, not a chicken. I thought the chicken might be missing somewhere else.

Before lunch break, while Pa was working at digging in the field, Mak snuck out of work to prepare the bird for lunch. She pulled off the feathers and buried them. Then she tossed the bird into the fire pit where I used to cook the grasshoppers.

When the bird was cooked, Mak rationed the bird meat among the three of us. She gave a small portion to Pa, some to me, and the rest was hers. The bird tasted great, like chicken.

When the communal chief saw us eating during lunch break, he accused us of stealing the chicken from Angkar. "Ah! *Mitt!* Where you get that chicken from?"

"What chicken? I didn't eat chicken. I ate an injured bird my son caught this morning," Mak said in defense.

Three Khmer Rouge ladies and two men threatened to report us to the Angkar Luer, and they threatened to kill our whole family.

Mak and Pa walked the Khmer Rouge to the place where she had prepared the bird. She showed them the feathers of the bird and said, "I am not betraying Angkar or anyone. I didn't steal anything from anybody." She was mad and nervous, trying to defend her life.

While she was quarreling, two other Khmer Rouge soldiers arrived. I sat on the ground, picking weeds and shaking. Sweat dripped down my head. I was afraid they would kill me. I was afraid they would kill Mak and Pa.

Pa stood firmly and talked face to face with the soldiers. "We work hard to serve Angkar Luer. What we ate was a bird not a chicken. You guys need to compare the color and the size of the bird's feathers with the chicken feathers. If these feathers look like chicken feathers, we accept Angkar's punishment."

Unlike Mak, Pa talked to the Khmer Rouge without showing any emotion. He talked slowly, clearly, and firmly.

After the Khmer Rouge soldiers saw proof of the bird's feathers, they stopped arguing with my parents and left, but with a warning, "If we catch you stealing, we will kill you and your whole family."

Revenge on the Black Ants

After the Khmer Rouge threatened to kill our family, Mak stopped taking me to work with her. My loneliness at home forced me find ways to entertain myself. I played with insects.

Most of the time, I played with the fire ants, tree ants, and black ants that crawled in front of our house. I was curious about their activities: the way they crawled, the way they carried food with their mouths, the way they built their colonies, the way they dug holes in the ground.

"Black ants, why don't you crawl in a trail like fire ants and tree ants do? You seem to crawl all over the place. Do you know where you are crawling?" I asked the black ants as if they could understand me.

One time while I was observing the fire ants marching along their trails, a black ant crawled onto my right foot and bit my ankle. It was a most painful bite. A burning sensation went through my foot.

I ran upstairs into the house to soothe it. I lifted my foot, spat on the wound, and blew on it to cool it off. I was furious and hated these black ants.

Minutes after my pain subsided, I found a stick to kill any black ants that crawled near me. Sometimes, I lured them to crawl onto the stick. Then I stood the stick on the fire ants' hole. The tiny fire ants went crazy and crawled onto the sticks to attack the black ants. I had lots of fun watching the black ants defend their lives.

My amusement with ants was mixed with hate because I had been bitten by them many times. When I got bitten by the fire ants, I destroyed their holes with the stick. Sometimes, I would pee on their holes and watch them drown in my pee. When I got bitten by the tree ants, I picked hard dirt and threw it at their nests to destroy them.

Life Skills: How to Tell Time with My Shadow

The Khmer Rouge continued to order my parents to work farther away from home and away from the communal cafeteria, so Pa and Mak were unable to walk and meet me for lunch every day. They had to find a way to teach me when I should walk to the communal cafeteria for lunch. Pa taught me how to read time by measuring my own shadow in the sun.

"Marin, stand in the sun."

He pushed my back slightly out of the shade of the tree. I stood facing the sunrise as he requested.

"Now, step on your shadow," he said.

I stepped on my shadow as he asked me, but the shadow moved away from me. I thought Pa wanted me to play a game with my own shadow. I had fun jumping and stepping on it.

"Son, just make a big step and try to step on your shadow's head."

Every time I took a step, the shadow continued to follow me. "Why, Pa? Why do I need to step on my shadow? I can't step on it. It is always walking with me."

Then Pa marked my standing position and my big long step.

"When your shadow becomes shorter to one step, it means it is time for you to walk to the communal cafeteria for lunch. Don't go there too early or too late."

The next morning, after the sun began to rise, ever so often I got out of the shade and measured my shadow. As the shadow rose higher in the sky, my shadow became shorter. When my shadow reached to one step, I began to walk to the communal cafeteria for lunch.

When I got to the communal cafeteria, I saw my parents walking from the opposite direction. I could see the happy smiles on their faces. They looked at me with surprise and were proud of me.

Moments later the communal chef rang the bell signaling lunchtime. I was starving so much that I didn't even talk to my parents. My mind was focused on food and thinking about what the communal chefs would serve. I hurried to line up with the children's group, which had about two-hundred people. My parents, looking exhausted and hungry, went to line up with the adult group of about one hundred, like they usually did.

Life Skills: Using What We Have

Living in the new thatch house, my parents had more time to see me. They had time to spend with me in the early mornings before they left to work and time to spend with me during lunch breaks. Pa used his free time to teach me how to survive without stealing from Angkar.

Moreover, the Khmer Rouge allowed my parents to bring working tools home. The three tools we possessed were a machete, an agricultural hoe, and a pair of *bonkee*, which is a dirt carrier made from rattan. With these basic tools, Pa became creative.

One afternoon, during lunch break, I saw Pa sitting by the middle post of the house. I walked from the mouth of the pond and stood next to him. "What are you doing, Pa?"

He didn't respond. He moved his head and looked at the field and bushes around the pond to see if anyone saw him.

When he didn't see anyone, he removed loose dry dirt with his machete and his hands. He dug into the ground until it was deep enough to reach his knees and removed a small object off the ground. He dusted it and blew off the dirt from it, and I saw a greenish metal box the size of a textbook. The box was three fingers deep.

When he opened the box, I saw small half-curved needles, medical needles, a few syringes, tiny glass bottles shaped like bullets, medicines, and tiny curved blades. My senses told me these tools were some sort of medicine and medical accessories, but I didn't know what they were used for and I wasn't nosey enough to ask Pa.

He removed all the curved needles out of the box and put them on the ground. He closed the box tightly and buried it back in the ground.

"Pa, why don't you put the box inside the house? Why do you need to bury it?"

He looked at me and said, "Son, I don't want anyone to know what we have. If the Khmer Rouge knows what we have in this box, our lives will be threatened."

I remembered that before the country fell under the Khmer Rouge control, two military men had come to our house and saluted Pa. They had requested that he get on the green military jeep with them and treat the wounded soldiers back at the government facility in Nakleung. That day, Pa had taken me with him and we had ridden in the backseat of the jeep. When we arrived at the government facility, Pa dressed in a white coat with a stethoscope hanging at his neck. I didn't know exactly what his profession was, but I saw him diagnose a few patients. Maybe he was a nurse. Maybe he was a medical doctor. Or maybe he was a surgeon.

After the box of medical supplies box was re-buried, Pa began to make a fire under our stilt house. When the initial smoke and flame disappeared from the fire pit, he picked the needles and heated them until they turned red. Then he took them out of the fire, placed them on the hoe, hammered them with his machete then crafted each needle into a fishhook.

That day, Pa didn't finish making the fishhook. He put out the fire by pouring a large amount of dirt into the fire pit to suffocate the smoke and heat. Then he went to his job.

Three days later, Pa made me a fishing pole from a bamboo stick and taught me how to fish in the pond in front our house. "Look, son! This is how you catch a fish. First, you cut a small piece of earthworm and hook it to a fishhook. Now, you can throw the fishing hook in the pond."

"Pa, do fish eat grasshoppers?"

He looked at me with a smile. "Some fish do and some don't. But most of the big fish do."

While I was watching Pa fish, he gave me the fishing pole and said, "This is your fishing pole. Hold it like this. Now, swing the fishing line into the water."

He stood behind me, held onto my hands, and helped me swing the fishing line into the pond.

"Watch for the float, son," he said. "When the fish bites, the float will sink in the water. Once you see the float sink, swing the pole onto the land."

The first day I didn't have any luck. Small fish nibbled all the bait and left me with an empty fishhook.

One afternoon, Pa hooked up the earthworms onto my fishhook and told me to swing the fishing line into the pond. While I was fishing, he walked to the other side of the pond. I saw the float sink deep in the water and my excitement jolted me to shout for my father.

"Pa! Pa! The fish is pulling! Fish! Fish is pulling!"

He instructed me with hand gestures. "Swing the fishing pole backward."

I swung the fishing pole hard and saw the fish fly overhead. It landed on the ground behind me. Pa rushed over to seize the flat fish, the size of his palm. The fish had dark gray scales and round black eyes. I stood and held the fishing pole, while Pa unhooked the fish.

"What type of fish is that, Pa?" I asked.

"This fish is called *trey-kranh*." With a small laugh and a big smile on his face, he said, "You did it, son! You did it! Now, you know how to fish." I was very *excited* and proud of myself.

The fish made me hungry. Pa didn't waste any time. He picked water-lily leaves and wrapped my fish in them tightly. Next, he picked clay from the pond and molded it over the wrapped fish. Then he did exactly the same to the other two snakehead fish he had caught. After he finished molding the three fishes with clay, he brought them to the fire pit near the termite mound and buried them in the ashes. Then he made a fire on top of the buried fish. Suddenly, Mak brought a kettle full of water to boil over the fire pit.

Burying the fishes in the ashes, and boiling water over the fire pit, weren't part of the cooking process. It was to conceal food from the Khmer Rouge. We hid whatever we had, especially food. Eating food outside the communal cafeteria meant betraying Angkar. The consequences could be torture or even death.

Once the fishes were cooked, Pa removed them from the fire pit and took them inside the house. Then he took a few steps back to close the door and he pulled down the shutters to half closed. The half-closed shutters illuminated a small amount of sunlight into the house, just enough for us to see our food. I sat in front of Mak and watched her crack the hardened clay open and remove the wrapped leaves. Steam and smell came out of the fish and permeated the house. My mouth started drooling like a starving puppy. My stomach began to growl, demanding food.

"Be patient, my son. I will feed you soon," Mak said.

She cut the fishes open and applied a small amount of salt on them. She cut off my fish's head, picked out the bones, and said, "Here, son, here is your fish. Eat it."

I finished the whole fish within seconds. My parents ate everything, including skins, eyes, bones, and guts.

After we finished eating our fishes, Pa opened the door and shutters to let the fresh air in. Mak grabbed all the trash and burned it in the fire pit to prevent the fishy smell from permeating the air.

Pa carried me to the pond and washed me. Then they went to work.

After they left to work, I was excited about fishing. I grabbed my fishing pole and continued fishing, but I didn't have any more luck.

Life Skills: How to Catch Eels

One day, I saw Pa carrying a whole bamboo stick on his shoulders. He dropped it under the stilt house. The bamboo was still green and fresh, and about ten meters long.

The next day, he brought three pieces of hollow bamboo, each piece less than two meters long. These three pieces of bamboo were to be used for eel traps.

Pa cut and shredded the long bamboo to make it appear like he was fixing the house, but he was really concealing the process of making the eel traps. There was nothing wrong with the house. The house was in good condition.

He cut the bamboo to reinforce the door frames and the stair guardrails. I could see that he didn't seem to care much about the guardrails. He reinforced them by merely tying them with vines. But when he made the eel traps, he was meticulous.

He poked the inner partitions of the bamboo to make it hollow. He left the last partition to keep as a seal. On the bamboo, he punctured several small holes about the size of my fingers to allow water to flow in and out. Then he crafted dozens of flexible flat bamboo sticks, the size of pencils, and wove them together. He made these woven flat sticks into a cylinder-cone shape to make the entrance for the eel traps.

I tried to help Pa, but I couldn't because it was too complicated and dangerous. Shredded bamboo could cut my hands. Besides, making the eel traps was a long process. It took my father a few lunch breaks to finish them.

Once every few days, Pa and I would sneak out into the swamp about half a kilometer from home. Before we went to deploy the traps, he caught a few snails or crabs and crushed them as bait. Once we arrived at the swamp, he sank the traps into the mud so they wouldn't float. Then he broke one or two small tree branches to identify the trap locations. In the evening, when he came from work, he went to the swamp to collect the eels. Each time he went, he had trapped at least one eel.

Pa prepared each eel by removing the slippery fluid from its body. He grabbed a fistful of ashes, applied it onto the eel, and squeezed the slimy fluid off. Then he cooked the eel by burying it in the ashes, as he had with the fish.

Life Skills: Edible Wild Fruits

Pa not only taught me how to fish and trap eels. He also showed me different kinds of edible wild fruits, seeds, roots, yams, leaves, flowers, vines, and seeds.

One time, while he was breaking a fruit seed to get the nut, he said, "Son, any kind of fruit that can be eaten by birds is safe for you to eat. The same thing with insects and seeds. If the birds can eat them, you can, too."

That phrase resonated in my head. I ate all the edible plants and insects. I never tried to eat earthworms, though. I felt they were gross, slippery, slimy, and disgusting.

One afternoon, Pa took me to the forest west of our house to find food. He found a big wild mango tree with lots of fruit. It looked exactly like a domesticated mango, but it was relatively small, the size of my big toe.

"Look, son." Pa pointed up at bundles of the small greenish fruit dangling on branches high in the air. "That is wild mango fruit. It is edible."

He picked up a stick about the length of his arm, positioned himself, and threw it at the fruit. He amazed me. With just one throw, he hit the fruit and knocked several of them down to the ground. I ran to pick them up.

"Stop, son! Don't pick them up! Don't touch the fruit with your bare hands. The fruit has a lot of sap. The sap that releases from the fruit can burn your hands."

Pa picked fresh leaves from other trees and gave a few to me. He placed the leaves on top of the wild mango fruit and picked them up, one at a time. He placed the fruit in his *kroma* and said, "This is how you pick wild mango fruit. Can you pick them like I did?" he asked.

Without answering his question, I picked the fruit exactly like he did. I picked a few. Then I stopped because it was too complicated.

"The fruit could burn your hands and your tongue," he explained to me. "You cannot eat this fruit like domestic mango because it has a lot of acid."

"Why do you pick them up if you cannot eat them?" I asked.

Pa didn't answer my question. After we finished collecting the fruit, we walked out of the forest and went back home. He cut the wild mango fruit and soaked it in water to drain out the sap. After they soaked in water for a long while, he cut them in half to remove the seeds.

The wild mango fruit tasted like domestic mangos. The green ones were sour, and ripened ones had a sweet and sour taste. We didn't eat much. Mak pickled all the fruit to preserve them for snacks.

A Formal Invitation from Khmer Rouge Soldiers

The second summer was approaching. The water in the pond had drained to half full. Tree leaves began to turn from light green to dark green. The Khmer Rouge began to change the dynamic of my family.

One afternoon, right after lunch, Pa was exhausted and took a nap inside the house. Mak and I sat on the stairs to catch cool air. While we were sitting, two Khmer Rouge soldiers with rifles hanging at their chests approached us. They were in their late twenties and had a dark- brown complexion, like me. Both of them looked slightly shorter than my father.

"Is your husband home?" one of the soldiers asked.

"Did my husband do anything wrong?" Mak asked them.

"No, there will be nothing wrong happening to him. Angkar Luer ordered him to work somewhere else," said the soldiers.

"Where will Angkar send my husband to?"

Mak probed them with several questions. Then she went into the house to wake up Pa. He got up and stood by the door, with his hands extended out, holding the door frames.

"*Soum-paek-av, haey-tov-jai-muy-ka-ngum,*" the Khmer Rouge soldier said. "Please put your shirt on and go with us."

"Going where?" Pa asked.

"We don't know yet," one of the soldiers said.

"Now, Angkar needed additional men to build a water canal," said another soldier.

"Where do we build a water canal?" Pa asked.

"Angkar will tell you where the work location is when you get there," the soldier said.

"Are you sure there will be nothing wrong with my husband?" Mak continued to ask, over and over again.

"Now, Angkar has a new policy to order men to work digging water canal," the soldier answered in a soft natural tone, while he picked fresh leaves from a small plant and blew it to make a musical sound.

Mak was very curious about the whole situation. "How many people are going?" she asked.

"Just several people. Two people from here, and a couple more people from another place." The Khmer Rouge responded in a calm way like nothing serious would happen to my father.

One of the soldiers walked past my house to request another man who lived a few houses away to come with him. Minutes later, the other man arrived at our house, with a hoe on his shoulder. Pa came out and walked down the stairs.

"Take the hoe with you," a soldier said and pointed to the agricultural hoe Pa had laid under the house.

Pa stooped over, grabbed the hoe, and set it on his right shoulder, with the blade hanging behind his back and his hand holding onto the hoe handle before him.

"When will my husband come back?" asked Mak. "When will the water canal be finished?"

"He will be back once the water canal is finished," said the soldier.

Pa rested his hand on my head. "Son, I have to serve Angkar. Angkar ordered me to work far away from home. Once my job is done, I will come to see you. Just stay with your mother, son," Pa said to me as if there was nothing to worry about.

"Let's go!" said the soldier.

As Pa walked away from home, I ran after him. "Are you going to work now, Pa? Are you coming back home tomorrow, Pa?"

He turned his head. "I will come home soon, son. Don't follow me. Go back to your Mak, son!"

"Come back home, Marin!" Mak shouted.

The Khmer Rouge soldiers walked right behind my father. Pa seemed to walk peacefully with the hoe hung on his shoulder.

But Mak seemed restless. She couldn't sit still. She sat and stood by the doorway of the house and watched Pa walk in front of the Khmer Rouge soldiers. Mak and I kept watching him until he turned to the oxcart road with trees blocking our view.

After Pa left, I saw a grim face on Mak. I could feel her sadness. She sat by the door, rested her head against the wall, and cried silently without tears. I didn't cry, but I felt sad seeing a strange expression on Mak's face. Her black wavy hair covered her skinny square face. Mak must have known something would happen to Pa, but I didn't know. I was too young to realize what might happen to him. All I knew was that Pa would work far away from home building water canals for Angkar.

My Stay at the Pediatric Hospital

After Pa left, my health deteriorated. My whole body swelled. My face was big and round, and my feet and arms were inflated like balloons. Out of curiosity, I pressed my foot with my fingers until it sunk to the bone. Then I let it go. The skin of my foot elastically inflated back up slowly to its original state. I did not feel pain, but I felt a lightness and numbness in my feet when walking.

The next day, my body deflated and no longer looked like a balloon. I turned from swollen fat to skinny. I was severely ill. My body felt weak. I couldn't sit down or stand up. Mak carried me on her chest and rested my head on her shoulder and took me to the pediatric hospital. It was located not far away from the rice warehouse where the Khmer Rouge soldier had strangled me for stealing rice.

Although I was severely ill, I was still conscious enough to see what was around me. When I got to the hospital, a female Khmer Rouge nurse assigned me a small wooden hospital bed near the door. Mak carried me to the assigned bed. The minute I got to the bed, I heard the sound of children crying. I saw a mother sitting and fanning her children. The hospital ward smelled stinky, like decaying wood.

Mak lay me down on the bed and arranged my head to rest on the folded *kroma*. Then she stood up and stretched her back to release stress and pain from her body. She took deep breaths and removed sweat from her face with a piece of cloth. After she was done stretching and wiping her face, she sat on the bed next to me. She put her hand on my head to feel my body temperature and said, "Son, I'm going outside to get some water. I will be right back." Minutes later she came back with a small metal container full of water. She wet a piece of cloth and washed me while I lay in bed.

The hospital had no doctor. The Khmer Rouge female chefs had roles as cooks as well as nurses. They provided food to the sick and injected medicine into children. The nurses provided two meals a day, lunch and dinner. The meals they provided were little better than those from the communal cafeteria: two small scoops of *bor-bor-peak*, a thick plain rice porridge, for lunch, and two small scoops for dinner.

I was very hungry, but I couldn't eat. My illness made me hate food. Every time Mak tried to feed me, the food smelled stinky, like rotten fish mixed with mud. Once the food got into my mouth, it tasted bitter and made me vomit.

The nurses injected medicine into my buttocks daily. I didn't know what the injection was doing. When the nurses approached me with a syringe and a big long needle, I cried for my life trying to hug and hold Mak. I screamed, "Help me! I am scared! Help me! Help me! Stop injecting me."

I began to hate Mak for holding me onto the bed and letting the nurse inject medicine into my buttocks. Sometimes the nurse pushed the syringe so hard that I could feel the needle hit my pelvis bone. I cried and shouted, pushing sweat out of my body.

The injection didn't help my illness, and both sides of my buttocks were sore from the frequent injections. I felt a sharp pain from inside my pelvis bones to the buttocks, so I couldn't sleep on my back. I slept either sideways or face down. Mak frequently wet the cloth to cover my body to keep me cool.

One time, when I saw a nurse coming up to me with a syringe attached to a needle, I exploded into crying again. Mak stopped the nurse from injecting the medicine. "*Mittbong*, please stop injecting medicine into my son's body. The injection has made my son's illness worsen."

The nurse argued with Mak. She raised her voice. "Do you want your son to die? Or you want your son to live? I work here. And I know what to do."

"I want my son to live. All he needs every day is enough nutritious food," Mak said.

The nurse looked at Mak with a disappointed face and walked out the door.

In my heart, I knew Mak was right. All I needed was good nutritious food to fill my stomach and heal my illness.

Without the injections, I gradually felt better each day and was able to eat. I was able to stand up and look at my skinny body, especially my flat and bony buttocks. I was so skinny that my rib bones were protruding. My head was all bony and bigger than my meatless body. My kneecaps were almost as big as my head.

As days went by, Mak took me outside the hospital to get fresh air under a shade tree. I felt better but not fully recovered. I couldn't walk. My feet felt stiff and numb. Mak held my hands and assisted me to take a few steps. She walked me slowly from one shade tree to another. I felt like a baby just learning how to walk.

While I walked, I noticed how small the hospital was. It seemed like the Khmer Rouge had converted an elementary school into a hospital. There were two buildings. The smaller building was used as a nurse compound and a kitchen. The bigger structure was used as a patient ward.

I didn't know how many days or weeks I stayed in the hospital. All I know is I stayed there until I was able to stand and walk again. I got better every day.

At some point, the Khmer Rouge nurses no longer wanted me to stay in the hospital. "I need both of you to get out of the hospital in the next three days," said one of the nurses.

"*Mittbong*, but my son is not completely healed. Can you let him stay here longer?" Mak said.

The nurse didn't care. She just walked away and ignored what Mak said to her.

When three days came, two nurses arrived and stood by the door. They told Mak to get me out of the hospital and go home, but Mak refused. "*Mittbong,* please allow my son to stay here for several more days," Mak begged the nurses. "I want him to stay here until he is completely healed. Once he is able to walk by himself, I will leave."

"This is the last time that we will tell you to get out of the hospital. If you don't leave within the next five days, the soldiers will come get you and your son out of hospital," said one of the nurses and walked out.

During the confrontation, I felt that I could read my mother's mind. I looked at her and thought, *Mak doesn't like this hospital. She hates it. She just wants me to have a better ration of food here. She also has all the time off to take care of me. If she goes back home, she will have to return to the hard labor at her job.*

The day after the warning, the Khmer Rouge nurses continued threatening us. They cut down our food ration from two scoops of rice porridge to one scoop.

"The food is only for sick children, not for caretakers," the nurse said while putting food in a yellow metal *chaan-srak*, a cylinder container.

Mak shared the one scoop of rice porridge with me. My starvation made me greedy. I didn't want to share with her. She begged me to share the food with her, but I didn't, and I had no sense of guilt saying no to her.

However, Mak had her own way to trick me. She wouldn't allow me to eat by myself. She preferred to feed me, instead. She used the spoon to scoop hot porridge from my bowl and blew on it to cool it off. Then she tasted a little bit to make sure it was cool enough to feed me.

On the fifth day of the deadline, Mak grabbed our few belongings and wrapped them in the *kroma*. We left the hospital and went back home.

Now, only Mak and I lived at home in the thatch house. Pa was gone. Vanny no longer came home to visit us. There was no information about them or where they were. I missed them and wished they would come home to visit me.

Mak's Journey to the Hospital

Mak didn't feel well. Her body swelled for a few days. Her arms, legs, and face were swollen like balloons. Her face was round and shiny, as if it was filled with air. Then her body went back to skinny. She decided to escape from the village and to stay in the hospital.

It was early morning. The sky was still dark. Mak woke me up and pulled my hand to get me out of the house. She held my hand and walked toward the same oxcart road where the Khmer Rouge soldier had escorted Pa. The morning visibility was low. We walked with the help of moonlight to guide our path. While I was walking, I noticed very few stars were still shining in the sky. There was a quarter moon. I heard roosters cooing as if they were calling for the sun to rise.

After a long walk on the oxcart road, the stars and moonlight disappeared and the sky was replaced with a grim sunlight. Then Mak and I encountered a huge water canal. It was as wide as a two-lane road. I thought, *Pa must have been building this canal.* The canal was long and endless. It was built parallel to the direction of the sunrise and sunset. I was amazed at the size and amount of earth that people had put together on each side to make the canal.

I walked behind Mak. As I looked back, I saw a huge, bright, red sun slowly emerging from the horizon. It rose straight behind me, with a reflection in the slow milky water. The sky turned from grayish to clear blue. My long shadow led the way to wherever the hospital was.

Mak and I walked almost half a day and didn't see a person on the berm along the canal or in the rice fields.

Then just ahead of us we saw that the berm had collapsed and water from the canal was gushing out into the rice fields.

Mak tried to think of a way we could get across the water to the other side. "Stay here, son. Mak will walk across the water to test the depth of the water and to test how strong the current is. And I will come back to get you."

She didn't walk across the current directly. She walked into the flooded rice field about seventy meters, then cut across it. The water was waist deep for me. But the current pushed her and made her fall many times. Finally, she made it to the other side. She walked up onto the berm and lay flat on her back.

"Mak, are you coming back to pick me up?" I shouted.

She didn't answer. I sat and watched her.

Minutes later, I shouted again, "Why are you laying down? Come back and help me cross the water!"

Minutes later, she got up in a sitting position, then fell on her back again. I kept waiting and waiting for her to wake up and talk to me.

"My son, I cannot come to get you. I'm very sick," Mak hollered, mixing the plea with coughs. "All I want you to do is walk the same path as I did. And I will instruct you from here."

I began to cry. "No! Come get me!" I demanded. "I'm afraid I might drown!"

She coughed, holding her throat, and shouted, "My son, I love you. You will be safe. The water is not that deep. Just walk into the water and I will direct you. If you don't walk into the water, I will leave without you."

She begged me and threatened from the distance. Maybe she used the threat with the intention of teaching me not to be afraid of the water currents. Or maybe she used the threat to force me to be more brave.

Whatever her intentions were, I didn't really care. I was frustrated with her and hated her at that moment. I cried and stomped my feet. After a long battle of arguing with her, I gave in and began to walk slowly into the rice field.

"Very good, son! Just keep walking toward the rice field and away from the strong current."

The water was waist deep for me. I felt the current push my feet and buttocks forward into the rice field. My feet stepped on the soft mud below.

"Keep walking straight, son! Now, stop! Turn to your left and walk straight across the current. Don't walk toward me yet. When I walked further, the water got deeper. And the current was much stronger. It made me nervous and scared. The water current was more cruel than I expected. It brought weeds, small branches, and wood skins to hit me. Suddenly, the strong current knocked my feet off the ground and pushed me farther into the rice field. I couldn't stand up to hold my position. And I almost drowned."

"Heeelp me! Mak! Heeelp!" I shouted. "Come to help me, Mak!"

I struggled to stand up, but I couldn't. I was scared and I thought I was going to drown in the shallow water.

Mak rushed into the water to rescue me. She lifted me up from the water and held me against her. She soothed me in the middle of the flooded rice field. She carried me on her waist and walked out of the water.

Mak was extremely exhausted. She dried the water off my face and sat me down on the ground. She coughed and sneezed, holding her stomach as if she was in great pain. After we rested for a while, we continued our journey to the hospital.

The sun rose straight above my head. My shadow became shorter, less than one step away. I realized it past lunchtime. My exhaustion and starvation forced me to cry for attention from Mak. However, as a child I wasn't aware of her illness. All I wanted was full attention from my mother to love me. I wanted her to provide me food. We had been walking more than half a day. My legs felt sore.

"Mak, please carry me."

She knelt, wiped off my tears, and said, "Son! I love you. If Mak was not sick, Mak would carry you."

After many hours of walking on the big canal, Mak began to turn south and walk on the rice-field levees. We walked past countless young rice fields. There were no roads, no buildings, and no villages around the area.

As we walked further, the environment changed from wet to dry. Some rice in the rice fields ripened. Some rice fields had just recently been harvested; others had nothing, only bushes.

When Mak saw ripened rice, she scanned the surroundings to make sure no one was watching. Then she got into the rice field, sat down pretending like she was about to pee, picked a fist full of rice and shoveled it into her mouth. She chewed, sucked all the rice juice, and spat the skin out.

I was thinking, *Mak told me not to steal anything from Angkar. Why did she steal rice from the rice field?*

Mak got out of the rice field, gave me a fist full of rice, and told me to eat like her. I tossed the rice into my mouth, chewed it well, sucked the juice, and spat out the skin. Actually, I knew this eating technique from a while ago, when the Khmer Rouge caught me stealing rice from the warehouse. I had never told Mak what happened.

"Son! Just chew a little bit at time. And don't eat too much. If you eat too much, you might get diarrhea."

"Yes, Mak," I said. But my starvation forced me to eat more.

After long hours of walking without food, we finally got to the Toul Ompil Hospital located on a flat hill. I had no idea what province, village, or district we were in.

Mak was admitted to the hospital. It was easy to get in. There was no registration or paperwork.

"*Mittbong*, I'm very ill. I need to stay in the hospital," said Mak.

"Just go find your own place and rest," said the Khmer Rouge. They viewed patients at this hospital as "rabbit sick," meaning healthy but pretending to be sick to get away from hard labor.

The condition of the hospital was much worse than the pediatric hospital where I had stayed. The hospital's physical structure consisted of bamboo, wood, and palm leaves. Hundreds of bamboo and wooden posts stood up supporting weaved palm roofs. The hospital had no wall. It had only a roof to protect patients from the sun, dew, and rain.

The hospital was big and crowded, with hundreds of patients, and there were no hospital beds. Patients slept on *kontaels* that were set on the ground. Others slept on hammocks. Most of the patients were women. Very few were children my age.

Mak squeezed into a small space with other patients and tied her hammock from one end of the post to another. She then rested. I sat by her hammock, crying and demanding food. She rested in the hammock and soothed me in many ways. "I know you are hungry, son. The food will be served soon." She positioned me to sleep next to her on the *kontael*.

After a short rest, I saw people rushing outside with spoons and bowls. It was time to eat. "Mak, wake up. People are going outside to get food," I said.

She untied a small pack she had brought from home, took out a spoon and a yellow metal *chaan-srak*, the deep cylinder food container, and gave it to me. When I saw the container, I was a bit surprised. I thought, *How could Mak steal that container from the pediatric hospital?* I remembered that container well. It had two sets of slots and had a small chip along the rim. The Khmer Rouge had used that container to put food in for me. Sometimes after we finished eating, Mak had used that container to scoop water to bathe me.

Without questioning the *chaan-srak*, I took it out of Mak's hand and ran outside. I sat on the ground in a long row with the rest of the people, put the *chaan-srak* on the ground, and waited for the Khmer Rouge chefs to put food in it.

Minutes later, several chefs walked out of the communal kitchen, carrying a huge and deep cooking pot. They walked along each row to distribute two scoops of rice porridge to everybody. The moment the chefs scooped the food and placed it into my container, I realized I didn't have a spoon. So, I used my fingers and scooped the food into my mouth. I finished the food within seconds, then licked the leftover fluid in the container until nothing was left. I licked it so well that it looked as clean as if it were newly washed.

After several days in the hospital, I ventured out into the fields and found a small stream to look for food, such as snail, crab, frogs, and fishes. When water dried out of the field, fish and other water creatures were vulnerable. They were isolated together in small potholes. All I needed to do was scoop them of out from the potholes, or I could simply kill them with the stick. Most of the time, I came back with a small fish and crabs for Mak. She was happy with what I got for her. Sometimes she hid them in a pillow and rested her head on it. I understand why she hid food in her pillow; there were many hungry mouths watching her.

Mak was very proud of me. I gave her the fish and snails I caught. She hugged me and kissed me on my forehead. "Son, I'm very proud of you. You are very smart. You know how to catch food," she whispered in my ear.

She looked at me with her hands running over my head, her face glowing, her eyes welled with tears of joy. Many patients in the hospital seemed to be proud of me. I overheard their conversation when they said I was a clever and considerate boy. Maybe they were thinking of having a child like me, or maybe they wished they could have a surviving son like me to find them food while they were sick in bed. Maybe they saw me and missed their own sons or daughters. I wished I could read their minds.

One afternoon, I walked into a shallow stream and caught two big snakehead fish the size of my forearm. They were the biggest fish I had ever caught. I was thrilled and anxious to show Mak. I secured the fish with the vines by tying their gills and mouth and carried them, running, back to the hospital to show Mak.

When I got there, I saw the awe in the people's faces. They were smiling. At the same time, I knew how little food they got and they probably wanted the fish from my hands to feed their hungry mouths. While I was walking toward Mak, they all turned toward me, looking at me and the fish. I was overwhelmed with their admiration. "Look at that boy! He caught a big fish." "That boy is very smart." "He is that young and able to find food for his mother." "Look at the boy! He is adorable. He got fish for his mother." "I wish I could have a son like him."

The echoes of their admiration made me proud of myself, and I approached Mak with a big smile. I sat in a kneeling position and whispered into her ear, while holding the fish over her to surprise her. "Mak, look! I got a big fish!"

I whispered in her ear many times, but she didn't wake up. I held the fish above her and whispered in her ear again, but she didn't open her eyes. Then I began to shake her harder and harder to wake her up. My voice raised louder, louder, and louder.

"Mak! Wake up! Wake up…! Mak! Mak! Wake up…….! Wake up…..! Wake up and open your eyes to look at what I got for you! Mak! Mak! Wake up and look what I for you."

I shook her violently, but she didn't wake up. Then other patients tried to help me wake her up. They shook her body and tried to open her eyes to look at me, but she would not wake up. She was dead.

I cried and shouted over her dead body. I hugged her, held onto her, and cried, pounding my head on her to wake her up. Patients who slept nearby came to soothe me. Khmer Rouge officials came over and took her body away from me. They put her on a carriage and carried her out into the open field in front of the hospital and set her on the ground. I cried violently and ran after her.

"Don't take my mak away from me! I want to stay with my mak!" I pushed the Khmer Rouge officials away as they prepared to take Mak away from me.

"Get out! Don't take my mak! I love my mak!" I screamed at them.

Several Khmer Rouge nurses grabbed me and tried to hold me still as they carried Mak to bury. I cried so hard. I stomped my feet. I kicked. I punched. I twisted and turned, trying to free myself from them. It didn't matter how much I tried, they held my legs, my arms, my hands, and my body to the ground. They carried Mak's body down the hill until she disappeared.

After Mak's body was out of sight, the Khmer Rouge released me. I got up quickly and ran toward her. They ran after me and dragged me back. They soothed me. They calmed me down. They gave me plenty of food: a plate of steamed rice, grilled fish, and a full bowl of soup. But I couldn't eat. I was still traumatized. I eventually got exhausted and ate the food that was set on the wooden platform. Once I finished eating, however, I continued to cry. Khmer Rouge officials bathed, soothed, and put me to sleep on a wooden platform, which they used as a bed.

In the morning, when I woke up, I still felt sad and empty. I cried again, missing Mak. The third morning, I was still traumatized, blubbering and moaning. I began to realize that my family had disappeared from me one at a time. First, my younger brother, then my sister, then Pa, then Mak. I felt alone, drifting like a falling leaf in the stream.

The Khmer Rouge took me to live with them. They called me *Mitt-Own*, a young comrade. I became the property of Angkar, the organization that had starved and separated me from my sister and my father. Angkar suddenly became nice to me.

Although they were nice to me, I continued to get mad. I hated them. My mother wouldn't have died if they had given her enough food or medicine. I had no mother, no father, no sister, no relatives to look after me. I didn't have anyone to call Pa or Mak.

PART II
My Desperate Survival

4

My Desperate Adventure to Anywhere

The third day after Mak died, I ventured out of the hospital farther than I ever had. I walked toward the sunrise where the Khmer Rouge had taken Mak's body to bury it. I tried to find the burial site, but it was impossible. All I saw were rice fields, bushes, and small hills.

Then I decided to search for Pa and Vanny. I had no idea where they lived, where they worked, or what group they were in. And I had no sense of where or how to find them.

My journey to find Pa and Vanny would depend on fate and luck. I walked on foot trails, oxcart roads, and rice-field levees to a village near the hospital. When I got into the village, I saw a boy about my age sitting on the stairs of a thatched house. He was watching a line of oxcarts, which were fully loaded with harvested rice, drive past him. It reminded me of living in the village where I had gotten caught for stealing rice from the warehouse. The way he watched the oxcarts made me remember how I had sat on the staircase in front of my own house and watched the Khmer Rouge soldiers escorting the men who were tied up.

The oxcart drivers drove north past me. So, I walked south in the opposite direction along the oxcart road, until the road intersected with a water canal. I took a short break at the canal and scanned the area near and far. Then I began to walk east along an old canal that had plenty of shrubs, weeds, tall grasses, and water plants.

This small, older canal was the width of a one-car lane. Parts of it had completely dried. Other portions of it had shallow water. While I was walking alongside it, I saw plenty of fish, frogs, and flying insects. But I wasn't interested in catching them for food. The misery of losing Mak had made me lose my desire for food.

The sun was in the middle of the sky. My reflection was shortened to one step of my foot. I realized it was lunchtime but I was not hungry. I was still numb and compressed by sadness. Countless sad memories of my dead mother flooded my thoughts. To divert my attention away from these thoughts, I looked at the rice field and beyond. But I didn't see people or cows in the rice field. All I saw were dead brownish rice straws.

After a long walk, I saw a person on the other side of the berm, walking in the opposite direction toward me. From a distance, I didn't know who he or she was. The person wore a *kroma* over the head to protect against the heat. I didn't know whether the person was part of the Khmer Rouge or not.

Once we approached closer to each other, though, I realized it was Vanny! "Vanny!"

"Marin! What…What are you doing here?"

Vanny ran across the berm to hug me. We hugged each other tightly with a giddy happiness.

"Marin, I'm very excited to see you."

"I'm very excited to see you, too. I haven't seen you in a long time."

"Where—where—are—are you going?" we asked each other at the same time.

"I'm going to look for Pa and you!" I said.

"Oh. I was going to visit Mak and you! I got information from the people who lived in our village. They said that you and Mak stayed in Toul Ompil Hospital."

Vanny pulled my hand and said, "Let's go. Take me to see Mak! I really miss her!"

Suddenly, my eyes welled with tears, which rolled down my cheeks, and I fell to the ground. My lips began to quiver, my jaw became tight, and I couldn't spit out the words.

"Why are you crying?" she asked.

"Mak is dead."

"What! What did you say, Marin? Did you say Mak is dead?" she asked me, stunned.

"Yes, Yes. Mak is dead."

"How did she die? When did she die? Was it Wednesday or Thursday?"

"She was sick and died in the hammock. I don't know what day it was, but she died three days ago."

Vanny began to cry violently, stomping her feet, screaming and shouting. She pulled my hands and asked me to show her Mak's burial site. "Take me to see Mak. I want to see her."

"No! I don't know where the Khmer Rouge buried her. I was looking for her body, too!"

We cried together and held onto each other's hands. I could feel Vanny's strong impulse of wanting to dig Mak's grave. She wanted to show respect for Mak's dead body.

After we were exhausted from crying, Vanny had one hand wrapped around my shoulders and said, "Come on, Marin! Come with me. You come live with me."

I had one hand wrapped around Vanny's waist and we walked side by side, like we didn't want to be separated again. We walked, talked, and cried.

"Oh! Where is Pa?" she asked.

"The soldiers invited him to work far away from home, digging a canal."

Vanny began to cry again. She cried louder and louder. Her forearm pressed on my neck.

After a day of walking, we finally arrived at Vanny's campsite. This camp was located in a vast field and had few shade trees. The camp had three small huts. The huts had no wall, only a roof to shield from the summer heat. Vanny removed her hand from my shoulders and held onto my wrist. She approached her group leader, Sareth, who sat on a platform inside the hut. Vanny called her Mittbong-Sareth. *Mittbong* means "older comrade." The leader's name, in this case Sareth, would follow after *Mittbong*.

"Mittbong-Sareth, this is my younger brother Marin. I want him to live with me. I met him along the water canal, while I was on the way to find my sick mother," Vanny said in a humble tone.

Mittbong-Sareth tilted her head. She scooped her long scattered hair off her face and set it behind her ears to clip it. Her distinct features would make me remember her forever. She was in her mid-twenties and had a light-tan complexion. She had a smooth, beautiful oval face and big brown oval eyes. Whenever she talked or smiled, two dimples appeared on her lower cheeks.

"What happened to your parents?" she asked.

"We have no parents," said Vanny.

Vanny began to cry and said, "My mak... my mak... just died a few days ago in the hospital. And our Puk (dad) died from working too hard serving Angkar." She cried and talked in a mumbling voice.

At that moment, I didn't know any better. I looked at Vanny and thought, *Vanny is lying about Pa's death. Pa didn't die. He is alive. How dare she say Pa is dead. I saw a Khmer Rouge soldier come invite him to work at digging the water canal.*

Mittbong-Sareth sighed and looked at us with sympathy. She got off the bamboo platform and said, "This is *Kang-Komarey*, a girl group. I cannot let your brother stay with you long. He could stay with you temporarily until I find the appropriate boy group for him."

"Thank you, Mittbong-Sareth," Vanny said humbly and we walked out of the hut.

Attending School

Vanny's group had recently moved from somewhere else. I had no idea from where. They had settled here a few days ago. Angkar didn't even have a work plan for them. The Khmer Rouge kept them busy by ordering them to build small levees in the rice field.

There were about a couple hundred girls in the group. Most of them were between ten and twelve years old. They were like girl scouts, except they did hard labor serving Angkar. During the day, they built small canals and rice-field levees. At night, after eating, they set *kontaels* on the ground to sleep. Vanny and I slept next to each other, like lovely siblings. Several other girls also slept on the same *kontael* with us. We cramped together like fish in a pothole.

After I had lived with *Kang-Komarey* for a few days, Angkar established a literature program to teach the girls how to read and write. There weren't proper school facilities, buildings, or classrooms. We studied under shade trees. There were several shade trees around the area. However, not all girls had the opportunity to study. There weren't enough teachers, blackboards, or shade trees to accommodate students.

The program had two levels: beginner and intermediate. Attending was all-volunteer. The Khmer Rouge taught one hour a day, right after lunchtime. Those people who were interested in learning walked to the shade tree where teachers set the blackboard. Individuals who weren't interested in learning took a nap under improvised shade in the field to renew their energy for work.

I was excited to learn. I walked to a shade tree designated for beginners. I sat on the ground with more than fifteen other girls, facing the blackboard and the teacher. The teacher was a young female Khmer Rouge in her early twenties. I didn't know her name. She had a dark complexion, round face, flat nose, and short straight hair hanging to her shoulders. She wore a completely black uniform: black blouse, black sarong, and black rubber sandals. She stood next to the blackboard with a rattan stick in one hand and white chalk in the other.

"Today we are going to learn how to write and identify Khmer vowels," she said. "Does anybody here know how many vowels are in the Khmer Language?"

She stood by the blackboard with her head turned to look at us. We students were silent and shy. Nobody raised a hand to answer her question.

"There are twenty-three vowels," she said, "and each vowel has a different sound. Today, we are going to learn all twenty-three of them."

She turned around facing the blackboard and wrote all the vowels from left to right. After she finished writing, she used the stick to point at each vowel and pronounced the sounds aloud. All of us repeated after her.

After reciting and repeating the written vowels, she erased the blackboard completely with a piece of cloth. Then she tested us by asking one person at a time to come up to the blackboard to write letters or vowels she would dictate.

"Comrade Marin! Come up to the blackboard."

I got up with a smile and walked past several people who sat in front of me. I stood next to the teacher with pride and enthusiasm in learning.

The teacher handed me a white chalk and said, "Write srak e, srak ei, srak ae."

I did and she said, "Excellent! Go back to your seat."

I had a good memory. I could write most of the vowels she dictated. Besides, Cambodian vowels seemed pretty easy to learn. One portion of the vowels looked like leaves. Another looked like small circles. Other portions looked like hooks. The rest looked like tree branches to form a different sound.

The tree's shadow moved slowly to the other side of sun. The one hour lesson was over. The whistle was blown signaling that it was time to go to work. Students got up and dusted their buttocks to remove the dirt, then walked to stand up in line before the *mittbong*.

There were about twenty female mittbongs in the *Kang-Komarey* center. Their responsibilities were to manage and control the girls from running away from the camp.

A *mittbong* walked alongside the rank-and-file and ordered everyone to line up at an arm length's distance from each other. The girls lined up as they were told to do. They stood behind each other, with their right hands touching the shoulder of the person in front them. One of the *mittbongs* walked to the pile of working tools and said, "Put your hand down!"

Everyone did exactly as told.

"Behind me there are *job-kap* and *bonkee*," said another *mittbong*. "These are the special tools you need for your work. You can choose whichever tool you want. You can pick *job-kap* to dig soil. Or you can use the *bonkee* to carry dirt."

The Khmer Rouge moved the girls one row at time and ordered them to pick the work tools of their choice.

Vanny picked up a *bonkee*, a woven rattan basket that was used to carry dirt. Some girls picked the *job-kab*, a square blade agricultural hoe. Then they all followed the Khmer Rouge into the field to build rice levees and a small canal.

While Vanny and her group were gone to work, I roamed the field with a stick to hunt for grasshoppers and crickets to eat. Sometimes, I picked hardened dirt to throw at dragonflies hovering in the surrounding area. Other times, I just chased after butterflies for fun. Or I wandered around in the open field, searching for wild fruit as a snack.

Attending school under a tree

Fighting a Khmer Rouge Official's Son

After I had lived with Vanny for three days, the Angkar held a huge conference at the camp. The Khmer Rouge workers built a temporary stage and set up microphones. This event drew a large crowd of people from different parts of the province. The majority of them were older males and females. Some groups were in their early twenties. Other groups were in their mid-thirties. They marched in long lines coming from all directions—east, west, north, and south. The Khmer Rouge ordered the people to sit single file and face the stage. They sat an arm's length distance away under the scorching sun. We waited for the Khmer Rouge's top official to arrive.

The sun continued to rise. People continued to come and sit in the field. I didn't have anything to do, so I walked and observed Khmer Rouge soldiers set several megaphone posts in the field. They set the megaphone high on wooden posts pointing toward the crowds who were spread along a meadow that was the size of three soccer fields.

While everyone was getting seated, Mittbong-Sareth escorted a boy to play with me. He was the son of the top Khmer Rouge official who would give a speech to the crowd. I didn't know his name. He wore a new black uniform. He had a red, white, and black checkered-pattern scarf wrapped around his neck, and black sandals. We were about the same age, the same height, and the same complexion. But he looked bigger than me.

His father stood on the stage and preached to the crowd. He said many things, but I couldn't understand a word. All I heard was the crowd clapping hands and raising their fists up, saying, "*Jaiy-yo! Jaiy-Yo! Jaiy-Yo!*" (Bravo! Bravo! Bravo!)

I didn't care about what his father was preaching. I was too busy playing a game with my new friend. We were hopping from one designated line to another, trying to prove who was the best. We played and laughed together like good friends.

While we were having fun, Vanny's leader approached us and

said, "You two get along very well. Marin, Angkar might take you to live with him. You can be his companion. You will be very lucky if he takes you with him."

I ignored what she said because I was busy talking and playing with the official's son. The boy and I walked away from the crowd to play under the shade tree where my class was.

"Let's throw dirt to hit the object," I said and walked to set a small piece of wood on the ground.

The rule of the game was that the winner would slap the loser's hand five times. After we played a few games, we had an argument and got into a fight. He pushed me, and I fell to the ground. Quickly, I got up and punched him in the face. My fist landed in his eye. He fell down to the ground, cried, and covered his face. He cried and shouted for help, but no one could hear him because the loud speech on the megaphones muffled his crying.

"I will tell my father to beat you up," he cried and ran toward the stage for his father.

At that moment, my instincts told me to run for my life by hiding in the bushes. My heartbeat was racing against my running feet. I ran fast and fell several times, but being frightened of being killed by the Khmer Rouge made my body reject the pain. I got up and ran again as fast as I possibly could. My adrenaline forced me to run fast from the bushes and hide along the rice-field levees. I crept and crawled behind the levees to make sure nobody could see me. My eyes scanned the field near and far to see if any Khmer Rouge soldier was coming to catch me. I ran as far away as possible so I wouldn't get caught.

While I was running, I looked in every direction trying to find a safe place to hide. But the only place was the forest a far distance away. Although I didn't see anyone chasing me, I continued to run into the forest to hide. My fear of being killed made me forget being tired.

Once I got into the forest, I could barely catch my breath. My body forced the air in and out through the mouth. My face was as hot as if it was caught in a fire. My throat was dried and ached. The temples in my head began beating in pain. My eyes started to blur and I had to lie down.

After catching my breath and the sweat dried on my body, I began to venture out into the woods. Not long after, I heard people talking and shouting. I followed the sound with caution and walked slowly, hiding behind bushes and trees.

I saw five Khmer Rouge soldiers, in their late thirties, fishing in a pond. They were working together doing *bach-trey*, a fishing technique that involves draining water out of the pond with buckets. Near the pond, there was a fire pit under a shade tree, which sent a small amount of white smoke into the air.

I sat silently in the forest, observing their activities. After they emptied the water in the pond, they walked knee deep into the mud to catch fish with their bare hands. Others used sticks to kill the fish, as I had. They caught several baskets of fish, placed them on an ox-cart, and drove off.

Staying in the Forest

After the Khmer Rouge fishermen left, I rushed into the pond to drink the murky water. My throat was aching and I needed to soothe it. I scooped the water with my palms and drank. Then I walked out of the pond to the fire pit, hoping to find scraps of food left over. But there were none, except fish bones buried in the ashes.

While I was standing near the fire pit, I heard the sound of brief movements in the muddy pond. My eyes scanned the pond like a crane, hoping to see something moving. Not long after, I saw a fish moving in the mud. I picked up a stick and walked into the pond to kill it. It was a snakehead fish about the size of my calf. The fish had done a great job of hiding from the Khmer Rouge fishermen, but it couldn't hide from me.

I didn't wrap the fish with lotus leaves or cover it with mud like my dad had. I simply put the fish straight onto the hot fire pit, and tossed and turned it until it was cooked. I took the fish out of the fire pit, brushed off the ashes, and ate it. I ate everything: the eyes, cheeks, tongue, gills, and guts. I tried to chew the bones, too, but my jaw didn't have enough strength to crush them.

That night, I slept on the ground by the fire pit. It was very scary being alone in the forest. I was afraid of the dark, loneliness, and night creatures, like wolves and tigers. My fears gave me flashbacks. I thought about the time I had gotten caught for stealing rice from the warehouse. I thought of how that Khmer Rouge soldier had attempted to drown me. I thought of how my whole family had almost gotten killed for eating the injured bird.

Trepidation led me to think of all sorts of questions. What would the Khmer Rouge do to me if I were to get caught? Would the Khmer Rouge tie my hands to my back? Would they tie me up against the tree and have the fire ants kill me? Or would they choke me to death like they tried to do before? What would my punishment be for punching a top Khmer Rouge official's son?

I looked at the sparkling bright stars and believed that angels and gods lived there. I believed that gods looked at me from above.

"Tevada," I said softly to the stars, "please help save my life and take me to live with you in Heaven. Tevada, would you please deliver a message to my dad that I am waiting for him in the forest. Please give him a direction so that he can come to get me."

Despite all my fears of being caught and of being alone in the darkness, I was exhausted from crawling and running. It didn't take me long to fall asleep. I slept like a log, unaware of my surroundings.

When I woke up, it was morning. The loud noise of birds calling and shouting in the forest woke me up. I continued to lie down by the fire pit and I scanned the fuzzy dark sky and my surroundings. I saw tree branches above my head as if they had protected me from the midnight dew. I turned my head to the left and to the right, hoping to see Pa sitting next to me, but I didn't see him. My disappointment with the gods and Tevada began. "Gods and Tevada," I said while staring at the sky, "I prayed to you last night to help bring my dad to me. Why didn't you bring him here? Why didn't you listen to me?"

Not long after, the fuzzy dark morning began to turn blue. When the sun rose above the treetops, I got up and dusted the dirt off my head, my face, and my body. Then I sat by the fire pit. I used a stick to remove ashes from the burning wood just to occupy myself from being bored. The sun continued to rise and the array of sunlight shone through the forest floor. I got up and walked away from the fire pit to explore the forest and find something to eat.

After walking about one hundred meters, I saw a small thorny bush twice as tall as me. It was full of ripe fruit that was round and the size of my index finger. The dark-red ripe fruit clung onto small thorny branches. I picked the fruit and tossed it into my mouth, one at a time. The ripe ones tasted sweet as candy. The pink-red ones tasted sweet and sour. I knew the fruit was edible because I used to eat it with my parents.

While I was picking the fruit, I saw a green snake in a position to bite me. Its head was coiled back against its body. It camouflaged well with the greenish bush. I wouldn't have seen it if it hadn't stuck out its tongue. Its big head, big wide jaw, and small neck led me to believe that the snake was deadly. Its body was about the size of my forearm. Its neck was smaller than its body and its head.

The moment I saw the snake, I pulled my hand back fast to my chest. My heart was pounding. Goose bumps appeared on my arms, as big as rice grains. I took a few steps backward slowly, then turned and ran for my life. While I was running away from the snake, a thought popped into my head. I had to kill that snake for food.

I picked a stick the size of my forearm, about a meter long, then I ran back and approached the snake cautiously. Despite my nervousness and fear of being bitten, I held the stick up over my head to beat it furiously. The snake fought back, trying to bite the stick, but missed. I beat the snake many times, but it crawled into the bush. I walked vigilantly, circling the bush a few times, looking for the snake, but I couldn't find it. I was disappointed with myself for being unable to kill the snake for lunch.

Although I failed to kill the snake, my hope of finding other food sources was high. With the stick in my hand, I walked from bush to bush and tree to tree, searching for edible fruit and creatures.

My venture got me out of the forest and into a tall grassy field. As I roamed in the field, I saw a muddy pond with several dead fish in it that were swamped with hundreds of fast and furious poisonous black ants. The black ants would bite anything that came across them. Despite their reputation for viciousness, I did not hesitate to rob a fish from them. I used a small stick, arm length, to move the fish from one place to another to get rid of the ants.

The ants were frantic and mad. They crawled and searched for their food in all directions. Quickly, I grabbed the fish, ran back to the fire pit, and tossed it into the fire. I twisted and turned the fish until it was cooked.

After having the fish for lunch, I was bored and restless. I scanned the horizon and walked away from the forest in the direction of the sunrise. After a long walk out of the forest, I saw a canal stretching across the grassy plane. I approached the canal and walked alongside it.

Many people at a distance were walking on the berm along the canal in my direction. From the distance, I couldn't differentiate between regular people and the Khmer Rouge soldiers. I thought the Khmer Rouge soldiers were looking to capture me, and my fear ignited. My heart jolted. My body was jittery. I scanned for thick bushes and tall grasses to hide. Without any delay, I ran more than one hundred meters away from the canal and hid in the bushes. Peeking through the tall grasses, I watched the people who were walking along the canal.

As they approached closer, I noticed it was Vanny's group. I was thrilled, but apprehensive. I was afraid the *mittbong* would hurt or kill me for hurting the top official's son.

After many girls walked past me, I saw Vanny walking with her small group of ten. I got out of the bushes and approached her. She was surprised to see me.

"Where have you been?" she asked with high anxiety, her hands on my shoulders. "I was very concerned about you! I missed you and looked for you!"

I was afraid to tell her about the situation, but she insisted. After her group walked past us, I whispered, "Yesterday afternoon, during the big conference, I had a fight with the top Khmer Rouge official's son. I punched him in the eye. He ran and cried to his father for help. He went to tell his father to hurt me. I was scared that his father would kill me. That's the reason I ran for my life and hid in the forest."

Vanny was shocked about what I did to the Khmer Rouge top official's son. She tried to soothe me and told me not to be afraid. While we walked, she pressed my head against hers and said, "All the top Khmer Rouge officials already left after the conference. It should be okay, now, because no one talked about it. But we must keep this silent to ourselves. And don't tell anyone what you did to the Khmer Rouge's son."

Even though Vanny said it was okay, I was still paranoid. I said to myself, *If I see any Khmer Rouge looking at me in a strange way, I will run for my life again. I will never let them catch me. I will keep my eyes and ears alert all the time to see if anyone is talking about me.*

When we arrived at the camp and Mittbong-Sareth saw me, my heart was hammering. But I pretended like nothing had happened. At the same time, I was prepared to run for my life.

She said, "How dare you, young comrade! You dare to fight with the official's son! You are lucky no one could find you that day. If someone were to find you, I don't know what they would do to you."

Once I heard that, I cautiously tried to distance myself from her to ensure that she couldn't come to catch me. I looked in her eyes. Then

I looked to my left and my right in attempt to run away again. But I was lucky. Mittbong-Sareth didn't want to capture or hurt me. She only gazed at me for a few seconds, then she walked away.

Separated Again

After the conference, Angkar had changed the leadership teams and the management style. They had shuffled people like a deck of cards and moved people to different work sites.

Angkar Luer ordered Mittbong-Sareth to lead other groups, so Vanny had new group leaders and they wouldn't allow me to stay with her group.

In the morning, I saw my sister line up with her group and march toward the direction of the sunset. I cried and ran after her. She stopped and ran to soothe me. She put her hands on my shoulders and said, "Don't cry, my brother. Everything will be alright. Don't follow me. You have to stay with your group. We have to do what Angkar tells us. Now, go back to your group. You will be alright."

While Vanny soothed me, a *mittbong* shouted from the distance, "Ah, Comrade! Come back to your group!"

Vanny turned her head to look at her new leader, then turned to me again with tears welling in her eyes.

"Come to your group right now, before I come to get you!" the Khmer Rouge shouted at her again.

With tears in her eyes, Vanny ran back to march in her group. I stood and watched her. She looked like she was feeling pain and helpless. My painful heart made me angry at those Khmer Rouge ladies for separating us. I wished my sister and I had the power to fight them. I thought if I were big as an adult, I'd punch her leader in the face, like I had the Khmer Rouge official's son. Eventually, I walked back to my group in tears, missing my sister and wondering if I'd see her again.

5

Living with the Kang-Jalat Group

A child my age would normally live with his parents. My case was different. I had lost my parents. I hadn't seen Pa since the Khmer Rouge soldiers invited him to work on the great water-canal project, and I didn't know if I had aunts or uncles.

Angkar did not have an appropriate group or institution to place me in, or at least they didn't have one in the area. So, Angkar had me live with the *Kang-Jalat*, a mobile group of young adults ages fifteen to twenty-five. There were thousands of people living in the *Kang-Jalat*, and the group was frequently moved from one place to another, pursuing work projects that Angkar assigned.

The Khmer Rouge ordered the group to move out of camp and march toward the forest where I had once slept. I grabbed a *bonkee* and carried it over my head to protect me from the heat. I walked barefoot in the scorching sun and followed the oxcarts that carried food supplies, water, and cooking utensils.

While I was walking, I became jealous of the Khmer Rouge because they rode on the oxcart and I had to follow the oxcart trail, not knowing when or where to stop for a break. I wished they would ask me to ride with them. Unfortunately, it didn't happen.

I walked past the forest where I'd attempted to kill the snake, and the field where I'd robbed the fish from the black ants. Long after the forest was completely out of sight, I heard a shouting voice through the megaphone, "Let's stop here! This is the site where Angkar Luer ordered us to build a water canal!"

At that moment, everyone stopped moving. The oxcart wheels stopped rolling and turned silent, and people turned their heads toward the direction of the sound of someone shouting.

I squeezed myself through the silent crowd to see who was talking. A man with a light-yellow complexion was standing on a termite mound, holding a megaphone in front of his face. I didn't know his name. He was as tall as my Pa. The man looked Chinese. He had slanted eyes and thick eyebrows. He stood side by side with several other Khmer Rouge soldiers under a huge shade tree. While he was talking, he walked with his knees turned outward, like a duck.

He walked from the termite mountain down to the field, where he ordered people to sit down in the field for a short conference. The man said many things, but I couldn't understand because he used a large vocabulary. All I heard and understood was, "We have arrived at our destination. We will build a water canal to direct the flow of water into the rice field. We will erect the canal to be as straight as a ruler." The rest of his speech, I didn't pay attention.

After the conference, the man ordered the people to get situated on this vast open field. The field consisted of wild grasses, small bushes, and trees. That afternoon, people began to clear grasses and bushes to camp at the site. Some people made small shelter from grass and sticks to protect themselves from the daily heat and midnight dew. I didn't make anything. I stood near an oxcart and watched the people clearing the land and making shelter.

Before sunset, the Khmer Rouge organized the people into groups of twelve and had them stand in a single-file line. Once the groups were formed, the project chief ordered the people to appoint a group leader within the group to represent them. While the people were picking their group representatives, the soldiers stood in the field, chatting among themselves, with their eyes on the people.

The project chief then shouted, "All group representatives who were appointed by your members must step forward!" The group leaders stepped forward and stood before their people as the chief ordered.

"These are your leaders!" the project chief declared loudly. "They are responsible for your group! If the group does not finish the job on time, they are held responsible! If a person is missing in your group, they are held responsible! You must work in a group and you must eat in a group!"

Now that the groups were formed and the leaders selected, the Khmer Rouge ordered them to clear bushes and cut down trees that would potentially block the canal project. While the people moved in a single-file line to work, the soldiers moved out into the fields and away from the people, and patrolled the fields to prevent and capture anyone escaping.

Receiving Special Treatment

During the first several days of the canal project, the Khmer Rouge were nice to me. I didn't know why. I thought to myself maybe they felt I was a lost and confused orphan. Perhaps they seemed to give me preferential treatment because I was the youngest and the smallest in the group.

The Khmer Rouge didn't order me to go to work. Even the Khmer Rouge cooking crews were nice to me. During meal time, they told me to eat alone near the kitchen, and they gave me a bigger ration of food than the rest of the people: a full plate of cooked rice and a bowl of soup.

So, I had lots of free time. As usual, I roamed the field to catch grasshoppers and crickets to eat. Sometimes, I chased after dragon-flies just for fun. But I couldn't catch them. They were too quick and too fast for me.

Sometimes, out of boredom, I would pick hardened dirt and throw it onto a field as far I could. Sometimes, I threw dirt to hit objects, testing to see how many times I could hit the object. Sometimes, I'd sneak up behind dragonflies, throwing the hardened dirt at them. Most of the time, I missed because they were too fast.

My First Time Working

About ten days into the canal project, the Khmer Rouge set stricter rules and forced everyone to work harder and longer, myself includ-ed. The Khmer Rouge no longer gave me preferential treatment. My free time playing as a child was over.

One afternoon, while I was chasing a dragonfly in the field, a soldier approached me and shouted, "Young comrade! What are you doing in the field?"

"I'm catching a dragonfly for fun," I responded.

"You need to build the water canal, like everyone else," the sol-dier said. He stared at me as if he wanted to hurt me.

Without saying a word back to him, I dropped the hardened dirt from my hands and ran to the work site where the soldier pointed.

When I got to my work site, the project chief measured a plot of land, one meter in width and five meters in length. "Young comrade, this is your plot of land. You need to dig three meters deep into the ground and carry dirt from here to the designated site," said the proj-ect chief.

One of his assistants who stood near him gave me a *job-kab*, an agricultural hoe to dig the soil. Then he also handed me a *bonkee*. "You need this to carry the dirt and pour it at the designated place."

I grabbed the hoe from the man's hand and raised it over my head to cut small chunks of the hardened soil. I scooped the soil to put it into the *bonkee* to carry to the designated site.

After I dumped the soil out of the *bonkee,* other people came to compress the soil. For the first hour of working, I felt brave and swollen with pride. This was my first time working. I was very proud of myself for contributing to the canal project. My job was fun.

However, hours later, after having worked under the scorching sun, I began to hate my job and the Khmer Rouge. I didn't feel as gratified or as brave. That day, the Khmer Rouge ordered the rest of the people and me to work without break until sunset. My body became weak. I often fell down on my knees. My hands were beginning to blister. My shoulders hurt, my heels were numb, and my back was stiff and aching.

The entire half day of work, I didn't finish my assigned tasks. I could barely dig one meter deep and two meters wide. Several men who had completed their tasks came to help me.

One man said, "This is ridiculous! I can't believe they ordered a child this young to build a water canal."

Kor-saang

As the days passed, the Khmer Rouge continued to force us to work competitively against other labor groups. The project chief walked from one group to another, and blew his whistle synchronized and in repetition to force us to work faster.

Sometimes, the project chief ordered us to sing revolutionary songs to energize us. But there was no break time. If anyone needed to use the restroom, they had to ask permission from the leader. If they took too long, Angkar would *kor-saang,* a form of punishment through a verbal warning, or even death.

Due to the newer stricter policies, I also was no longer eating separately. The Khmer Rouge integrated me into the group. They ordered me to eat with the people in my group. Some people in my group seemed to feel sympathetic for me; they shared a small portion of their own food with me. A man in my group scooped a small chunk of fish from his soup bowl and put it in my plate.

"Here is my food. Just eat it," he said.

Another man scooped a full spoon of his soup and put in my plate, but he didn't say a word. Although I endured harsh treatment from the Khmer Rouge, I felt a sense of loving and caring from my group.

During meal time, the people didn't talk to each other. Maybe they were exhausted and didn't know what to talk about. Maybe they were disgusted and speechless about the system they were trapped in, which made them *kor-saang* each other.

At night, right after we had our meal, the Khmer Rouge ordered each group to have a meeting. I rushed to sit with my group, who formed a small circle. I listened to them *kor-saang* each other. In the meeting, the assigned group leader reported, "I know you heard about people running away from the group last night. Those who run away I consider *kmang*, the enemies of Angkar. They won't escape from Angkar, because Angkar has many eyes, like a pineapple. Angkar will catch them and *kor-saang* them."

After everyone got the general news, the group leader opened the floor for everyone to critique each other or report on each other. In the meeting, everyone addressed each other as Mitt, meaning comrade.

"I would like to *kor-saang* Mitt—for going to the restroom too long. I don't want you to repeat this action," said one young man.

"Thank you for seeing my mistake," the reprimanded man countered. "I will not repeat this action again. I would like to *kor-saang* you back for talking and complaining about work during work hours."

"Thank you for correcting my mistake. I will not talk or complain during work time."

"I would like to *kor-saang* Mitt," another man said, "for scooping more than one spoon of soup during lunch this afternoon."

"Thank you for your critique. I will not repeat this action again," said the man.

During the meeting, the group leader concluded, "If you are *kor-sanged* many times by many people I will report you to Angkar Luer. I don't want to do this. But if you don't change your behavior or your actions and people continue to *kor-saang* you, I have to report to Angkar Luer. I have no other choice. That is Angkar's order," said the group leader.

I had never heard people *kor-saang* me. And I had never *kor-sanged* anyone. All I wanted was to finish this stupid meeting and stop *kor-saanging* each other so I could go to sleep.

Once the meetings adjourned, people rushed to find a place in the field to sleep. I slept on the *kontael* with a few older women near the communal kitchen. Some people slept directly on the ground. Others used a *kroma* as a blanket or folded it and used it as a pillow. Others used the *kroma* as a floor mat to sleep on.

One night, I was extremely tired from work. I lay down like a cow on the ground, attempting to sleep. The project chief assistant saw me and approached me with a stick in his hand. "Young comrade, get up. Go sleep over there under the oxcart." He pointed to the oxcart that was parked near the communal kitchen. I got up to a sitting position and looked at the oxcart. It was made entirely of wood. On the underbelly of the oxcart, I saw a small pile of dried rice straws that were used to feed the cow. I got up and didn't say a word. I walked to the oxcart and crawled under it. I was happy to sleep under the oxcart. It felt like a home. The two oxcart wheels served as a protective wall. The underbelly of the oxcart served as a roof to protect me from the midnight dew. And I used those dried rice straws as my bed cushion.

From that night on, I continued to sleep under the oxcart. Every night before I fell asleep, I gazed at the bright stars through the wheel and asked Tevada and Mak's spirit to protect me. Some nights I prayed to Tevada for help. *Tevada, if I were to be in* Kong-Jalat *for a long time, I wouldn't want to grow up to be an adult. I want to remain young and small as I am today. Being the smallest and the youngest may bring empathy from the Khmer Rouge. Moreover, if I were to make a mistake, I would receive less punishment from the Khmer Rouge.*

Every day before sunrise, the Khmer Rouge blew a whistle to wake the people up to get ready for work. Each morning, the Khmer Rouge distributed two canteens of water for drinking and washing. The canteen was the size of a man's thigh.

The men and women used their water conservatively. They washed their faces by pouring a small amount of water into their palms and applying it to their faces. Then they pressed their hands against their cheeks side to side, then up and down, to make themselves fully alert. Others wet their *kroma* and applied it to their faces. There were no toothbrushes or toothpaste. Some people used small pieces of charcoal from the fire pit in the communal kitchen to rub against their teeth; many used ashes or sand, applied it on their fingers, and rubbed their teeth side to side.

I never brushed my teeth. I only rinsed my mouth with water and washed my face. Most of the time, I didn't even want to get up. But I was afraid that if I didn't get up and line up with my group, the Khmer Rouge would punish me.

While I was busy washing my face and getting ready for work, the whistle blows became shorter and more frequent. Whenever this happened, everyone abruptly stopped what they were doing and rushed to line up single-file, one arm's length behind each other, in their groups. Then they marched in two long lines along the unfinished water canal to continue working where they had left off.

I was always late to line up because I hated the job and everything the Khmer Rouge ordered me to do. The Khmer Rouge did not *kor-saang* me for being late.

The First Holiday

About two months of the canal project had passed and it was about to be completed. Thousands of people were still digging in the soil, building the two berms on either side of the one long canal.

The canal project was still about one kilometer from being finished when the holiday arrived. I didn't know what the holiday was. The Khmer Rouge cooked a lot of food and allowed workers to take a few days off, with permission to visit their loved ones.

I didn't really care what holiday it was. All I knew was it liberated me from the hard labor and gave me the chance to eat enough. The communal chefs cooked *khor-trey,* a sweetened fish soup, and a dessert made from green-bean seeds and sticky rice. It was served "all you can eat" style. There was no restriction on how much anyone could eat. I didn't care much about the dessert. All I ate was my favorite *khor-trey* and rice. Not knowing when I would be able to eat again, I devoured as much food as I could. After I finished eating, I could barely walk. My stomach was so full that it felt like it was about to explode.

During that holiday, I missed Pa, Mak, Roth, and Vanny. I wanted to visit Vanny, but I had no clue where she lived. If I knew where she was, I would have requested permission to visit her.

However, I noticed that this holiday was eerily quiet. I didn't see people celebrating, and there was no music. There were no people singing or dancing. The people sat under the shade of the trees and spoke quietly with each other. Women took turns combing and cutting each other's hair. Others took turns picking lice off their heads, and crushed them with their fingernails.

Some men rested in the shade alone. Other men sat facing each other, playing the game called raik, a Cambodian checkers. Although they told me what the game was, I had no idea how it was to be played. They didn't have a checkerboard, so they drew many squares in the dirt to imitate a checkerboard. One player used small sticks, shorter than my finger, for his moving pieces. Another player used small pieces of hardened dirt to differentiate from his opponent.

I was captivated with the way they played the game. So, I sat next to them and watched them take turns moving their pieces.

"Pu, how do you play the game?" I asked. In Cambodian culture, calling someone *Pu* means uncle. Anyone ten years older than you is considered *Pu* as a form of respecting age status.

They turned their heads and looked at me. "I don't know how to explain it to you," said one man. "All I can tell you is that it is difficult for you to play." Then they turned their heads back, with their eyes focused on their moving pieces.

"Can I play too, Pu?"

"You are too young to play this game. You just sit and watch us play," said the man.

I watched them play, disappointed. *Why won't they teach me how to play the game?* I thought. *If they taught me, then I could play it. I don't think that game is difficult.*

After I watched them for a long while, without understanding the complexities and subtleties of the game, I began to get bored. I walked away and tried to catch dragonflies for fun.

My Separation from Kang-Jalat

Once the holiday passed, the Khmer Rouge forced the people to get back to work and finish the last portion of the canal. Thousands of workers dug and mounted dirt. As time passed, the water rations were reduced to one canteen per person.

Suddenly, the first monsoon rain began pouring from the sky, washing the sweat and dirt off the people's bodies. The rain slipped through the hard soil and made it easier for people to dig and scoop the soil into their *bonkees*. The wet soil made the job easier and faster, so we could finally finish the canal project.

Angkar Luer relentlessly pursued the canal project to direct the flow of water into the rice fields. When one canal was finished, they moved people to another location to build more canals. The projects were endless.

Once this water canal was finished, the Khmer Rouge separated me from the rest of the people and sent me to live in Toul Somphy Village. I had no idea where the village was or how far it was from the camp where I had been living.

Not long after lunch, the project chief ordered his lower-ranked comrade to prepare an oxcart to take me to the village. The well-built, twenty-year-old comrade got two big cows and set them in the yoke. He got on the oxcart and said, "Young comrade, get on the oxcart."

Without any delay, I ran to the oxcart and got onto it. I was excited that I had the opportunity to ride on an oxcart for the first time. I sat behind the oxcart driver. He jerked the leash around the cow's head and whipped the cow's rear end, forcing the animal to move.

I felt great on the oxcart. I enjoyed the bumpy ride and the sound of the oxcart wheels squeaking.

On the way to the village, the driver frequently forced the cow to run, making the oxcart bounce on every object on the path.

The man was quiet. If I didn't talk to him, he wouldn't talk to me. Out of curiosity, I decided to speak to him by calling him Pu.

"Pu, how long does it take to get to the village?" I asked.

He didn't answer me right away. It seemed like he was thinking hard. Minutes later he said, "The way I drive, it doesn't take long. You will get there before sunset."

After he drove along this long stretch of grassy and bushy landscape, we finally arrived at the village. But the man didn't take me directly to the communal center. Instead, he took me to a pond. It was about half the size of a soccer field and was surrounded by cashew nut trees and *kro-sunk*, a type of thorny tree with hard and round green fruit. He stopped the oxcart and got off.

"What is this place called, Pu?" I asked.

He ignored my question. "Get off the oxcart and walk behind me," he said.

I had no idea what he was doing, but I obeyed his orders. I jumped off the oxcart and walked behind him, approaching the pond.

Then I spotted a shirtless soldier standing under a shade tree. He was scanning the field. When I got to the pond, I saw three other soldiers holding their rifles below the waist, with the gun barrels pointed down. The three soldiers appeared to be in their mid-twenties. When I saw them, my heart began pounding and my body started to shake. I was scared they were going to kill me. But I continued to walk behind the oxcart driver and I tried to show no signs of fear.

The oxcart driver approached the three soldiers and said, "Mittbong, Angkar Luer ordered me to bring this child to live in this village. I would like to ask your permission to speak with your superior."

The three soldiers probed the oxcart driver with a few questions. Then one of them walked us to a forty-year-old man who was sitting on a tall stool and getting his hair cut by an older soldier.

The oxcart driver approached the forty-year-old soldier and said, "Mittbong, Angkar Luer ordered me to bring this child to live in this village. He is truly the Angkar's son. He is a great worker. He works hard like an adult. The project chief is sending him here to live with the children's group."

After the oxcart driver formally introduced me and himself to the soldiers, my fears began to fade and my pounding heart began to relax. But I told myself not to trust these soldiers. My instincts told me that these were the soldiers who punished people. They were the ones who captured people to *kor-saang* or to kill. I hoped they didn't know I had hit the Khmer Rouge official's son in the face. And I hoped they wouldn't punish me.

A Strange Haircut

After the Khmer Rouge soldiers finished cutting their hair, another soldier with scissors ordered me to sit on the stool. At first, I felt paranoid. In my mind, I began to raise questions. Was he going to hurt or kill me with the scissors?

"Come here, young comrade! Come sit on the stool and let me cut your hair," the soldier said, waving his hand.

I crept toward the stool cautiously, my eyes focused on his body language, my fear mixed with assertiveness.

While I was on the stool, I turned my head to watch his hand movements. I was afraid he would kill me with the scissors.

"Young comrade! Stop moving your head and stay still." He positioned my head straight.

He ran the comb through my hair and began cutting it. At that point, I felt safe and I stopped moving my head from side to side.

I set my eyes on the pond. The water was half full and slightly milky, but I could see the reflection of the clouds moving across the sky. In the pond, there were water lilies and water plants floating. Every few minutes, water rippled from water creatures. It made me want to catch them for a snack.

While he was cutting my hair, he asked me many questions. "What kind of work did your dad do?"

"I don't know."

"Was your dad in the military?"

"I don't know."

"Do you have an aunt or uncle?"

"I don't know."

"Did you ever see your dad wear a military shirt?"

"I don't know."

"How old are you?"

"I don't know."

"Are you five years old? Six? Or seven years old?"

"I don't know."

"You are funny, little comrade. All you know how to say is, I don't know…. I don't know…. I don't know…... You don't know anything, ah?" he said with laughter.

While he was cutting my hair, all the Khmer Rouge soldiers were giggling and laughing and said to me, "You look great with this hair style."

I didn't know what my hairstyle looked like. They didn't let me see in the mirror. I ran my fingers over my head, and the right side felt shorter than the left. I ran my fingers again and grabbed my long bushy hair. "Why does one side of my head have longer hair than the other?" I asked.

One of the soldiers said, "Just keep it that way. It looks nice on you." Then everyone started to laugh. I thought it was funny, so I laughed with them.

While I ran my hand through my hair, I looked around the area. I didn't see the oxcart driver. He had left without saying goodbye to me.

"Bring him a set of clothes!" an older Khmer Rouge soldier shouted at his comrades who were chitchatting under another shade tree.

"Throw away your shorts and put new clothes on," said one Khmer Rouge to me.

I took off my shorts and put on the brand new black uniform.

"These clothes are too big for me," I said with a laugh. The pants couldn't hold onto my waist.

"Ah, these pants are too big for him," said another soldier. "Let's find a string to tie his pants."

One of the soldiers found a string and tied it around my waist to prevent my pants from falling down. Then he folded my long-sleeved shirt up to above my elbows. "You look handsome, young comrade. You looked like Angkar's son," he said with a laugh.

Minutes later, I saw a man who resembled Pa walking toward the pond. "The village chief is coming," he said and pointed to a man who was approaching.

The village chief looked slightly shorter than my Pa; however, his dark complexion and thin frame reminded me of my dad. The village chief approached the soldiers and talked to them briefly. Then he called me, "Young comrade! Come over here." He signaled me to walk toward him.

"Go with the village chief," said the Khmer Rouge soldier.

"Come back in the next couple of days," said the soldier who had cut my hair. "I will cut the other half of your hair, and I will give you another set of uniforms."

I walked behind the village chief along the narrow rice-field levees, without thinking of what lay ahead.

6

The Toul Somphy Village

When I arrived at the Toul Somphy communal center, I didn't see anyone. All I saw were three long huts. Two huts faced each other and another one faced the sunrise. These huts had no front wall. Inside each hut were bamboo platforms that served as beds. The platforms sat on bamboo posts, about one meter above the ground.

That evening, I saw many girls return back from work to the center. They walked single-file on the rice-field levees and from different directions. Most of the girls look tired and hungry. Their feet and arms were covered with dried dirt. This made them look white.

My eyes scanned the girls from the distance in hopes of finding my sister. Many girls walked past me, but I didn't see Vanny.

Then there was the last girl group walking from the west to the communal center. As they approached closer to the center, I saw a girl with a light-yellow complexion, wearing a *kroma* over her head. From the distance, her round face resembled my sister, but I wasn't sure.

I approached her and shouted, "Vanny! Is it you?!" At that moment, I could feel my face glow with excitement. My spirits were up. My heart was energized with joy. I felt like somebody had lifted me off the ground. I ran toward her. It was Vanny!

Vanny squeezed herself out of her group to hug me. "I missed you, Marin. How did you know that I'm here? And how did you get here?" she asked.

"The canal project chief sent me on an oxcart to this village. Then the village chief brought me here," I responded.

She removed her hands from my body and put one of her hands on my shoulder. Then we walked side by side, like best friends. She ran her other hand through my hair.

"What is wrong with your hair?" she asked.

"One of the soldiers cut my hair. He said this style looked good on me. Then he gave me a new set of clothes," I said, with hand gestures running over my hair. "The soldier told me to go back to him again in the next couple of days to cut the other side, and he will give me another pair of clothes."

My hairstyle not only caught Vanny's attention, it was also noticed by her peers. When everyone saw my crooked hairstyle, they smiled and laughed at me. I was flattered and laughed along with them. I felt like I was a funny and loveable boy.

Vanny walked me to the water well and scooped water to bathe herself and me. Then we rushed to the communal cafeteria for dinner. During dinner, the Khmer Rouge didn't give us enough food, but we both still felt happy seeing each other.

Evening turned into night, and Vanny took me to her hut to stay with her. There were approximately two hundred girls living in the communal center. No boys. I was the only one.

Vanny and her peers arranged a place for me to sleep. They unrolled the *kontael* and lay it on the bamboo platform to serve as the bed. Then they set up the mosquito net to prevent mosquito bites.

The Khmer Rouge assigned four girls to sleep on each platform. "Tonight, my brother and I will sleep in the middle of the bed. You three sleep on the edge of the bed," Vanny said.

Her intent was to prevent me from getting mosquito bites. There were millions of mosquitoes breeding here. Without the mosquito net, the girls who stayed in this village could be killed by the swarms of mosquitoes. I slept in the middle next to Vanny, and I could hear the mosquitoes' buzzing sound, like a swarm of bees.

The girls used all sorts of techniques to try and kill the mosquitoes and to prevent them from biting. They made a fire pit under the platform to produce a high volume of smoke to repel the mosquitoes. They used palm leaves as fans to chase them away. When all else failed, they tried to smack them with their palms. No matter how hard they tried to protect themselves, they still got bitten. While I was half asleep, Vanny's bedmates were tossing and turning. Then they were mumbling and complaining to my sister, and they got into an argument. Vanny and her bedmates quarreled with each other for wanting to sleep in the middle.

"Today I was supposed to sleep in the middle," said one of Vanny's bedmates, "but your brother took my place."

"I just met my brother today. I miss him. And I love him. I want him to be safe and sleep next to me," Vanny said.

"Why don't you sleep at my spot and let me sleep next to your brother," said her bedmate.

They argued back and forth over the same things, but Vanny refused to move me from sleeping in the middle. And she refused to take someone else's spot. I loved my sister. I thought she must be a fighter like me.

I slept on the bed next to my sister, sandwiched tightly. I felt guilty for hearing the girls argue over me. But, at the same time, I wanted to have a good night's sleep near my sister.

Night turned to morning and I had a good night's sleep. I woke up and got off the sleeping platform. Vanny held my hand and walked me to the water well near the communal cafeteria. On the way there, I heard many girls complaining about mosquito bites. They scratched their arms and feet with madness. One of the girls grouched and mumbled to Vanny, "Look! Look at my arms! I have a lot of skin bumps from the mosquito bites!"

Vanny and I briefly looked at the girl's arms, then walked to the water well to wash our faces. The water-well area was crowded with girls waiting their turns to scoop water to wash their faces.

Vanny let go of my hand and said, "Marin, go to that wooden post over there. Just wait for me over there. Let me fetch some water to wash our faces."

I did exactly as I was told. The minutes I stood near the wooden post, a swarm of tiny flying insects hovered over my head. I felt annoyed and frustrated by the buzzing insects. I used my hands to fan over my head to get rid of them, but they kept coming. I slapped over my head, hoping to kill them, but they dodged me every time.

Minutes later, Vanny returned with a half-full bucket of water. I noticed a swarm of flying insects also hovering over her head. It appeared like they were searching for an opening spot in her hair to suck her blood.

"How do I kill these stupid insects over my head," I asked.

"That stupid insect is called *mo-mung*. Everyone hates them, but nobody knows how to get rid of them," Vanny said.

The insects followed me everywhere. They followed me to wash my face. They followed me to work. They followed me to the restroom. When they bit, it sent a strong itchy signal to my nerves, which made me want to pull my head off. Even when people wore a *kroma* to cover their heads, they still got bit. The only way to get the insects to disappear was to wait for the hot sunlight to clear the morning cool moisture.

When the sun rose past a distant tree top, several *mittbongs,* their ages ranging from fifteen to eighteen, walked near the water well. A few of them had sticks. One of them shouted, "It is time to work! Hurry up with what you are doing and line up!"

At that moment, my sister and her group rushed to line up in front of their *mittbong* for the body count. There were fifteen female mitt-bongs. Vanny stood in a file of twelve people. She put her right hand behind her peer's shoulder and spread out an arm's length away.

I was an extra person, but maybe they didn't care. I stood behind Vanny and put my hand on her shoulder. After the body count, their *mittbong* briefed them about their next work assignment and where they would be working.

They commanded us and led us row by row to march into the paddy rice field. One of the *mittbongs* stopped me and ordered me to *dork-somnab*, a job that required pulling paddy rice for replanting.

I hated them, but I had to obey their orders. If I didn't, they might punish me.

Separated Once Again

I stayed with Vanny for two nights. We barely had the chance to interact or socialize. When she came from work, she rushed to the communal cafeteria for dinner. After dinner, she took her turn wash-ing herself and went to bed. We met only at bed, talking about Pa and Mak. We really missed our parents.

The next morning, our *mittbong* approached me and said, "You are not going to work today. You stay here and wait for Angkar Luer."

"Who is the Angkar Luer?" I asked.

The *mittbong* didn't respond. She ignored my question and walked away from me.

I waited around the communal cafeteria and looked over the greenish rice paddy. From where I was, I could see the pond where the soldier had cut my hair. I thought, *Maybe Mittbong wants me to wait for the soldier who cut my hair so I can get another uniform?*

Not long after everyone went to work, I saw the village chief speaking to the communal chef who was washing pots and pans at the water well. He was about fifty meters away and I didn't pay atten-tion to what they were talking about.

After a brief conversation with the communal chef, the village chief shouted to me and waved his hand, signaling me to approach him. "Young comrade! Come over here!" I approached him, and he said, "Come with me."

"Where are you taking me?" I asked.

"I am taking you to work at a different place, in Baeng Pong Village."

"Could you wait?! Let me tell my sister first," I told him and I ran to look for my sister.

"Young comrade! Come back! Don't go!" he shouted and waved his hand to come toward him. "Someone else will tell her!"

"But!... I... I want to tell her myself."

"Don't go! Just come with me!" he shouted.

I walked toward him in disappointment, tears building up in my eyes. I was upset, but I didn't say a word. I followed him but avoided getting close to him, because I was afraid he might grab me and hurt me.

Guarding a Cucumber Farm

I walked past many green paddy rice fields into the forest and approached the oxcart road to Baeng Pong Village. Once I got out of the forest, there was a huge cucumber farm in the middle of nowhere. The farm could fit as many as ten soccer fields.

The village chief introduced me to Rith, a dark-complexioned midget boy. He stood under a shade tree and watched over the cucumber farm. He was slightly taller than me. Rith was thirteen years old. He had short wavy hair, no front teeth, and a flat nose.

"You work with Mitt-Rith. You two watch over the farm. Make sure there is no animal destroying the farm. And make sure no one is stealing the cucumbers."

"Yes," we answered at the same time.

The village chief left us at the site to monitor the farm. Then he began his walk along the oxcart road to the communal center.

Rith held a slingshot in his hand as if he was ready to shoot any creatures that entered the farm. The slingshot was made from small tree branches that had a web like a letter "Y". I thought Rith was smart. He used black, flat elastic rubber straps from Khmer Rouge sandals as the slingshot string.

Rith talked to me as if he was the Khmer Rouge. He addressed me with the word *Mitt*, which means comrade. So he asked me to call him *Mittbong-Rith,* meaning *older comrade Rith.*

"Mitt-Marin, let's walk inside the farm," he said as he led me into the young cucumber farm.

When I entered the farm, I noticed the cucumber plants were in their infant stage. Most of them had produced leaves, but they had barely developed vines, let alone flowers.

"Mitt-Marin, your responsibility is chasing after the birds. You must prevent them from landing in the farm," Rith said in a commanding tone, while raising his slingshot to shoot in the air as if he wanted to show off. "If you see the birds attempting to land in the farm, you must shout and throw dirt at them."

"Yes," I responded softly.

At lunchtime, Rith walked me to the communal cafeteria, where my hairstyle caught everyone's attention. Workers turned their heads, stared at my hair, and giggled among themselves.

The dynamic of the group in this village was different from Vanny's group. The group leaders weren't as rude. People could laugh and joke around with each other. Boys and girls could live in the same communal center, but they couldn't sleep in the same huts. There were more than one-hundred-twenty people living in centers; the majority of them were girls. Their ages ranged from what appeared to be fifteen to nineteen years old.

Rith and I were the smallest and youngest. We slept in the same hut. Usually in the morning, Rith woke me up. He forced me to wash my face and ordered me to go to work. We walked through an area where tall bamboo trees grew around the empty concrete space, the size of a soccer field, to the farm.

At the farm, Rith assigned me to pick hardened soil to make it into a round shape and to use as slingshot palettes to shoot the birds. Although he didn't see any creatures in the field, he shot the slingshot for fun.

"Marin, if you see a snake in the farm, just let me know. I will kill it with my slingshot. If you happen to see king cobra, just run and shout for help."

"What does a king cobra snake look like?" I asked.

"It looks like a regular snake, but before it bites, it raises its head up, enlarge its neck, then strikes. It is the deadliest snake. If it bites a person, that person would die instantly."

"Have you ever seen a king cobra snake before?" I asked.

"No, I have never seen one. I only heard people talk about it. If I see one, I will kill it with my slingshot," said Rith.

Rith and I guarded the cucumber farm for a long time, from the infant stage until they produced a long strand of vines and flowers. Some of them began to develop yellow flowers and bear young fruit. During that time, workers in the village made human puppets from rice straw and placed them in the farm to prevent birds and other animals from entering the farm. They also spread the rice straws to keep the soil cool and to prevent the cucumbers from spoiling.

A few of the Khmer Rouge soldiers approached us. "You two must report to Angkar if you see anyone entering the farm and stealing the cucumbers."

"Yes, we will report to you," I said.

"We are great workers," Rith added. "We will not let anyone steal the cucumbers."

From the first day that I guarded the farm, I did not come across anyone entering the farm, except the two of us. We were the ones stealing cucumbers from Angkar. When the cucumber fruits got big- ger, we walked the farm and picked the best quality ones for food. I ate them almost every day. I ate them until I developed hiccups.

Guarding the farm was the easiest job I ever had. I had fun chas- ing, throwing dirt, and shouting at the birds. Rith and I developed a strong bond. He taught me how to use a slingshot. He loaded the hardened dirt palette and handed the slingshot to me. I used all my power to pull the string of the slingshot, but I couldn't do it because I didn't have enough strength.

Rith had not killed a single bird with his slingshot. He did not have enough strength to pull the slingshot a sufficient length back- wards to get a power shot. Every time he saw the birds land in the farm, he snuck up behind them to shoot them for food. But Rith was a terrible shooter. Ever since I'd met him, I had never seen him kill one bird with the slingshot.

When the cucumbers matured, hundreds of women came to pick them and loaded them onto dozens of oxcarts. It took them about ten days to pick the cucumbers. After they finished harvesting, Rith and I had nothing else to do.

I Can't Believe What I Just Ate

After the cucumbers were harvested, I had no work and no re- sponsibilities. Meanwhile, Rith and I had the opportunity to venture around and explore food sources in the village. Sometimes, we snuck into rice fields to catch some fresh water snails, frogs, and fish.

After months of working with Rith, my hunting skills had devel- oped. My eyes were as sharp as an eagle. I could see any movement in water, on land, and in the air.

One morning, I went to hang around along the water canal. I scanned every surface in my surroundings. I saw small fishes jumping up and down in the milky shallow water. I jumped into the water to catch the fish, and caught a dozen of them with my bare hands. Most of the fish were flat and small, the size of my palms.

While I was busy catching fish, Rith went into the field that was surrounded by a bamboo forest. The bamboo had grown in a rectangular formation, as if it was a naturally grown fence. There was once a building structure in this field, but it was completely destroyed. I could only see a concrete floor and a few broken concrete posts. Rith made a small fire pit on the concrete near one of the posts to roast the food he had caught.

"Mitt-Rith, what are you roasting?" I asked.

"I'm roasting a rat," he said.

"Look what I caught." I showed him the fish.

While Rith was cooking, the village chief approached us. The minute I saw him, my heart pumped fast. I could feel my sweat roll down me. I got a flashback. My mind took me back to the rice warehouse where I had been caught stealing the rice. I remembered how my entire family had almost been killed for eating the injured bird.

"Rith, hide the food! Put out the fire! Put out the fire, now! The village chief is coming! He walked toward us! Hide the food! Hide the food now!" I clenched my face.

Rith refused. "Don't look at him! Just pretend like you don't see him! He is not going to punish us!" he said.

I tried to hold myself together, pretending not to be scared.

"What are you two doing?" asked the village chief.

"Oh, I caught a rat and I'm roasting it," Rith said with confidence. The village chief watched Rith toss and turn the rat over the fire flame, then he left.

I felt so relieved. This village chief was very nice. He was not as mean as others in the Khmer Rouge. I had not seen any Khmer Rouge as nice as him.

After the village chief left, Rith shared his food with me. He gave me one front leg and one hind leg of the cooked rat. He ate the rest. I was suspicious of the "rat." My experience told me it wasn't a rat because the skull of this creature was too big and too round to be a rat. I knew a rat head's was smaller and was shaped like a cylinder cone.

"This is not a rat! It doesn't look like a rat," I said.

"You are right! It is not a rat! What do you think it is? You guess!"

"I don't know!"

"Does it taste different from other meat?" he asked bluntly.

"No! Not at all! It tastes like bird meat. What is it?" I asked again.

"It was a baby cat," he said.

When he told me that, I was in shock. I could not believe I had just eaten a baby cat. I knew he told me the truth. While I was catching the fish, I had heard the cat crying.

In fact, I used to see that baby cat running around the area, but I had never thought of killing it for food. I loved cats. When I was a child, I used to play with a cat at my home. A cat was a human's best friend. They were gentle and fun to play with. That baby cat had been skinny and had a long tail. It had dozens of black spots on its body. Now, I would never hear the cat "Meow, Meow, Maaaw."

After realizing that I ate the cat, I felt lost, confused, guilty, and sad. Why did I eat that cat? Why did Rith kill that cat? Why could he not kill fish, frogs, or grasshoppers, like me? Why didn't he venture out further to catch frogs and snakes? I couldn't believe I ate a baby cat. No matter how starved I was, I wouldn't kill a cat for food. If he had told me the truth, I wouldn't have eaten it. Now, I would feel guilty for the rest of my life.

Rith warned me not to tell anyone that he had killed the cat for food. "If anyone knows about this, I will be in trouble and you will be in trouble too, because you ate the cat with me. I will beat you up if you tell anyone," he said.

After we finished eating the cat, Rith put my fish into the fire pit and we shared the fish. While I was eating the fish, I was still thinking about the cat. Then I asked Rith, "Why did you kill the cat? Why don't you catch fish, like me?

"What? You don't like it? If you don't like it, spit it all out," he said bluntly in a furious broken voice and he threatened to hurt me. "If I hear you telling someone about us eating a cat, I will kick and punch you in the face."

I shut my mouth and promised him to keep it a secret. But that memory burned in my head forever.

My Injury

It was my fifth day of being jobless. I was bored and decided to roam around the area, hoping to find something for a snack. Then I came across a wooden bridge that was built over the water canal.

Just for fun, I climbed on the bridge guardrail and stood on it. Then I saw a fish jump out of the water. I couldn't resist catching it for food. I stood motionless and waited for the fish to surface again. Not long after, the fish emerged.

Without foreseeing any danger, I jumped into the water to catch the fish, but my feet hit objects in the water. The excruciating pain sent shockwaves throughout my body. My legs were crippled and unable to move. My heart was beating like a drum. I cried for help while being submerged in the water.

I thought I was going to drown. I struggled to push myself out of the water to breathe. Gasping for air, I tried to get out of the water by swimming to the shore, but I couldn't. Half of my body was still submerged in the water, and the slow current was pulling me back into the water. I cried and shouted for help, but no one heard me. With the current pulling me into the water, I tried to find and hold onto any objects to stay ashore.

Minutes later, there was a young communal chef walking to the restroom near that area who heard my desperate cries for help. She ran to me and dragged me out of the water. Then she ran back to the communal kitchen and called for more people to come help me.

While she was gone, I looked at my legs and saw that both of my shins were cut to the bone. Blood flowed out of the wounds and soaked my feet.

Minutes later, all the female *mittbongs* who worked in the communal kitchen arrived. "What happened to him?" asked one of the girls.

"I think he jumped off the bridge and his feet hit the foundation of the bridge," said the girl who had dragged me out of the water.

Several girls came and carried me to the communal hut. They lay me down on the woven bamboo platform near the kitchen and cleaned my wounds. I cried and shouted for Mak and Pa to help me.

The girls tried to soothe me and told me not to move. Then one girl shouted, "Does anyone know how to treat his wound? Can anyone find people to treat him?"

In that confusing moment, I overheard the girls talking about finding an herbalist to help me. One of the girls who stood next to me said, "You stay here with the boy. I will find an herbalist to treat him."

After a long while, the herbalist came. He was a man in his late thirties. He looked at me and my wounded feet briefly. Then he turned to the girls and asked, "Can anyone help me boil a pot of water? I need to boil the herbs to clean his wounds."

Minutes later, he stepped away and I overheard him say to the women that he was going to clean my wounds and cast each foot with bamboo sticks.

Not long after the herbs were cooked, the herbalist brought the herb pot and set it near me. I saw the hot steam rise out of the pot. The man stirred the fluid inside the pot to force it to cool faster.

"Now, it is warm enough to clean his wounds. I need your help to hold him in place," said the herbalist to the girls.

They did exactly what he said. Some of them held onto my feet, arms, and head to prevent me from moving.

The moment the man applied the herbal medicine on my wounds, the excruciating pain stung from my toes to the tip of my hair. I screamed and shouted. Sweat gushed out of every pore of my body. My eyes went blurry.

No matter how loud I screamed or how hard I tried to move, the girls didn't free me. They held me down tightly on the platform until the herbalist finished his job.

That night, I was severely ill and could not get up. My body temperature was growing increasingly hot. I felt the heat, the dryness, and the weakening of my body. My whole body was full of pain. The lady chefs were my nurses. They became my sisters and Mak. They took turns taking care of me, feeding and washing me. They treated me like one of their own younger brothers. I didn't know their names or their backgrounds. I called every one of them *bong*, a formal way of calling someone older than myself.

I was unconscious, but I don't know for how long. I didn't know how many days I was sick. When I woke up, I saw the woven bamboo cast on my feet and felt unbearable pain from my heels to my head.

Every several days, the herbalist came to remove the casts and to clean my wounds. He boiled tamarind leaves and mixed them with various ingredients as a cleaning solution. As usual, every time he cleaned my wounds, a few people held me down, in place. They held my head, my body, my arms, and my feet so the herbalist could clean my wounds. I cried for my life, shouting for Mak and Pa to help.

As time passed, my feet got better but they weren't completely healed. I could barely walk and I had to use tree branches as walking sticks. I was able to move only in small steps.

The herbalist removed the casts off my feet to reveal my wounds. I could see the white shin bones and the rotten flesh. It stunk. My wounds attracted flies. Every time they landed on the wounds, it felt painful and itchy. I was mad at those flies and hated them. I wanted to kill them one by one until they were eradicated from the area so they wouldn't annoy me again.

My wishes came true. The herbalist gave me a small amount of shredded dried tobacco leaves to apply on my wounds. The leaves would protect it from the flies. Every time the flies landed on the shredded tobacco to search for my rotten flesh, they got poisoned. They fell off to the ground and were unable to fly. They flipped over with their limbs up and spun on their backs. Some of them flew to hit objects. Others crawled slowly on the ground. As a child, I had fun watching them suffer. I caught the flies and dropped them by the fire-ant trails.

Injuring my foot was the longest physically challenging experience I had endured. It took approximately four months for my feet to heal.

PART III
Year Three of the
Khmer Rouge Regime

7
Living in Hell

The new rainy season set in. Thick white clouds built up in the sky, and it often poured rain all day and all night. The rain gave new life to the plants and creatures. Weeds, grass, vines, and trees turned from brown to green. Crabs, frogs, toads, and shell snails emerged to enjoy themselves after many months of hibernation in the ground. I had learned all of this from my dad, from Rith, and from observation.

When the new season set in, Angkar Luer began to shuffle people again. They separated and integrated people into groups and moved them to different places. The Khmer Rouge ordered me to move in with a female group, whose ages ranged from fourteen to eighteen. There were approximately thirty people in my group. I didn't know why the Khmer Rouge didn't put me with the children's group or a boy group. Didn't they have children's groups in the village? I wondered.

Being the only boy and the youngest one in the group, again I felt like a baby cow lost in the herd. I was confused and unable to foresee what lay ahead. In spite of my confusion, however, I continued to move with the group to a location I didn't know.

After more than a half day of walking, my group arrived at a destination. I didn't know the name of the village or the province. I had never heard people question or talk about it.

The landscape was surrounded by an ocean of rice fields and marshes. To the north and the east of the communal center, hundreds of rice fields stretched to meet the horizon. To the south of the center was plenty of thick vegetation and tall trees. This was the place where the Khmer Rouge soldiers lived to guard prisoners. They lived along the river about a kilometer away from where I lived.

While I tried to get myself situated to the assigned shelter, I noticed the place was similar to the Toul Ampil Hospital, where my mother had died. All the shelters had no walls, only bamboo posts to support the reed roof from falling. The rectangular shaped huts had no walls, no platform, and no beds.

About an hour after I got myself situated, a group of about fifty women arrived. The majority of them were in their late twenties. I had no idea where the Khmer Rouge had moved them from.

When they approached closer to the communal center, I saw a boy with a light-yellow complexion walking among the women. His thick, straight black hair reminded me of my younger brother, Roth. The moment I saw him, I went outside the hut and wanted to talk to him. But I didn't because I was afraid the Khmer Rouge might punish me.

While he was standing in formation for the head count, I tried to look at him many times, attempting to catch his eyes. His face finally turned toward me. Our eyes caught each other and locked for a brief second. I smiled at him, but he turned his face away and looked down to the ground as if he were afraid of me. I thought, *Maybe he too has no parents and got lost in the crowd like me.*

I continued to look at him until our eyes caught again. Then we looked at each other as if we wanted to talk and to play together. But we couldn't because we were afraid of the Khmer Rouge hurting us.

That evening, the Angkar Luer ordered everyone to a meeting outside the shelter. The boy walked outside the hut and sat on the ground. I went to sit next to him. "What is your name?" I asked.

He didn't answer right away. He ran his fingers over the ground.

Then he grabbed a small amount of dirt and squeezed it tightly. "Vichet," he responded, stone-faced.

"My name is Marin," I said.

After everyone was seated, Angkar began to give a speech. I didn't pay attention to what Angkar preached. I picked up a twig and drew whatever came to mind on the ground. I wrote a few vowels that were shaped like elongated leaves. The rest of the drawings were circles. I had learned these circles and vowels under the shade tree with Vanny's group.

The meeting was over and Angkar Luer assigned a new team of Khmer Rouge to lead us. I would later learn the names of my new leaders: Mittbong-Mai, Mittbong-Seouth, and Mittbong-Vel. These three Khmer Rouge comrades were about the same age, in their mid-twenties. Mittbong-Vel was the most noticeable for me. She was the only female and had a dark complexion like me. She had a flat face, flat nose, and full cheeks. Her eye sockets were white and clear, and her pupils were shiny black, like black emeralds. Her black collar-shirt was decorated with colorful buttons—red, white, black, and blue. My collared-shirt barely had five plain buttons. Her collared-shirt had more than fifteen buttons, from the neck down. It seemed to me that the colorful button was fashionable among the female Khmer Rouge.

Minutes after our group was formed, Mittbong-Vel gave a brief speech. "Today, I am glad you are part of my group. We will work hard together to serve Angkar Luer. And we will obey Angkar." As she spoke, she walked from one point to another with a stick in her hand. "Those individuals who disobey or violate Angkar Luer will be considered *kmang* (enemy)."

Then Mittbong-Seouth stepped in and stressed some of the rules. "We are the eyes and ears of Angkar Luer. Whatever we say you must pay full attention and obey our rules." Mittbong-Seouth didn't look mean or cruel. He had a light complexion, a thin belt, and a soft voice. But his appearance could be deceiving. Mittbong-Mai didn't give a speech. He walked around and looked at everyone as if he wanted to torture one of us.

In the morning, the Khmer Rouge ordered Vichet and me to line up with the rest of the workers for the body count. Then they forced us to walk single file along the canal to work in a designated paddy rice field to plant rice.

"Marin, you work in this rice field! Vichet, go to work in the rice field over there!" said Mittbong Seouth.

Planting rice was not easy. The job required standing in deep mud with my back hunched over. It was the most uncomfortable position to work. After long hours of working without any break time, my neck started to stiffen, my back began to ache, and my lower spine began to burn and irritate. From time to time, I positioned my back up in a standing position to stretch. Every time I stood, sharp pain occurred in my head, causing me to faint. My eyes became blurry for minutes. I closed my eyes and stood still for a moment. Then I opened my eyes again, hoping the blurriness would go away. It worked, but I still hated the job.

At lunchtime, the Khmer Rouge ordered everyone to walk back along the same canal to the communal center for lunch. After lunch, they ordered us to form a single file again, walking along the same water canal to finish the work where we had left off. I continued to work until dusk.

When the rice planting stage was over, I was happy and hoped I would have nothing to do—but I was wrong. The Khmer Rouge ordered me to work on the west side of the fields, to pull weeds out of the rice field to ensure the healthy growth of rice. Pulling weeds out of the rice field was a simple and easy task, but these paddy rice fields were infested with leeches of all sizes: big, small, long, and short. I hated leeches.

I heard people say horrifying things about the leeches. They said that the tiny leech could creep into a human's genitals and rectum to lay their eggs. Once the eggs hatched, the babies would feed on the human blood from the inside to make the people sick and eventually die. The awful images I imagined terrified me to death. I was more afraid of the leeches than I was of the Khmer Rouge.

One morning, Mittbong-Vel ordered me to work in a designated rice field. "Comrade Marin, you go to work in that rice field." She pointed to the paddy rice field that had lots of weeds. I didn't go into the field right away because I was scared of the leeches. I walked around the rice field a few times, buying time, looking for a potential spot that had no leeches.

"Comrade Marin!" she shouted from a distance. "What are you doing walking around the rice field? Get into the rice field and pull out those weeds now!"

I walked into the water thigh-deep to pull out the weeds. Minutes later, a leech swam toward me. I shouted and splashed the water at the leech. The leech moved away from me a few meters, then turned and started swimming toward me again.

"Get away from me, you stupid leech! Just get away from me! Get out of my sight, you stupid leech! Get away from me! Don't come to me, you stupid leech! I will kill you! I will kill you! I will kill you, you stupid leech." As the leech continued to come, my fear and anger continued to build up.

The leech was stubborn. It didn't matter how strong I was. I splashed water at it, and it continued to approach me—and the more I splashed the water, the more I alerted the other leeches to come toward me.

First, I saw one. Then two. Then three. Then four came straight at me. Minutes later, five more leeches were swimming up and down and lunging toward me.

I screamed, I shouted, I yelled, and I cursed at the leeches, until I felt my throat dry. Despite all that splashing and yelling, it didn't work. I ran onto the rice-field levee, the only dry land in the area. I sat on the levee and I didn't go back into the water.

Now, I had two fears. The first fear was the leeches, because they were sneaky, creepy, slippery, slimy, sticky, disgusting, gross, stubborn, and elastic. I was afraid of them latching onto my penis or getting into my rectum to kill me from the inside out.

My second fear was the Khmer Rouge. I was afraid they would punish and kill me for not doing my job.

I sat on the levee and prayed to Tevada, to the evil spirit, to Mak for helping me kill the leeches, but they never did.

To Keep You Has No Benefit

It was winter. This time of the year, the rain poured down from the sky furiously. The rain wet my clothes all day and all night, and my only pair of clothes never had a chance to dry. Germs and bacteria got into my skin, and I developed water rashes, which created tiny blisters from my waist down. Also, the rain made it harder for me to see the leeches swimming toward me.

At night, I slept on the ground inside the hut. From time to time, the heavy midnight rainstorms soaked me completely. The rain, strong winds, loud thunders, and the flashes of lighting frightened me and I had nightmares. Despite the frightening conditions, however, I continued to sleep in the pothole of water, covering my ears with my hands, clenching my legs and arms together like a fetus in a mother's womb. *Tevada, please stop the wind, the rain, and the thunderstorms!* I prayed.

Early the next morning, with the skies gray and visibility still low, the Khmer Rouge blew the whistle to wake me up and ordered me to go to work. I went to work with wet and dirty clothes, like a pig just out of the mud. Most of the time, I didn't get enough sleep, and I felt grouchy and frightened about everything.

My fear of the leeches became overwhelming. I was more afraid of the leeches than I was of the Khmer Rouge. Because the leeches dominated the water, I became afraid of the water. I was afraid to walk across the water canal to do my work; at the same time, I was afraid of being killed by the Khmer Rouge for not working. My crying didn't get any sympathy from the Khmer Rouge. In fact, it got the Khmer Rouge leaders becoming even more impatient with me.

One cold foggy morning, I had a headache and a stomachache. I cried on my way to work. I told them about my sickness, but they didn't believe me. They thought I had "rabbit sickness," the term they used to accuse people who were not sick and pretended to be sick.

"You have rabbit sickness! You are not really sick. You pretend to be sick because you are afraid of the leeches and you don't want to work!" Mittbong-Soeuth yelled at me.

They pushed me to walk faster along the canal. Then they kicked me into a water canal that was infested with leeches, and accused me of *kaun-ar-neaytun*[1], referring to me as the son of a merchant.

"Stop crying, *kaun-ar-neaytun!* If you don't stop crying, I will kill you right now! You cannot get out of the water," Mittbong-Mai said with a hoe in his hand.

I bit my teeth, squeezed my eyes, wiped off my tears, and held my breath to stop crying.

The Khmer Rouge leaders appeared to hate me so much that they wanted to get rid of me. They even used the phrase *tuk-kor-men-jomnegn, dogjegn-kor-men-kart.* "Look at Vichet, he has never cried like you," said the other Khmer Rouge soldier. "Whatever I ask him to do, he just does it. A child like you, *"tuk-kor-men-jomnegn, dogjegn-kor-men-kart."*

At first, I didn't understand what the leader meant by that phrase. I thought they were teaching me how to add and subtract. I was confused. In Khmer, the words mean the following: *Tuk*: keep or to keep. *Men-jomnegn*: no profit. *Dogjegn*: take away or subtract. *Men-kart*: no loss. What they said translates to: "To keep you has no benefit. To take you out is of no loss." I later learned that the phrase was often

---

1   The word *kaun* means son or daughter. The word *neaytun* means merchant. The Khmer Rouge combined the two words and twisted the meaning. It means the son of an aristocrat or the son of a capitalist.

used before they killed a person.

"You stay there! Don't get out of the water!" Mittbong-Seouth said and left after issuing the warning.

I was horrified. My body shivered and my teeth rattled against each other like a rattlesnake rattles its tail. I was neck deep in the water, and I slowly moved to shallow water.

I felt something on my left arm, below my armpit. When I raised my hand up, I saw a huge horse leech, the size of my big toe, latched onto my lower armpit and ribcage. I snatched the leech off my body with my right hand, threw it in the water, and ran for dry land, horrified.

My body continued to shake like a newborn puppy. I crawled up out of the water and sat down to hold myself. I clamped my feet and my hands together against my body to stop myself from shivering.

I saw two Khmer Rouges walking toward me. I lay face down on the ground and crawled slowly back into the water. I was lucky they didn't see me sitting on the berm of the canal. Once they approached me, they ordered me out of the water to follow them to work.

Taking Revenge Against the Leeches

Every time the Khmer Rouge forced me to get into the rice field, my body shook like a newborn puppy. I was frightened that the leeches would get into my stomach. When I worked in waist-deep water, I frequently walked to shallow water or dry land to check my penis and make sure there were no leeches latched onto it.

When the Khmer Rouge saw me standing on the levee, they shouted from a distance, "Marin! Get back into the rice field right now!"

I walked slowly back into the water to prevent huge water ripples that would alert the leeches. While walking into the water, I had countless death wishes for both the Khmer Rouge and the leeches.

The situation got even worse. I had a lot of pain in my stomach, and the frequent burning sensation in my stomach forced me to go to the restroom. I hoped the leeches weren't inside my stomach eating my flesh. I was frightened and thought I was going to die. I evaded my work responsibilities and sat on the dry land, pretending to release my bowels.

One of the Khmer Rouge leaders saw me and shouted from the distance, "What are you doing, young comrade?"

"I have a stomachache and I am releasing my bowels."

"How long have you been doing it? I saw you sitting for too long! Go back to work now! Or I will punish you!"

Though in my heart I cursed her, I walked into the rice field slowly, to prevent the water from rippling.

After a long while in the water, I felt my foot become itchy. I lifted it out of the water and saw a huge black leech latched onto me. My heart pounded fast and I ran for my life to dry land, shouting, "Help! Help! Help! Help! Somebody help me! Help! The leech bit me!"

As I ran, I could feel the leech bouncing on my foot. I got to the berm, sat, and rubbed my foot, kicking and stomping the ground, trying to get rid of it. It didn't matter how hard or how fast I stomped my foot, the leech stuck to me like glue.

"Help! Help! Help me! The leech bit me!" I shouted.

I was disgusted at the leech's body filled with my blood. I was afraid to touch it with my bare hand. I grabbed a fistful of dead grasses and dried soil to apply to the leech, snatched it off my foot, and threw it hard down onto the ground.

"You...fucking...stupid...crazy leech. I will kill you!" I shouted at the leech with clenching teeth and fists.

I took revenge by using small sticks to nail the leech down to the ground to prevent it from getting back into the water. My blood squirted from its body all over my feet. I left the leech to bake in the hot sun.

"Tell your mom, your dad, your baby, and your friends not to bite me. If they do, I will kill them like I killed you!" I shouted madly at the leech.

The leech bite didn't hurt. It felt a little itchy. When its body stuffed itself with my blood, all I could feel was something heavy stuck to my foot. I hated leeches, because they were sneaky, creepy, slippery, slimy, sticky, disgusting, and gross.

I was brave enough to kill the leech, but I was afraid to get back into the water. I was scared that more leeches would bite me again.

My Punishment

While I was killing the leech, Mittbong-Vel, the group leader, approached me. I wasn't aware of her approaching.

"Comrade Marin! Why are you not in the rice field?" she asked, standing in front of me with a stick in her hand.

I stood up and said, "I...I...I...I was afraid of the leeches."

"Comrade Marin! Is the leech bigger than you or smaller than you?" she said and pointed her stick to my chest.

"Smaller," I said softly with fear and tears building in the corners of my eyes. At the same time, I was furious. I clenched my fists and toes. I wanted to kick, punch, and push her into the water that was infested with leeches. I wanted to leave her in the water and have the leeches kill her.

"I cannot hear you! Mitt Marin! Is the leech bigger than you or smaller than you?" she shouted at me.

"It is smaller than me," I said.

"It is smaller than you. So, why are you afraid of it?"

"I...I...I..." I tried to find words to explain it to her, but my thoughts were jumbled and not a word came out of my mouth.

"*Kaun-ar-neaytun!* You don't know how to work. You are afraid of leeches. What am I going to do with you? A child like you, Angkar *tuk-kor-men-jomnegn, dogjegn-kor-men-kart*," she said.

She said all these fancy words and I couldn't understand what she meant.

"Now, Angkar has to punish you. I will give you three spanks with this stick. If you cry or shed any tears, I will hit you three times and count it as one. The total spanks would be nine spanks."

She bent toward me and set her stick on my shoulder. "Do you agree, comrade Marin?"

I didn't answer her. I stood for a while thinking of the possibilities of running away. I looked around to the east, west, and north. All I could see was a green paddy rice field stretched to the horizon. Almost all of these paddy rice fields were infested with leeches. Hiding in water infested with leeches was not an option. Running south was not a good option, either. The soldiers would butcher me like firewood. Or maybe they would arrest me and torture me like they had the prisoners who had tried to escaped. I had also heard another story of a Khmer Rouge soldier cutting off a prisoner's legs with an ax for attempting to escape.

My only choice was to accept her condition. "I...I agree," I said softly, biting my teeth as my brain boiled in anger.

She ordered me to count with her. She grabbed my hands, turned me around, raised the stick high in the air, and hit me in the lower back.

"One!"

"One."

"Two!"

"Two."

"Three!"

"Three."

Every spank that landed on my body was painful and made me jolt—but I didn't cry or move my hands to soothe the pain.

"Go back to work!" she shouted.

I clenched my teeth in anger, biting my lips in excruciating pain. I walked into the rice field, rage swelling inside me, and thought of what it would take to get revenge.

I prayed to Tevada in Heaven and the devils dwelling in Hell to help me kill Mittbong-Vel. *Tevada, please create lightning and strike her in the head. If you don't want to kill her, would you please make me as big as her so I can break her neck with my strong kick. Evil, please crack the earth open, drag her to Hell, and toast her like I did the grasshopper. Tevada, why don't you create lightning and strike her in the head? Why do you allow her to spank me? Why didn't you pull the stick out of her hand?*

At lunchtime, Mittbong-Vel announced to the group, "I am very proud of our young comrade, Marin. He could stand three spanks without dropping a tear. He is truly the Angkar's son."

When I heard that, tears built up in my eyes. I was pissed off. Tension built up in my throat and almost made me choke. I cursed at her in my heart and hoped lightning would strike her during her speech. I clenched my fists and wanted to break her jaw. At the same time, I was frustrated at Tevada for not using his power to make me as big as an adult so I could fight her.

Getting Sick Leave

One day after I was punished, I was severely ill and could barely walk to work. I had many blisters. The cause of the blisters from my waist to my toes was probably from staying in the water so long.

I had been working the flooded rice fields and was sleeping in mud inside the hut. The blisters were as big as rice grains. They were itchy and painful, especially on my upper thighs and my genitals.

While people washed their faces to refresh themselves and got ready to line up for the body count, I approached Mittbong-Mai, Mittbong-Seouth, and Mittbong-Vel, who were in the fields talking to each other. I was in pain and walked frog-like toward the Khmer Rouge leaders.

"Mittbong," I said, "I cannot go to work because I am very sick."

Mittbong-Mai and Mittbong-Seouth looked at me as if they wanted to kill me. "What!" said Mittbong-Mai. "You are not sick! You have rabbit sickness!"

I was mad and stripped naked in front of them.

Mittbong-Vel stood still, appearing to be sickened by my body. Her eyes scanned and inspected the condition from my waist down. "You can take several days off from work," she said softly as if she had sympathy for me. "When the blisters disappear, you must go back to work."

I felt relief and happy for not having to go to work. I felt at ease, not having to see the disgusting leeches at the work site.

That morning, after everyone left to work, I took off my pants and my shirt to wash in the canal. Then I placed them over small bushes to dry. I was naked and bored. I entertained myself by throwing dirt into the water. But most of the time I had a small stick in my hand to kill grasshoppers and crickets for food.

When I had collected a handful of them, I walked to the communal cafeteria and threw the dead insects into the fire pit. I used a small twig to toss and turn the grasshoppers until they turned red, like cooked shrimp. Then I took them out of the fire, dusted off the ashes, and ate them. My starvation made every piece of food that I ate delicious.

That afternoon, while I roamed alongside the canal, I spotted a snakehead fish in a small pothole in the rice field. With the stick in my hand, I snuck into the rice field to kill it. I wrapped the fish with water-lily leaves, mummified it with clay, and buried it under fire. I had learned this cooking technique from Mak and Pa. After the fish was cooked, I took it to the berm beside the canal, broke the clay open, removed the leaves, and ate it without letting anyone see. The fish was juicy and tasty. I ate everything, including the eyes, the brain, the tongue, the gills, and the guts.

On the second day of my absence from work, I continued to stay dry by exposing my naked body to the sunlight. When a blister hit the sun, I could feel the itchy dryness of my skin, and a few blisters popped. A tiny amount of clear fluid came out of the holes, and the pain and the itchiness made me want to scratch the rashes all over my body. But I couldn't because I was afraid I would get an infection. So,

I controlled myself by rubbing my thighs together to soothe it.

In spite of the itchiness and pain, I continued to catch insects for food. My eyes scanned the surrounding area to see if any grasshoppers, crickets, or frogs were hopping within my sight. Once I spotted them, I killed them for food.

Late that second morning, I didn't put my clothes on. I caught some insects and walked to the kitchen fire pit to cook my food. While I tossed and turned my food over a burning piece of wood, a forty-year-old woman chef walked in. I didn't see her coming from behind.

"What are you doing here, son?" she asked. "Why aren't you at work?"

My body jolted. I turned my head toward her. She stood approximately three meters behind me. Her dark wrinkled face and curly long hair made me feel uncomfortable. I looked her in the eyes. She had both hands on her waist, and she looked at me as if she wanted to kill me and throw me into the fire pit.

Before I could even answer the questions, a younger lady chef interrupted and said, "Oh, that boy is ill. Angkar gave him the permission not to work for several days."

The older lady Khmer Rouge chef dropped her hands from her waist and walked out of my sight without saying a word. Minutes later, she came back with a used *kroma* in her hand and walked a steady pace toward me. I stood up, ready to run away from her.

Then she said to me in a softer tone, "Here is my *kroma*. Take it and get out of the kitchen. It is time for me to cook now."

I walked a few steps toward her, reached my hand to the *kroma*, looked at her briefly, and said, "Thank you, aunty."

I wrapped the *kroma* around my neck. Then I turned around to remove the half dozen grasshoppers and crickets from the fire pit. I placed them in the *kroma* and walked out of the communal kitchen.

I walked along the canal and ate the insects as snacks. After I finished eating, I removed the *kroma* from my neck and tried to wear it on my waist, like many adult males did. I tried to wear it many times, but it would not hold onto my waist. It kept falling off. I tried to visualize how my dad and other older men wore the *kroma* by rolling a small portion of the cloth tightly to the waist. After much trial and error, I was finally able to wear it, but it looked clumsy.

The Treatment of Prisoners

On the third day of my absence from work, while sitting in the hut where I slept, I witnessed horrific events. I saw Khmer Rouge soldiers escorting male and female prisoners from the south to construct a rice warehouse and a small hut near my sleeping hut. I have no idea what that other hut was used for. Maybe the Khmer Rouge used it as their command post, or simply to protect themselves from the rain and summer heat. The prisoners' arms and necks were locked with wooden devices that they carried across their shoulders like a yoke. They were chained to one another and marched in a line of ten or less. Their legs were chained together, too, leaving them just enough space to walk in small steps.

When the prisoners arrived at the work site, the soldiers removed the locks and the yokes from their necks, but their hands and feet remained locked and chained to each other. Some prisoners had their necks chained to their feet, restricting their steps even more. The Khmer Rouge worked them to death. There were no restroom breaks; they urinated and released bowels in their pants while they were working. I saw one man with feces splattered on the back of his pants, and flies swarmed his wet buttocks. I never saw them taking a lunch break, either. They had only one meal a day, probably dinner. Every time I came to the communal center for lunch, I saw them carrying logs, digging holes, sewing wood, and carrying dirt from one point to another.

The prisoners were bony. I could see their ribcages. Their stomachs sank deep inside almost touching their back bones. Their thighs had no meat, only skin attached to the bones. Their heads were bony and they had no flesh on their cheeks. Their eyes sunk deep into their heads. They were as skinny as me during my stay in the pediatric hospital with Mak.

During the fourth day of my sick leave, my own rashes began to dry, but were not completely healed. I touched my thighs and buttocks and felt a roughness on my skin like fine sandpaper. But it didn't hurt. Every time I rolled my palms over the surface of the blisters, dead skin came off, like ashes flying off me. I looked at the sun and prayed to the heavens. *Tevada, please leave blister marks on my body. Please keep the blister marks as evidence to prove to the Khmer Rouge that I'm still sick. I don't want to go to work in the rice fields infested with leeches. I want more sick days off. Please help me.*

It was afternoon. Everyone had already left to work. I was sitting in the hut where I normally slept and thinking about nothing. Then I saw a soldier escort a woman prisoner from her work site and force her to sit in a kneeling position on the muddy soil. She was less than thirty meters away from me. She was in her mid-thirties and skinny. Her eyes sunk deep into her eye sockets, and her half-torn pants revealed the light-yellow skin attached to her bones. Her pants barely held onto her waist.

Her hand shook when she re-tied her pants. The Khmer Rouge placed the tip of a rebar (the size of a chopstick) on one side of the woman's shoulder and pushed her to sit down. She turned her head and, with a pale face, looked at the rebar on her shoulder.

"Sit down right here! In a kneeling position!" said the Khmer Rouge soldier.

With shivering lips, the woman begged the Khmer Rouge not to hurt her. "Please don't kill me."

My body shook as I watched her. Her eyes blinked rapidly and she cried without tears.

She looked at me as if she wanted me to be the eyewitness to this horrific and unjust event.

The soldier removed the rifle from his chest and pointed it to her back. He repositioned his stance and said, "You stupid lady! You betrayed Angkar Luer! You must be punished!"

I didn't know what type of crime she had committed to betray Angkar. I prayed to both Tevada and Evil to help her and to kill the soldiers.

"You are betraying Angkar," said the soldier. "Now, I have to punish you by whipping you ten times with this metal rebar. If you show signs of pain, I will whip you three times and count it as one. If you scream or shed tears, I will kill you. You must count with me when I whip you," said the soldier.

He raised the rebar up in the air and swung it down onto her back. "One!"

"One."

"Two!"

"Two."

"Three!"

"Three."

"Four!"

"Four."

"Five!"

"Five."

"Six!"

"Six."

"Seven!"

"Seven."

"Eight!"

"Eight."

"Nine!"

"Nine."

"Ten!"

"Ten."

Treatment of prisoners

When I heard the metal rebar land on her bony back, a flashback struck in my head. It was like how Mittbong-Vel had whipped me with a stick. Each whip that landed on the woman, it made my body jolt. The woman didn't cry or scream, but her body jerked every time the iron bar landed on her back.

After the ten whips, the soldier stepped aside, wiped sweat off his forehead, and looked at the woman to see if she was crying. Then he shouted, pointing a stick at her, "Get up and go to work!"

She pushed on the ground with her hands and struggled to get up. She clenched her face to hold the pain inside her, and she walked slowly back to work.

When I saw this inhumane treatment of the prisoners, the beating and the torturing, I began to realize a few things. I began to realize that my father was dead. If Pa were alive, he would come to find me and get me out of this dreadful place.

I remembered when Vanny had taken me to live with her and she had told Mittbong-Sareth that Pa was dead. She had told her leader that Pa had passed away during hard labor, building a canal.

If Pa were alive, I wouldn't want to see him living in prison like this. I would prefer to see him dead by hurting or killing one of the Khmer Rouge soldiers. Maybe Pa did fight back with the Khmer Rouge and they didn't spare his life.

The Brave Daughter

During dinnertime on the fifth day of my sick leave, I saw the woman who got beaten by the soldier. She was working alone, sitting in a squatting position while crushing rocks with a hammer. The rocks were used for building a foundation for the rice warehouse.

The woman's ankles were chained loose, just enough for her to walk in small steps. Her neck was latched to a large wooden pole. People who arrived from work turned their heads and looked at her briefly with sad faces. They were frightened and couldn't do anything.

Helping her escape could mean risking the lives of people in the entire village. Everyone not only appeared to be exhausted from work, but they were probably also feeling traumatized for what they saw and experienced.

The food was almost ready to be served. People began sitting in a small tight circle in groups of ten. They sat in a squatting position, with their plates set on the ground before them. I also sat in the circle. I sat and faced the woman prisoner. Then I noticed that she moved her body toward my group.

The communal chefs walked from one circle to another to scoop food from their large cooking pot and put them onto people's plates. When the food was in my plate, I could read the woman's body language; she wanted to snatch the food from us and shovel it into her mouth. But she couldn't. I imagined that her starvation forced her to catch every smell of food that she could sense.

While we were eating, a girl sitting next to me took a fistful of the cooked rice, ran toward the woman and shoveled the rice into her mouth. Then the girl quickly ran back to her seat like nothing had happened.

Suddenly, I saw tears build up in the girl's eyes and roll down on her cheeks and drop into her own rice bowl. Everyone looked at the girl in shock. The girl wiped the tears in her eyes and said softly to herself with shivering lips, "That is my mother."

At that moment, my eyes went blurry from my own swollen tears. My throat and jaws were tense. While I felt sad and scared, I was also proud of the girl's heroic action. I thought, what would happen if she saw her mother being tortured by the Khmer Rouge soldier? Would she cry? Would she grab the metal rebar from the soldier? Or would she kill the soldier with the machete or a hoe?

The girl was lucky, because the soldiers didn't see her feeding her mother. If they had, both she and her mother would be instantly killed. It could be worse. The Khmer Rouge soldiers might even have killed all of us for aiding the prisoner.

The Khmer Rouge punished a woman

The Escaped Prisoners

After my sixth day off during my sick leave, the blisters on my body disappeared. It was completely healed—but I was unhappy. I preferred to be sick so I wouldn't have to work in the rice paddy and face the leeches. I wanted to have the freedom to play as a child. I didn't want to be a work slave. My fears of being tortured by the Khmer Rouge, and working long hours dealing with the leeches, had traumatized me.

I began to have a revulsion and disappointment with Tevada for not keeping the blister marks on my body to prove to the Khmer Rouge that I was still sick. Again, the Khmer Rouge forced me back to work. My life would force me to continue facing the horrors of the leeches and the Khmer Rouge.

That evening, the sky looked grim. Gray clouds built up in the sky and sent drizzle onto the earth. The soils were wet and turned from grayish to dark brown. After dinner, I saw Khmer Rouge soldiers tying two male prisoners back to back to a bamboo post inside a small newly built hut. The tied prisoners were less than twenty meters from where I slept. Their hands and elbows were tied to their backs to prevent them from possible escape. Their ankles were chained and their bodies were tied with a rope. The Khmer Rouge soldiers left the prisoners there without guarding them and went to their base.

That night, I slept sideways, with a *kroma* covering my face, and pretended I had a deep sleep. I peeked through the *kroma* and watched the prisoners struggling to move. I saw their chests protrude whenever they tried to breathe. I heard them cough and moan as if they were in great pain. My exhaustion didn't allow me to watch them long enough. My eyelids slowly closed and I fell asleep.

Night had turned to morning. I was half awake and I heard rumbling footsteps and the sound of people arguing. I thought I was dreaming. Then a strong shouting sound pierced my ears.

"Where did you tie them up! Do you know which way they ran to!"

My eyelids began to open and I moved my head in the direction of the shouting. I saw one Khmer Rouge soldier on horseback. Another soldier got off a horse and walked to the small hut where the two prisoners had been tied. He looked at another comrade who was standing in the hut near him and shouted, "How could the prisoners escape from this place?" He returned to his horse, jumped onto its back, and said, "Let go! Let's find those two prisoners and drag them back here!" The two soldiers jolted their horses, signaling them to move west.

I noticed that the sun was still hiding in the horizon. I got up in a sitting position and watched other prison guards walking in the sprinkling rain, looking for a clue as to where the two prisoners had escaped. The soldiers looked for them furiously.

One of the prison guards said, "I will kill them. They not only escaped, they also stole two of my horses!"

While I was sitting, I turned my head and looked at the people in the hut where I had slept. I saw depressed faces all around me. No one was talking, but their heads were turned in one direction, watching the Khmer Rouge searching for clues by tracing footprints in the mud.

When I looked at Vichet, he still lay on the ground as if he were imagining things. He had one hand resting on his forehead and his eyes were looking up at the ceiling. It seemed to me like he felt depressed like everyone else in the hut.

Not long after the soldiers on the horses left, two of the prison guards approached the hut and said, "Today, nobody goes to work! We have to find out who helped our enemies to escape!"

Nobody answered. People looked at each other, mumbling in denial.

Another soldier moved his head side to side with hatred on his face as if he wanted to kill all of us. "No one can escape from Angkar! Angkar has many eyes like a pineapple. Whoever helped the enemies escape will be punished to the extent of the Angkar law." Then he turned around and walked to the hut where the prisoners had been tied.

It was midmorning. The sprinkling rain had stopped, but the sky continued to look bleak. Thick and thin gray clouds shielded the sunlight from shining onto the village.

While the ground was still wet, I walked outside of the hut to urinate by a small bush. At that moment, I saw the soldiers dragging the two prisoners behind the horse through marshes. I was scared and ran back to the hut, without realizing I had urinated in my pants.

Once the soldiers brought the prisoners to the site, they got off horseback and ordered the prisoners to stand up. But the prisoners couldn't get up. Both of them lay down on the ground as if they were dead. The soldiers pulled them by the hair and forced them to sit in a kneeling position for interrogation. The soldiers untied the prisoners' hands at the front, then yanked their hands behind their backs and tied their hands and elbows to secure them from another possible escape.

One of the prison guards approached the hut with a rifle at his waist. He stood outside the hut and briefly stared at the people. "I want everyone to get out of the hut and stand in front of the prisoners!" he shouted.

Everyone rushed out of the hut in fear. I walked behind the people, with my hands clenching my stomach to prevent my body from shaking.

While I was standing and watching the prisoners, the soldiers said to the crowd, "We caught our enemies who attempted to escape from Angkar! Now, we brought them back for interrogation! We want all of you to take a good look at them!"

"Who helped you escape from here?" the soldier asked the prisoners and pointed a military knife at individuals in the crowd.

"Not me. Not me. Not me. Not me," the answers came from various individuals as the knife was pointed at them.

The soldiers asked the prisoners many times, but not a single word came out of their mouths.

Then another soldier pulled a knife from his waistband and pointed it at the prisoners' throats. The two prisoners didn't seem to be afraid. One of them moved his neck toward the tip of knife and said, "Kill me now, *ar-juy-maray!*"

The soldier grabbed the prisoner by the hair, tilted his head up, and stabbed the prisoner in the shoulder blade. The prisoner's body jolted. With his mouth and eyes wide open, he screamed, then clenched his teeth in excruciating pain.

The soldier pulled the knife out from the prisoner's shoulder, and blood squirted out following the tip of the knife. The soldier cleaned the knife with dirt to get rid of the blood. Then he stabbed the prisoner again—in the throat and chest.

I was frightened and cold. It seemed like my soul flew out and escaped my body. I stood on the muddy ground, but I didn't feel my feet touching the wet ground. My body shook. My teeth rattled. I felt a sharp pain in my stomach. Everything in my system was pushed out to my throat. I turned my head away to throw up, but only the air and the saliva came out of my stomach. I folded my arms and squeezed them tightly to my chest to hold my body and soul together.

When I turned my head to look at the prisoners again, I saw both of them fall dead onto the ground, soaked in their own blood.

"This is what happens to those who betray Angkar. Nobody can escape from Angkar. Now, the enemies are dead. All of you can go back to work," the soldiers said to the crowd while standing over the dead men.

On the way to work, I kept replaying in my head what I had just witnessed. The picture of the prisoner screaming with his mouth and eyes wide open appeared in front of my face. The image haunted me. I was scared and shivered again. I shook my head violently from side to side to make it disappear from my head.

My head was numb. It seemed like it was filled with compressed air. I couldn't think of anything clearly. When I got to the work site, I stood still in the rice paddy as if I was dead.

I suddenly lost any sense of fear for the leeches. Now, my worst fear was being killed by the Khmer Rouge.

A Haunted Canal

A few days after the two prisoners were killed, the Khmer Rouge ordered everyone to work in different locations. After the morning head count, Mittbong-Mai said, "Today Angkar Luer is very proud of you. You have accomplished incredible work. But Angkar Luer needs all of you to do more."

Then Mittbong-Vel interrupted his speech. "All the women groups will go to work farther east. You need to follow them to the new work site." She pointed to four other Khmer Rouge leaders who stood behind her.

After the woman's group left to work, Mittbong-Vel and Mittbong-Seouth ordered my group to follow them. While we were on our way to work, Mittbong-Vel said to me and Vichet, "You two must work in the same rice field where you left off yesterday. Your work is not done yet. I could still see a lot of weeds in the rice paddy."

Once I heard the order, I exited out of the group and walked back into the rice paddy. I slowly dug my feet into the water, trying not to alert the leeches. At the same time, I thought of killing Mittbong-Vel and the rest of Khmer Rouge. I wished I could fight them and force them to do my work. My anger reached a boiling point and I got mad at Tevada.

Tevada, why didn't you give me the power! Could you give me guns and bullets so I could kill the Khmer Rouge!

While I thought about death wishes for the Khmer Rouge, I saw Vichet walk into the next rice paddy, which was about one hundred meters away from where I was working. In my mind, I thought various questions. Did Vichet ever get angry at the Khmer Rouge? Did he ever think about fighting or killing the Khmer Rouge, like me?

The escaped prisoners

After Mittbong-Vel and Mittbong-Seouth walked farther out of sight, my antagonism began to subside. I had a lower sense of fear because, this time, nobody monitored me while I was working.

That evening, I noticed that the sky was overcast. It was still hot and muggy, but the air was thinner than usual. The sky prohibited the wind from blowing into the village. I was hungry and exhausted. I took frequent deep breaths to renew my energy.

Not long after, I saw the Khmer Rouge leading my group farther from the communal center. Vichet and I got out of the paddy rice field to join the group. We managed to arrive at the communal center first, before the woman group. When I got there, I sat and waited for the food to be served. But the communal chef didn't serve us because everyone had not yet arrived.

The Khmer Rouge ordered the women to take what appeared to be a short-cut route by walking through a chest-deep water canal. It was routine for women to clean themselves after work. The women went to wash themselves to remove dirt and sticky stains from their bodies. As they washed themselves and walked through the water, they accidently touched several dead bodies that were floating in the slow current of the water canal.

While I was waiting in the hut for the food, I heard the women shouting in horror along the east canal. "*Kamorch! Kamorch! Kamorch*[2] in the water!" The several ladies screamed while running to the hut.

Their screaming sent a shockwave of fear through everyone to run for their lives. They ran and crashed into each other, and jumped over each other like a group of village children being chased by a furious tiger. Some of the women fell into the rice fields. Others fainted in shock. Several collapsed just meters from where I stood.

Those who had reached the hut breathed fast and spoke about what they had seen. "I accidently touched the head of *kamorch!*"

"I saw something floating, but I didn't know what it was. And I

---

2   Kamorch in Khmer refers to dead bodies, or ghost.

didn't think it was a *kamorch*."

"I accidently grabbed the *kamorch's* head."

"I saw that one *kamorch* had no head!"

"I only saw the head floating, but no body. I almost touched it."

My body got goose bumps as big as a grain of rice, and I shivered from the inside out. At that moment I no longer felt starvation. My fear was mixed with curiosity. I walked to the hut, with my heart pounding, where I stood and clutched a bamboo post. Terrified, I watched the women.

The women who arrived at the hut first used whatever means they had to soothe their fellow workers. The only means of remedy they had was *kors-kajol*, a form of treatment that involves scratching with a coin on a skin surface to stimulate blood and body temperature.

"Does anyone here have coins and tiger balm for *kors-kajol?*" one of the ladies asked with shivering lips.

Then a few ladies said, "There are no coins or tiger balm! Just use spoons to *kors-kajol*."

They ran back with spoons and a bowl of water to stimulate the patients who had fainted or were unconscious. They applied a small amount of water to their fellow workers' bodies and used a spoon to scratch them. They scratched the women's backs along the ribcage, on the triceps, on the forearms, on the upper chest above the breasts, and behind the neck. They scratched until the skin turned bruise-red.

Some women stroked and massaged the others' arms, legs, and heads, hoping they would feel better. Others cracked finger joints, toe joints, wrist joints, and ankle joints to help the women regain consciousness. Others grabbed a small amount of a woman's hair and pulled it with just the right amount of force to make a cracking sound. Whatever methods they used to save each other's lives, it was impressive. This could have been the breaking point for many of these women. Many had died from overwork, exhaustion, or even panic attack. Today, no one died.

8

The Second Holiday Celebration

The weather changed from rainy to windy breezes. The clouds were thinner, whiter, and ascended higher in the sky. The rains no longer poured down from the sky in a fury. Some rice plants turned from light green to dark green and grew taller and bigger. The water in the canal and rice field became shallower.

As the weather changed, the Khmer Rouge also shifted their attitude toward us. They increased our food rations and gave us three days off for a holiday.

This was the second time I experienced "the holiday." I still didn't know what holiday it was or what it represented. All I cared about was that I could eat as much food as I wanted. It also was "all you can eat." There was a lot of food during that holiday: fried rice, *nom-bagn-jok* (Cambodian freshly made noodles), and dessert.

Again, during this holiday, the Khmer Rouge issued permission slips to the people to visit their loved ones. More than half of the people at the center got the permission slip. People who didn't know where their relatives were had to stay at the center.

I missed my sister and wanted to visit her, but I still didn't know where she lived. At night I prayed to Tevada to help me dream of locating her. But I slept like a log and there was no dream. I was disappointed with Tevada for not helping me to locate Vanny.

People who stayed in the center interacted with each other, as if they had forgotten about the killings, the starvation, the bodies in the water canal. As during the first holiday I experienced, now also the women took turns grooming each other, searching for lice. Some of them made soap from fermented ashes and leaves for washing their hair. Others boiled their clothes to kill lice and bacteria. Then they washed their clothes to make them look new again.

These women were very nice. One of them approached me and said, "Young boy, your clothes are too dirty. Take them off and let me wash them for you."

Without any hesitation, I took off my pants and collared shirt and gave them to her.

She grabbed the clothes from my hands and put them into a big boiling pot. She used a stick to stir my clothes for a minute or two, then she took them out of the pot and washed them thoroughly. I thanked her for helping me.

These ladies treated me as if I was their son. They bathed and shampooed me with liquid soap from the ashes and crushed plants that they made during the holiday.

At night, people celebrated by playing musical instruments made out of pots and pans. A few young men who came to visit loved ones made an impressive *skoe-dei*, an improvised music drum. The men also used *thass*, a large round metal food tray, to cover a dug hole, with some room for air to get out. Then they stood a foot-long stick the size of their finger in the center of the *thass*, placed a string on the stick, and tied both ends of the string to the ground. They adjusted the tone according to how tight the string was on each side, and played by using two drumsticks to hit the string and the *thass*. When they hit the *thass*, it sounded like a drum; the string sounded like a bass-guitar.

The rest of the people hit spoons, cookware, plates, and bowls to make rhythm. Some women simply clapped their hands. I enjoyed listening and watching them play music. I tapped my feet and moved my body along with the music, but I didn't dance.

The people sang and danced, temporarily leaving behind all their trauma.

The Khmer Rouge didn't allow the people to sing rock 'n' roll or any romantic songs by the legendary artists Mr. Sisamouth and Ms. Rosarey Sothear. Only Khmer Rouge revolution songs were permitted. The lyrics of the Khmer Rouge songs were about hard work and praised Angkar. Not many people knew how to sing those songs.

Then there was a lady who started singing "*Uy-komleng-chak-chongkess,*" which translates "Ouch! Don't tickle me, I'm tickled." This beautiful song by Rosarey Sothear, a legendary female singer in Cambodia, was my favorite. I rocked along with the music, sang and danced with the rhythm. I remembered that Mak and Pa had played that song for me to dance and had watched my funny and cute moves.

After I sang and danced about half the song, the Khmer Rouge came and said to us, "Do you all want to die?"

Suddenly, the party came to an end. The music stopped. Everyone stood frozen for a few minutes, then began to sing the revolution songs.

I was disappointed with the soldiers. Why didn't they allow us to sing? Were they stupid? Didn't they know how to sing and dance? At the time, I didn't know that my favorite song had flirtatious connotations.

Permission to Find My Sister

The holiday was over and people returned from visiting their families. In the hut, they shared their experiences about their trips. One of the ladies said to me that she had seen Vanny in the Toul Somphy Hospital. "Marin, you need to visit your sister. She is very ill and skinny."

I had no idea how she knew my sister. But she described Vanny's physical description and it seemed to match: long straight hair, round face, light-yellow complexion. I was thrilled with the information. I was sad to hear that Vanny was severely ill, but I was anxious to ask permission from Angkar Luer to go visit her. Even so, immediately I approached Mittbong-Vel who sat in the hammock.

"Mittbong-Vel, I know where my sister lives. I would like to ask you permission to visit my sister Vanny."

"How do you know about her?" she asked.

"One of the ladies who lives in my hut told me that she lives in Toul Somphy Hospital. My sister is very ill. I want to visit her."

Mittbong-Vel got off the hammock and looked me in the eyes. "When do you want to visit your sister?"

I was impatient. "I want to go now."

Mittbong-Vel stooped down to my level and looked at me in disbelief. Then she pointed to the sun. "Marin, look at the sun. It will set anytime soon. I cannot let you go right now. Besides, I have to ask Angkar Luer for permission."

That afternoon Mittbong-Vel went to her superior and requested a written letter for me. Permission was granted.

The next morning, Mittbong-Vel gave me a new uniform: a black collar-shirt, black pants, and a red *kroma;* the pants were big and had no pockets. I took my old clothes off and put on the new uniform right away. I looked great and felt proud of myself. I felt brave and strong, like the Angkar's son. I felt safe from being hurt by the Khmer Rouge.

The communal chef wrapped a small amount of steamed rice and dried fish with lotus leaves and tied them to my *kroma.* "This is your lunch, son! Don't eat it too early. If you do, you might be hungry in the evening."

"Yes," I said.

Then Mittbong-Vel gave me a rolled piece of paper, the size of a cigarette. She rolled it into my waistband and said, "This is a letter from Angkar Luer. Don't lose it. If you meet mittbongs along the way or in the village, just show them this letter. They will provide you food and give you a place to sleep."

"Yes," I answered.

"Now, you can go to visit your sister." She pushed my back slightly.

"Yes."

"Just walk straight along that canal." She pointed north.

That morning, the sky was clear blue. I could feel the cool breeze from the south pushing me to walk faster. The canal was slightly bigger than a one-car lane. It pointed straight toward the northern horizon.

I passed countless green rice fields, and took a short rest for lunch and drank water from the canal. I continued my lonely journey to find Vanny.

The sun moved above my head. It was hot and humid. Sweat poured from my body and frequently made me thirsty. I was fortunate that there was still plenty of water in the canal. I was able to scoop water with my palms to drink it and splash it on my face and body to keep me cool.

As I continued to walk further, I noticed that the landscape of the rice field changed from light green to dark green, then to golden red. A light-green color indicated young rice fields. When the rice matured, they turned dark green. When they bore seeds and ripened, they changed to golden red.

I was overwhelmed by the beauty of the sky and earth. In the evening, the sun moved past countless scattered thin clouds to rest. The western horizon slowly turned from blue to golden red. The golden rice plants danced slowly with the direction of the wind blowing.

While the sun worked its way west, countless flocks of small birds flew west as if they were having fun chasing after the sun. Storks and cranes flew in a formation as if they were trying to find their places to sleep. Hundreds of swallows flew individually, maneuvering and zigzagging just above the rice fields, to catch flying insects to eat.

Thousands of giant bats flew silently toward the east to scavenge for food. I was overwhelmed by these creatures and wished I could fly as freely as they did.

As I continued walking, I saw several ladies harvesting rice. I shouted, "Aunty! Do you know where Toul Somphy Hospital is?"

One turned around, looked at me, and shouted from the rice field, "What did you say, son? Son, I couldn't hear you clearly. Can you wait for me a little bit?"

Several minutes later, she got out of the rice field, walked up onto the dry land, and approached me. With her left hand, she held a *kondiev*, a curved blade device used for harvesting the rice. With her right hand, she removed the *kroma* from her head and wiped the sweat off her face. Her hair was smeared and unorganized. Her face looked dark and a bit wrinkled. She looked like she was in her mid-forties. She was taller than Mak and as dark as I.

"Son, where are you coming from?" she asked. "Or where are you going?"

"I came from over there." I pointed to the direction I had walked from. She looked where I pointed. "Aunty, I wanted to find my sister. Someone told me she is staying in the hospital at the Toul Somphy Village."

"Where are your parents, son?"

"I…I…I have no parents. They are all dead."

"Hmmm…" She sighed. "What are your parents' names, son?"

"My dad's name is Yann, and Mak's name is Yim."

"Aren't you afraid of wild animals, like wolves and tigers? I won't let you continue your journey, because it is very dangerous to walk at night," she said in a serious, concerned tone. "There are many wild animals and creatures out there. You must stay in the village. In the morning when you get up, you can continue your trip."

She took me to her group leader, a younger lady who stood in the communal cafeteria. I took the handwritten letter out of my waistband

and gave it to the leader. After she read it, she gave me food and let stay me in the village.

After I finished eating, the old lady stripped me naked and bathed me. She treated me like a son. She prepared a place for me to sleep by unrolling a *kontael,* and she set up a mosquito net. That night I felt so special because I had the opportunity to sleep in a house, on the floor, and with a mosquito net to protect me from mosquito bites.

In the morning before she went to work, the woman took me to see the chefs and she requested some food for me to continue my journey. The chef gave me three scoops of steamed rice and a few *trey-chlogn-ang,* a type of stick fish that is grilled. She wrapped the fish and rice in banana leaves.

The old lady walked me to the canal to see me off. "Son, walk safely. You must be cautious on the way, because there are many wild creatures out there."

"Goodbye, aunty," I said.

"Take care, my son."

We walked in opposite directions. I went to the north and she went to the south.

By midmorning, I walked past the village and the rice fields. I noticed that the canal was built straight and cut through the vast grassy field that was mixed with bushes and large trees. I continued to walk along the canal without knowing when or where it was going to end. There were no signs of people in sight.

While I was walking, the sound of bird calls echoed through the sky. Then a fear of being alone began to creep into my mind. I picked up a stick the size of my arm length to protect myself from wild creatures. At that time, I had no idea what a wolf or a tiger looked like, but I had heard people talk about them as being mean and ferocious.

Despite whatever negative image I had of them, my fear of being alone was much greater than being scared of wild creatures. In my mind, I thought that if I were to see animals I would chase them and kill them for food. I didn't care if it was a wolf or a tiger.

It was afternoon. The sun was still rising high in the sky when the earth began to cool down a bit. The breeze swept on my face as if welcoming me to meet my sister.

Then I saw smoke coming out of a roof and dancing in the wind as if congratulating me for my arrival at the Toul Somphy Village.

As I approached the village, I saw several long huts built under trees, but I didn't see anyone. I walked into the hut where the smoke was coming through the roof. Upon entrance, I saw two female communal chefs preparing food. They didn't see me coming behind them.

I approached them from behind and called for attention. "Mittbong! Mittbong! Mittbong!" I said repeatedly, but they didn't hear me. They were busy talking while pulling pots and pans from a small platform in the communal cafeteria.

Then one of the ladies who held a big zinc pot turned and saw me. She was stunned for a moment and said, "You scared me, young comrade! Where did you come from! Why didn't you say something for our attention?"

"I called for your attention a few times, but you didn't hear me. My name is Marin. I got permission from Angkar Luer to visit my sister, Vanny, who lives in this village."

The other chef, who had a *kroma* wrapped around her hair, turned, looked at me, stood up with a cleaver in her hand, and walked toward me.

I asked, "Mittbong, is this Toul Somphy Hospital?"

Instead of answering my questions, the two chefs looked at each other, then at me with curiosity. "Where are you coming from, young comrade? And who are you coming with?"

"I came from over there, a village near the river. I have been walking for two days just to find my sister. Here is a permission slip from Angkar Luer." I tried to take the paper out of my waistband to give it to them.

The two ladies were in their mid-twenties. The one with the cleaver took the paper from my hand, unrolled it, and looked at it. "I don't know what is being said in this letter, because I don't know how to read it." She gave the letter to the mittbong who had the cooking pot. "Do you know how to read?"

"No, I don't know how to read. This is Toul Somphy Village," she said to me, "but there is no hospital in the village."

"What does your sister Vanny look like?" the chef with the cleaver asked.

"She has long, straight hair and a light complexion."

They looked at each other. "There are many girls living in this communal center. I don't know all of their names. Well, you have to wait," said the chef with the pots. "The girls will come back from work anytime soon."

They went back to cooking. I walked outside of the hut, sat under a shade tree, and waited with the hope of seeing Vanny.

When the sun began to set, I saw several lines of girls walking from different directions toward the communal center. The majority of them carried a machete on their shoulders, which they used to cut bushes to make fertilizer. There were about two hundred girls living in this center. My eyes scanned each one of them, but I didn't see Vanny. I was disappointed.

The communal chefs provided me dinner. They gave me the same amount of food as the rest of the girls: two scoops of steamed rice and a scoop of soup. The group leaders ordered me to sleep on the same bed with the older girls, who set mosquito nets and had me sleep in the middle. They loved me like their young brother.

More than ten girls approached and asked me questions. They came one after another, as if they were taking turns interviewing me. They asked me many questions. Where are you from? What is your name? How old are you? What is your sister's name? What is your Mak and Pa's name? How did you get here?

After a while, I got tired of answering the same questions. I closed my eyes and pretended to be sleeping. My mind wandered. I imagined myself talking to angels to help me locate my sister. But there were no signs of locating Vanny.

When I woke up in the morning, the communal chefs wrapped food for me to take, and the group leader walked me out of the communal center. "You have to go back to where you live. There is no hospital in this village. If you were to continue to walk farther, you wouldn't find anybody, only the jungle. There will be no road and no canal."

"But I want to see my sister. I want to continue my journey along this water canal. I miss her and love her."

"Young comrade, this canal ends about one kilometer from here." She pointed north.

I looked at that direction. All I could see was thick blurry trees at a great distance that stretched to the horizon. It was a major disappointment. I couldn't believe that the lady who had returned from "holiday" had given me false information. I had walked two days just to find my lovely sister. Now, I felt hopeless and depressed. My face went numb, and I couldn't feel the tears rolling down my cheeks and building up in the corners of my lips.

When I walked back to my group, my depression was mixed with frustration. I punched and kicked at the air with ferocity. I hit the bushes with sticks to release my irritation, and prayed to Tevada in Heaven. I demanded that Tevada bring my sister to me. But he did not.

9

Defying Life and Death

Abandonment and Survival

Angkar Luer had a new mission for the people: to work on sugarcane farms and corn farms in the remote areas for three months. I overheard people say that the new work site was far. It would take them two days of walking to get there.

Vichet and I were not included in this new work project. The evening before the Khmer Rouge moved people out of the village, I saw Vichet sitting inside my hut. He was about ten or twenty meters away from me. While he was preparing a place to sleep for the night, I saw Mittbong-Mai and Mittbong-Seouth walk from the communal kitchen and approach him. They stood in front of him, and he tilted his head upward to look at them.

"Vichet," Mittbong-Seouth said to him, "we will be leaving tomorrow morning. You and Marin will watch over the rice field." Mittbong-Mai briefly looked at me, then said to Vichet, "We will come back when the rice in the fields bear seeds. Our job at the corn farms will be finished within three months. Once we finish our job, we will come back to the center. I want both of you to stay here and wait for us until we return."

They both cracked into a small laugh and ordered Vichet to follow them to the kitchen.

At that time, I had no perception of time. I didn't know how many days were in a week, how many weeks were in a month, or even how many months were in a year. All I knew was day and night, rain and shine. However, staying at the center until the rice bore seeds seemed like a very long time. I thought the two mittbongs must be joking. It never came to me that they were seriously abandoning Vichet and me in the village to survive on our own. I thought they just wanted to scare us for fun.

The next morning, I continued to think that the Khmer Rouge soldiers were teasing me. Then the whistle blew. The people grabbed all their small belongings and lined up in two long lines for head count.

Vichet sat in the hut, with his back leaned against the bamboo post. I ran to stand behind one of the lines. When the Khmer Rouge finished with the head count, they ordered the people to walk toward the glowing sunrise. The people began to walk orderly by following each other's footsteps, and I followed them.

After I had walked about fifty meters, Mittbong-Seouth pointed at me and shouted, "Go back to the hut! You can't come with us!"

I stopped as he commanded, and I watched the people moving away from me. After they were one hundred meters away, I ran to follow them. Mittbong-Mai chased me back to the hut, and I began to realize that the Khmer Rouge were serious about leaving the two of us to survive on our own.

At that moment, fear began to strike in my nerves, and my head was traumatized with all sorts of fear. I was afraid the Khmer Rouge soldiers would torture and kill me like they had the two prisoners. I was scared the soldiers would cut off my head and throw it into the canal, like the group of women had seen. Because of all that Rith had told me about dead people haunting the living, I was afraid that a headless dead body floating in the canal would come to haunt me in the daylight and at night. I had once stayed in the forest by myself, but I hadn't experienced the kind of terror I had seen in this village.

This trauma pressed me to get out of this village, and I began to cry and run after them again. They chased me all the way back to hut. I ran and cried, begging the Khmer Rouge to take me with the group. "Please let me go with you. I don't want to stay here. I'm scared to live here," I begged.

"Go back to the hut now!" they shouted with clenched faces.

As the people moved farther and farther away from me, I ran after them again.

"Go back! You stubborn kid! Stop following us!" Mittbong-Seouth shouted and chased after me with a stick in his hand.

I cried and ran back to the hut.

Then Mittbong-Mai and Mittbong-Seouth were tired of chasing me back and forth from the line to hut. So, Mittbong-Mai chased me again and caught me by the head. He whipped my legs, threw me to the ground, and beat me all over my body. "Do you want to die this way, *ar-juymaray!*"

I cried. I screamed. I shouted. I kicked. I twisted and turned to free myself. I ran back to the hut in agonizing pain all over my body. I was horrified.

I cried all day near Vichet. He sat quietly, looked at my bruises, and watched blood dripping from my body.

In the afternoon, while I was still crying, Vichet got up, walked to the communal kitchen, and started cooking. He cooked rice and roasted *prohok*, a fermented fish. After the food was cooked, he shared the food with me equally.

The Khmer Rouge had put Vichet in charge of us, and not me, probably because he was smart. Perhaps he was two years older than me, or maybe he was just more mature and taller than me.

Vichet was also meek and a bit of a follower. Whatever the Khmer Rouge told him to do he would do it. From the first time we had met, he and I had never had the chance to talk or to play with each other. The Khmer Rouge had put us to work in different rice fields. Now, Vichet would manage my life. He would decide what to eat and the amount of food I should be eating.

The Khmer Rouge had left Vichet half a sack of rice and a small jar of *prohok,* a fermented fish. They also gave him pots and pans, bowls, spoons, a machete, and a lighter left behind in the communal kitchen. The intentions of the Khmer Rouge were clear: They wanted to kill both of us in a subtle way. They probably thought we would be dead after the food ran out.

The first few days, I was both bored and scared, and I was afraid to walk out of the hut. At night, Vichet and I slept on the ground huddled next to each other like cats and dogs do.

As the days passed, my fear faded. During the days, we would roam the field to search for food and eat whatever we could find. After many days had passed, we refined our survival skills. We no longer ate grasshoppers, crickets, and centipedes. We ate fish, snails, and frogs, which were more plentiful and easier to catch. Catching fish in the rice field that had water rising to our knees was easy. I had learned and perfected the well-trap technique that I had learned from my dad.

I dug a small well, waist deep, in the rice field. I elevated the mud around the well to prevent water from getting in. Then I scooped the water out of the well. Once I finished scooping the water out of the well, I made a smooth surface around the well to make the fish slip into the well.

Then I dug three holes, one in each rice field. Each hole was the size of a barrel. I dug it about a meter deep, and built a levee around it to prevent water from getting out. I then scooped the water out, smoothed the levee surface, and built it three inches above the water. I left it overnight. No fish bait was required.

In the mornings, I went to collect fish from the well. Sometimes I caught catfish, but most of the time I caught snakehead fish.

I wondered how the stupid fish fell into my trap. Maybe they were goofing around with each other and accidentally fell in the well? Maybe they liked to play on the smooth surface around the hole? Perhaps they mated on the smooth surface and accidentally fell in the hole? I wished I could understand their minds.

Vichet and I became best friends. We shared everything that we caught.

One morning, he killed a big centipede near our fire pit. He beat the hell out of the creature and tossed it into the fire. We had it for breakfast. It tasted like over-toasted crab meat.

One drizzling morning, I sat by the fire pit inside the hut. I was bored and was playing with the smoke, catching it with my palms. While I was entertaining myself by the fire pit, I saw a snake the size of a broom stick, over a meter long, crawling over a dead log with small branches. I shouted and pointed, "Vichet! Snake!"

Quickly, I ran to the communal kitchen, grabbed two crooked long sticks the width of my wrist and gave one to Vichet. He ran behind me toward the snake. In fear and bravery, we beat the snake. We killed it.

"This snake is not as poisonous as a king cobra. Maybe a frog killer snake, a type of snake that hunts for frogs," Vichet said, like he wasn't sure what kind of snake it was. Whatever Vichet said I believed. I didn't know any better.

That mid-afternoon, Vichet and I prepared the snake for lunch. He cut the snake head off and tossed it into the fire pit. The head of the snake slowly burned and turned into ashes. While Vichet held the snake, he asked me to help him. "Marin, can you help me hold the tail of the snake? I want to slit the snake's belly open."

"How do I hold it?" I asked.

"You hold it with two hands and pull it tightly."

I did what he instructed me to do. I grabbed the tail of the snake with both hands and pulled.

When Vichet slit the snake's belly open, the snake's tail began to move as if it wanted to grab onto my wrist. I was nervous and dropped the snake. "Vichet! The snake is still alive. Maybe its soul is still trapped in its body."

Vichet continued to sit, firmly holding both the knife and the snake. He said, "The snake is already dead," he said, "but the nerves of the snake forced its tail to move."

After the belly of the snake was slit open, Vichet removed its internal organs and put them into the cooking pot. His hands were soaked in snake blood, but he didn't wash his hands. Then we skinned the snake by pulling it in opposite directions. I held onto the snake by the neck as tightly as possible, while Vichet pulled the skin from the neck all the way to the tail, to reveal the white meat underneath. Vichet chopped the snake into many pieces, placed them into the pot with the guts and the veins and boiled it. It was a lot of snake soup for two people. The snake meat tasted like chicken; it was bony, but we chewed everything, including the bones.

Vichet and I had lots of freedom and stayed well-fed. We could sleep as long as we wanted. We didn't need to work. All we thought about was what we were going to do for play and what we were going to eat the next day. Whenever we got bored, we caught male crickets for a cricket fight. If they wouldn't fight, we forced them to fight by yanking their antennas and spinning them several times. Then we put them back in the pot and watched them fight. We tossed the losing crickets into the fire and had them for a snack.

After many days passed, the food supplies that the Khmer Rouge had left for us were about to run out. So there was no more cooked steam rice, and Vichet only cooked plain rice porridge that was in a sack the Khmer Rouge had given us. I didn't care much. I ate whatever Vichet cooked. Moreover, I had a new source of food: The rice in the field got older and turned from light green to deep green; and the rice was pregnant, bearing young seeds in the tubes. I picked the pregnant rice and ate it. It smelled like grass and tasted like raw rice milk.

The Hot Chilies Competition

It was approximately three months since Vichet and I had been left alone at the village—and the others returned. Their return made me worry. I was afraid they would abuse and torture me again.

When Mittbong-Mai and Mittbong-Seouth saw us, they were surprised we were still alive. "You two are tough kids," Mittbong-Mai said.

The first day of their arrival, the Khmer Rouge began to abuse us again. They served us a full bowl of soup mixed with the hottest chilies. They crushed half a dozen tiny red chilies in the soup, then ordered Vichet and me to eat for competition.

"This is your celebration for being able to survive on your own. When I count to three, you have to eat all the soup," Mittbong-Seouth said.

Vichet and I sat facing each other in front of our soup bowls, waiting for the signal to start. On the count of three, we began to eat.

The first scoop of food in my mouth was burning hot and made my eyes tear like a monsoon rain. I continued to eat and slurp, though my nose poured clear mucus. My head went numb, my eyes got blurry and teary, and my ears couldn't hear anything. No matter how spicy it was, though, I continued to eat until the bowl was completely empty.

I finished first and ran to the communal kitchen to drink and cool off my mouth and head. Then I stood outside and opened my mouth wide, trying to catch my breath.

The Khmer Rouge were laughing among themselves. I was furious, and wished death upon them. I wanted to kill them with my spoon.

I prayed to the Evil who lived in Hell to crack the earth open and pull them to the lowest level of hell. "Evil, whenever you pull the

Khmer Rouge to Hell, please crush hot chilies and smack it on their faces and spread it around their eyes. I want to see them cry with irritating blindness. Devil, please have them bitten by furious and poisonous snakes and let them die in pain."

All the dreadful wishes I had for the Khmer Rouge never came true. But one afternoon, Mittbong-Mai was bitten in the foot by a huge blue-headed centipede. I was happy and wanted him to suffer. I was proud of that centipede for taking revenge for me.

Mittbong Mai's foot was swollen and turned blue. He couldn't even walk. His painful foot made him feel uncomfortable sleeping on the hammock, so he slept on the ground near me. He buried his injured foot into the ground, believing the cool dirt would help ease his pain and heal it faster. He cried and moaned, like a child crying for his mother. While he moaned and screamed, I covered my head with a *kroma* and laughed quietly.

I had fun watching Mittbong-Mai suffer, and I wished another centipede would come and bite his other foot. My wishes of death for the Khmer Rouge became stronger. I wished the centipede would send its whole family to bite the rest of the Khmer Rouge leaders who had hurt me.

The Tiny Rascal Workers Group

Less than ten days after the Khmer Rouge forced me to eat the hot chilies, Angkar Luer transferred Vichet and me to live with the *Kang-Komara*, a group of boys ages eight to twelve.

Angkar Luer had recently moved the boy group from somewhere else and placed them to live by the mouth of the river, which was about a kilometer away from where the soldiers lived. The only route to the *Kang-Komara* camp was to walk along the water canal to the east. Mittbong-Seouth walked Vichet and me along the east canal to the *Kang-Komara* living quarters.

While I was walking along the canal, a flash of bad memories resurged in my mind. I remembered Mittbong-Mia and Mittbong-Seouth chasing and beating me with sticks along this canal. The horrific memories made me withdraw now and walk slower, trying to distance myself from Mittbong-Seouth. Vichet walked right behind him, but I stayed twenty meters farther behind. Mittbong-Seouth was in a bad mood, and I felt he wanted to hurt me. I would not let him catch me this time.

After about half an hour of walking, we arrived at the *Kang-Komara* site. I was excited and scared at the same time. This was the first time I would experience living with a children's group, and I didn't know how the new Khmer Rouge would treat me.

Upon arrival inside the hut, I saw more than one hundred boys ages nine to thirteen. Some were conversing. Some were taking naps. About a dozen were sitting on a platform, looking at Vichet and me.

While I was observing the boys, I heard a shout: "Are those the two boys that Angkar Luer sent to us?"

Instinctively I turned my head and saw one *mittbong* coming out of a smaller hut, approaching Mittbong-Seouth.

Mittbong-Seouth giggled a bit and said, "Yes, these are the two boys."

Minutes later, two female *mittbongs* and another male *mittbong* came out of their huts to speak with Mittbong-Seouth. All the four *mittbongs* were about the same age, in their mid-twenties.

While they were conversing, I stood next to Vichet and observed our new living conditions. It was a bit better than the place where we had moved from. The huts had three walls, one in the back and two on the sides. Both structures had a woven bamboo platform that was raised two meters above the ground. The bigger hut was used as a living quarters for us boys, the smaller one was for the *mittbongs*. The two huts faced the river and the sunrise.

That evening, the *mittbongs* told all of us boys to get out of the hut and to stand before them. Everyone did exactly as they were told.

Then one of the male *mittbongs* said, "Today, we can relax. We will begin working tomorrow. We will take care of rice, the rice plants in the field, and fixing rice-field levees. We must work in groups."

One of the female *mittbongs* looked at the boys and said, "Today we will divide all of you into four small groups. Once the group is divided, you must stay with that group. You must eat with that group and sleep in the hut with that group. And you must go to work with that group."

After the groups were divided, a *mittbong* handpicked a group that he or she wanted to manage. My group was chosen by Mittbong-Bross, a buff, dark-complexioned man of a thick medium build. Vichet was not in my group. He was chosen by a lady *mittbong*. Because of this division of groups, he and I didn't have the opportunity to talk to each other anymore. We would see each other, but we were separated the whole time.

The next morning after our arrival, the whistle blow forced everyone to wake up and to stand in line for a head count. We all rushed to the river to wash our faces. I washed my face and rinsed my mouth like everyone else. Then I rushed to line up with my group and face Mittbong-Bross.

Mittbong-Bross ordered, "Put your hand behind each other's shoulders and form a straight line."

I stood behind the other boys, one arm's length behind them.

"Next to me is a pile of working tools," said Mittbong-Bross. "There are *bonkees* and hoes. You must choose a tool to work with."

I picked a *bonkee* because I thought that digging with the hoes would be the harder task. With my tool, I marched along the rice-field levee to search and destroy bushes growing in the field. My group wasn't just cutting bushes; we were also fixing rice-field levees and controlling the flow of the amount of water in the field. We were like a tiny rascal engineering team. If the rice field had too much water, we cut the rice-field levee open to drain some water out. If the rice fields were too dry, we broke a small water canal to make the water flow in.

But I was not an obedient boy looking for broken levees or bushes. I was good at looking for food—in the bushes, on trees, and in the ground.

The King Snake

One morning in the soft muddy field, I spotted a small hole the size of my wrist. I thought either a crab or a frog lived in it. I inserted a twig into the den to test its depth and to track the direction of the hole.

The den was two arm-lengths deep. I began digging the hole with a piece of wood and scooped the dirt out. After I dug deep enough, I inserted my hands into the hole to grab whatever was in it. My fingers touched something soft. I thought it was a frog.

When I got it out from the muddy hole, it was a snake the size of a drum stick. Before I noticed, it bit my right middle finger, and a small amount of blood came out of my wounded finger. My heart hammered hard and fast, and sweat began to drip down my head.

Being frightened of death jolted me to kill the snake with the stick in a frenzied manner. I was scared and thought I was going to die soon. I used to hear people say, "When the king cobra snake bites you, you will die in a short period of time. You can't even walk past a distance of two rice fields for help." I ran several steps away from the den and screamed for help.

"Help! Somebody help me! I got bitten by a snake. Help! I will die soon! Please somebody help me! I don't want to die!"

Three boys heard my screaming and shouting and ran toward me. "What kind of snake is it?" one of the boys asked.

"I don't know."

"Where did it bite you?"

"Here." I showed them my bleeding middle finger.

"Does it hurt?"

"Yeah….no…not really. It hurts a little bit."

"You are not going to die. The snake had no poison," said one of the boys.

"Are you sure I'm not going to die?"

"Where is the snake?" the boys asked.

"Near the den. I killed it."

We went to the den and one of the boys grabbed the dead snake and said, "This *is pous-channa-morm* snake. It is the king snake. You are lucky being bitten by this snake."

I was crying and confused with what he was saying. I quickly wiped off my tears and asked him, "What do you mean I'm lucky? You mean I am not going to die tonight?"

"Once the king snake bites you, no other snake will dare bite you again. I wish I had been bitten by the king snake," he said. "Now, you have to shout in every direction, declaring that the king snake has bitten you."

The way he said it sounded convincing. Whether it was true or not, I believed him. I ran about twenty meters from the den in every direction and started shouting as loud as I could.

"All snakes living in the rice field, in the swarm, and in the forest, please hear me now! My name is Marin! You cannot bite me! Because the king snake just bit me!"

I ran in all directions—north, south, east, west—and shouted the same message several times until my throat dried and became itchy.

While I was shouting, I noticed the three boys were working together to cook the dead king snake I had killed. By the time I finished shouting and screaming, the snake was almost cooked. They toasted and turned the snake in the freshly made fire pit that contained small twigs and dead grasses. Once the snake was cooked, the boys rationed it. "Marin, you get the biggest piece because you are the one who killed the snake," said the boy who cooked it.

After I finished eating the king snake, I began to realize I wasn't going to die. My finger was no longer bleeding, and my heart was beating at a normal rate. My fear of death had dissolved.

A Tug-of-War with Snakes

It was midday, and I was exhausted from a day of hard work. The group leader called all the boys in the field to line up for the head count and to march to the communal cafeteria for lunch. I was at the end of the line. Behind me was my group leader.

While I was walking, I saw a rice plant moving from side to side as if an animal was walking in the field. It was a strange movement. At that moment, I pretended to have a stomachache and I asked my leader for permission to go to the restroom. With one hand I held onto my stomach and, with the other, I held my buttocks, pretending this was a real emergency. With a frowning face, I said, "Mittbong, I need to release my bowels. Please let me go."

"Go ahead. Don't take too long," he said.

Quickly, I ran onto the rice field to locate the strange movement. I sat down, pretending to relieve my bowels, and scanned the area. I saw a snake the size of my thigh crawling slowly over the soft muddy rice field. It was about two meters long. Its belly was twice as big as its body. Maybe it was pregnant or maybe its stomach had too much food. The snake had shiny blue scales, like peacock feathers. Its head and neck were about the same size. I followed it and learned about it. And I realized it was a *pous-chanamorm*, the type of snake that had bit me. But I was not 100 percent sure.

I remembered the moment when the boy had told me, "When *pous-chanamorm* bites you, no other snake would dare to bite you again." I believed what the boy had said, but at the same time I was skeptical. Although I had mixed feelings, I continued to follow the king snake. I looked for a stick or a stone to kill it, but I couldn't find any.

Then I thought of another technique of killing the snake with my bare hands, by grabbing its tail and swinging it hard to the ground. My determination was strong. I jumped to grab the tail of the snake with two hands and quickly dragged it backward several steps. I lifted up its tail in an attempt to slam it to the ground. But when I lifted its tail above my chest, the snake turned its head toward me, coiled its neck and lunged at me with a wide-open jaw. I jumped backward quickly and released it. It missed biting me by centimeters. My reaction was as quick as the snake's strike.

I was nervous. My heart was beating fast. But I was determined to kill the snake for food. My instincts told me that if I were to kill the snake and bring it to my group, everyone would respect me and would be proud of me.

The snake continued to crawl forward. I continued to grab its tail and pull it backward in an attempt to kill it with my bare hands. Every time I got its tail, it struck at me wildly.

Minutes later, I saw another snake that was the size of a broom stick. It was crawling less than ten meters behind me. It crawled fast in the opposite direction of the other snake. I didn't know what type of snake it was, but I ran after it and grabbed its tail and tried to kill it. The moment I touched its tail, it raised its head, widened its neck, and lunged at me. I quickly jumped backward.

Then I began to realize it was a cobra. I had learned about the cobra from Rith. When he and I had guarded the cucumber farm, Rith had talked about how deadly the king cobra was. Now, here I was confronting one of the deadliest snakes.

The cobra was much faster and brutal than the *pous-chanamorm*. Its head arose and it faced me. It widened its neck to show me it was brutal and deadly. But my temptation to kill it for food was stronger. After several attempts to kill the cobra, the snake stood its ground, ready to attack me.

I ran back to find the *pous-chanamorm,* and again tried to kill it with my bare hands, more than ten times. But the snake was too big and too heavy for me to kill, and my attempt was not successful.

So I ran back to the cobra and tried to kill it again. But I couldn't. I ran back and forth many times, but I couldn't catch both snakes. I ran until I got exhausted and could no longer chase after them.

Then my body began to shake, and sweat began to drip from my forehead and every pore of my body. I felt cold and weak, and I couldn't walk. I collapsed in the rice field near the canal, exhausted, hungry and thirsty.

I crawled to the canal to drink. I drank a lot of water and washed the sweat off my face. Then I scooped water with my palms and splashed it onto my body to cool myself. I crawled out of the canal and rested under a small shade tree, where I fell asleep.

Saved by the Khmer Rouge

While I was asleep, the shade slowly moved and left me baking in the scorching sun. When I woke up, I couldn't move my body. I couldn't move my head, my arms, or my legs. I tried to open my eyes, but I couldn't see anything. All I could see was a blurry bright light. I felt like I was going to die.

I could hear the sound of my own mumbling and moaning for help. I moaned for Mak, Pa, Roth, and Tevada to save me from dying. But they didn't help me. My eyes remained shut. My ears remained open. I listened to the slow heartbeat from my chest.

Then I heard a shouting that sounded like it was from a dream. "Aaah! Aah! Aaaah! Aah! Get up. Ah! Aah! Drink water!" It felt like somebody moved me. Minutes later, I felt splashing water on my face and my body, and my eyes began to open slowly. I saw a blurry shadow sit me down against him. When I was fully conscious again, a young man in a black uniform fed me water and shook me awake.

"Can you sit down? Can you stand up?" he asked.

"Hmmm...no...noo," I responded in a fussy and exhausted voice.

The young man wrapped his hands around my body, stood me

up, and carried me on his back. He carried me along the paddy rice levees and water canals until he reached his thatch house. He took me inside and lay me down on a platform.

Then an old lady came in and said, "Sophal, who…is it? Who is that child? Where….did you get him from?"

"Mother, I found him by the water canal under the scorching sun. At first, I thought he was dead. When I approached him closer, I heard him mumbling for help. If I didn't help him, he would have died."

"Go to the communal kitchen and ask for rice. I will cook rice porridge for him. Hurry up! Go! Go!" said Sophal's mother.

Sophal rushed out of the house and ran to the communal kitchen. After he left, I managed to turn my head and look at his mother. She was starting a fire. I couldn't see her face. All I saw was the back of her head and a portion of her back. She had straight black hair below her shoulders, and a *kroma* tied to her head. She had a dark-brown complexion like her son, Sophal. She looked healthy and strong.

I turned my eyes in every direction, trying to study what was inside the house. It was about five meters by eight meters, built from palm leaves and wooden posts. The kitchen was basic and simple, with a small fire pit elevated about half a meter above the ground. There were a few pots and pans hanging on the wall next to a pile of firewood. The entire house was open; no wall separated the platform on which I lay.

I watched smoke rise from the clay stove, and Sophal returned with a small amount of rice wrapped in a *kroma* and gave it to his mother. "Here is the rice, mother."

"When you went to get rice from the communal kitchen, did anyone ask you anything?" she asked.

"No."

"Don't let anyone know we have a person in our house."

"Yes, mother."

While Sophal's mother waited for the porridge rice to cook, she stripped me naked and cleaned me with a wetted cloth to remove dirt off my body. I felt sensitive and sore, like I suffered a severe fever. She finished washing me, wrapped a blanket around me, and had me sit beside Sophal.

"Sophal, can you hold him?" she asked. "Let me get the food to feed him."

Sophal got on the bed and sat me up. He leaned my back against his feet to keep me from falling.

The rice porridge was ready. Sophal's mother poured it onto the plate, crushed a boiled egg and mixed it in.

I was starving. My eyes locked onto the food. I could barely control myself when I saw the hot steam come off the plate and permeate the house. I wanted to grab the plate and gulp it all down.

"I know you are hungry, son," said Sophal's mother, "but you have to sit still. I will feed you." She fed me one spoon at a time until the plate was completely empty. After I finished eating, they put me back to rest.

That night, my body temperature grew increasingly hot. My whole body was sensitive and sore. When I coughed and sneezed, aches ran through every part of my body. Sophal's mother pulled off my blanket, positioned me face down, and set her leg over my feet to prevent me from moving. They began to *kors-kajol*.[3] She applied a tiger-balm ointment along my ribcages and spine, and scratched me with a smooth-edged coin. It was painful. I cried and told her not to scratch too hard.

"Aunty, please don't scratch me too hard. I hurt."

"I know it hurts, son. You will feel better when it is done."

She finished the *kors-kajol* on my back, then rolled me over and started to scratch the front of my body. She scratched my chest, my stomach, my forearms, and my thighs. She scratched until dark red marks appeared on my skin.

---

3 Coining, a traditional healing remedy for fevers or cold.

When the *kors-kajol* was done, my chest and arms looked like somebody had tortured me methodically with a whip. There were red marks about an inch apart from each other along my ribcages, my chest, and my stomach. After she finished the *kors-kajol*, she put me back to sleep again.

Sophal and his mother were Khmer Rouge, but not hardcore. They had to have a heart to care for a child like me and save me from dying.

In the morning, I was able to crawl onto the woven bamboo bed, and I sat by the wooden post of the thatch house. Two days later, I felt better and was able to walk. I wanted to wander around outside of the house, but Sophal's mother wouldn't allow it. I could only get outside of the house to urinate or to use the bathroom. She didn't want anyone to see me. She was afraid Angkar would accuse her of abetting the enemy. According to the Angkar, anybody who escaped from the group was considered an enemy.

One night, Sophal's mother used a kettle to boil herbal drinks. I leaned against the middle post of the house and watched her. Sophal sat on the platform next to me, with his feet hanging to the ground. His mother asked me many questions.

"What is your name, son?" she asked me while removing the *kroma* off her head.

"My name is Marin."

"What is your Mak's name?"

"My mak's name was Yim. And she…she died in the hospital," I said in a somber tone. I missed Mak.

Sophal's mother turned around, added more firewood into the stove, and checked her herbal kettle. Then she turned back around and hung a *kroma* over her shoulder. "What is your dad's name?" she asked.

"My dad's name was Yann. He died of hard labor, building the canal."

She sighed with a long breath. "Oh *Preah Oey* (oh God). Why did our country become like this?" she said with sorrow and sympathy in her face. "Do you have brother or sister?" she asked.

"Yes, I do. I have a younger brother, but he died. And my sister, she is still alive, but I don't know where she is at."

"What year were you born? Do you know what animal sign?"

"I don't know. I don't know my age. I don't know what year I was born."

"Son, what group do you live in? I have to send you back to your group. If Angkar Luer knows you are living with me, we will be in trouble."

Sent Back to the Tiny Rascal Workers Group

After nine days of living with Sophal and his mother, they decided to send me back to my group. I was terrified that my group leader would punish me, maybe even kill me. I sat and held onto the wooden post of the house, shivering and not wanting to leave.

Sophal's mother went outside of the house. A moment later, she came back and called Sophal to step out of the house and talk to him. I overheard their conversation.

"Son, you have to tell his leader not to hurt him. You have to take him to his group now," said the mother.

Despite what I heard Sophal's mother say, my fear was not abated. The moment I walked out of Sophal's house, I had horrific flashbacks of all I had seen and experienced. I thought about all that the Khmer Rouge might possibly do to me. Would they accuse me for betraying Angkar? Would they accuse me of being their enemy? Would they put me in prison and lock my neck in a yoke like they did those prisoners? Would they stab and kill me with a knife, like the two prisoners who escaped from the hut? Would they whip me with the iron bar, like they did the emaciated lady prisoner? Would they tie my neck to the wooden post, like they did the lady prisoner? Would they whip me and kick me and force me to stand in the canal that is infested with leeches, like they did to me before? Would they strangle me by the neck, like they did when I was caught stealing rice from the warehouse?

The flashbacks were intense and overwhelming. It made me tense and shaky. My eyes began to blur as if people were pouring muddy water over my face. I wiped my face with my hands and realized it was my tears. I felt like my heart was no longer beating. I could feel my soul slowly escaping from my body. Half of my upper body felt light, like a balloon filled with air. My head felt numb. My ears couldn't even hear my own crying. The lower half of my body felt heavy. When I walked it felt like thick heavy bricks were cemented to my feet. Every step I took, I felt heavy. This was the first time I ever felt this way.

After a long morning of us walking, Sophal approached my group leader who was standing in the field not far from where I had tried to catch the snake. When I saw my group leader, my body felt light like my soul flew out of my body.

I began to walk slower trying to distance myself from Sophal. My horrible thoughts of punishment continued. Would my leader kill me by tying me up to a tree filled with fire ants? Would he punish me by tying me up and throw me into water infested with leeches?

As Sophal talked to my leader, I began to tremble. I thought of running away. I didn't know what Sophal was telling my group leader because I was more than one rice field away from them.

After Sophal had a brief conversation with my leader, he turned and called me, "Marin, come here!" He waved his hand, signaling me to approach. I began to cry and refused to walk toward them.

"Why are you crying?" Sophal shouted.

"I am afraid my leader will beat me and kill me like they did the two prisoners."

"I am here. Nobody is going to hurt you," Sophal said.

I walked slowly toward him, whining, and shaking like a rabbit.

"Stop crying," said the group leader. "I will not hurt you."

I wiped off my tears with my palms and forearms and stopped crying.

"Here! Take the hoe and go to work with them," said my leader.

He handed me a hoe and pointed to the boys who were cutting bushes. I felt relieved.

All the boys had their eyes on me and asked, "Where have you been the last several days?"

I didn't tell them the whole story. All I told them was I was severely ill.

Sophal walked back to his place. I wondered why he didn't allow me to stay with him? What kind of job did he do? I wondered. What kind of power did he have?

I could have a job like him. Just walk around and save children like me. From all the Khmer Rouge leaders that I knew, I respected Sophal the most. He saved my life, and he told the other leaders not to hurt me.

10

The Tiny Rascal Engineering Team

My New Job As a Bird Chaser

Many days after I returned from Sophal's home, all rice in the rice fields bore seeds. The fields turned from green to golden red. When the rice changed color, the temperature also changed from warm to freezing cold, especially at night and in the morning. There was no more rain, and the water in the rice fields began to dry.

My job position also changed, from maintaining the rice fields to chasing birds away. My new responsibility was to shout, scream, and yell at the birds, preventing them from landing on the rice fields. If one flock of birds was to land in a rice field, all the rice crops would be gone in minutes.

Every morning, flocks of birds flew from west to east in search of food. In the evening, before sunset, thousands of birds flew in flocks over the rice fields, coming in like a thick black cloud, moving fast and zigzagging in the sky. The flocks of birds in the evening were much larger than the morning flocks.

Our group leader warned us not to neglect our work. "If anyone allows birds to land on the rice fields," he said, "Angkar will punish them to the extent of Angkar's law."

I was assigned to the two rice fields near where the baby snake had bitten me. When I saw birds flying over the rice field, I ran onto the rice-field levees, screamed, shouted, yelled, and threw hardened dirt at them, to prevent them from eating the crops.

Evening was the busiest time. When birds migrated back to their nesting sites, they took every opportunity to refuel their energy along the way. They tried to land in every rice field to eat.

I worked from dawn until dusk, until no more birds flew over the rice field. I liked this job. It was fun. Millions of birds were afraid of me. I wanted to kill them for food, but I couldn't. Every time I threw hard dirt at them, they dodged and flew away.

Wolves Attack

The rice was ripe and healthy. Each rice stem bore countless seeds, and turned from green to gold. The vast rice field looked beautiful, like a thick golden carpet laid over the ground.

At this time, the Khmer Rouge moved the elderly women groups from different places to harvest the rice. Every day, when I walked to my work sites, I saw the women harvesting the rice and loading it onto oxcarts.

After the rice harvest season was over, the Khmer Rouge began shuffling people again. They integrated me with a young adult group and moved me to work in many different places with different tasks. Each task was short and lasted several weeks. One task was to dig a large pond to get water from the ground for drinking. Another task was to build rice-field levees. Not long after the rice-field levees were completed, the Khmer Rouge assigned me to cutting *derm-kontri-ang-ket*, a type of bushy plant that the people used to make natural compost.

After my temporary tasks were over, the Khmer Rouge ordered

me to watch over the pumpkin and yucca farm. It was about the size of seven soccer fields and located in a remote place. To the north of the farm was a jungle; to the south, east, and west of the farm was grassy land.

I worked with five adult males. Four of them were in their late teens. I don't remember all their names because I called everyone *Pu*.

The only person whose name I can remember was Phoeun. I called him Pu Phoeun. He was in his late twenties, had a light-brown complexion and wavy hair. He was the oldest and the tallest person in our group. The Khmer Rouge chose him to be the group leader.

Although the pumpkin and yucca farm was in a remote location, the Khmer Rouge soldiers occasionally came to check to see if anyone had escaped from elsewhere and was hiding near the farm. Sometimes, they checked on us to see if we were working. However, Pu Phoeun outsmarted the soldiers. When he saw Khmer Rouge soldiers patrolling the farm, he ordered all of us to work hard by pulling weeds and softening the soil. Then when the soldiers left the site, he ordered us just to walk and patrol the farm.

Pu Phoeun understood the dynamics of the group. He encouraged us to share whatever we caught in the farm. Sometimes people caught snakes. All six of us lived in a hut, which was approximately five meters wide and fifteen meters long. The hut was built of bamboo, with walls made of palm leaves, and a roof made of reeds. It had four shutters and an entrance, but no door. Inside the hut was a platform we used to sleep on; it was one meter above the ground.

By day, the farm seemed safe and peaceful. But at night, this place belonged to scary creatures: poisonous snakes, wolves, and tigers. Packs of wolves howled from many different directions. Nocturnal birds flew over our hut and shouted loudly, like they wanted to chase us out of their territory.

At night, we were all scared, especially since there was no moonlight and low visibility. As the days passed, it seemed like more and more wolves were getting closer to our hut and howling even louder. We were afraid to sleep on the platform. We were afraid the wolves and tigers would come and attack us during our sleep. So, Pu Phoeun requested hammocks from Angkar Luer, which he distributed to us. We tied the hammocks high above our beds, almost touching the roof.

One time, at midnight in complete darkness, wolves and wild dogs appeared and moved toward our hut. It seemed like they wanted to kill us. They howled and called their members from different directions. They came from the east, the west, the north, and the south. We could hear their footsteps approaching the hut, rubbing their bodies against the reed wall, playing with each other.

I was frightened and clenched onto my hammock silently. I held my breath and hoped the wolves wouldn't come into the hut. My skin developed goose bumps as rough as sandpaper. My lips shook and my body trembled. I prayed and called the souls of Mak and Pa for help.

Suddenly, there was a strong and loud drum beat. Booom! Baboom! Barroom-boom! Baboom! Baboom! Barroom-boom! Baboom! Mixed with screaming and shouting, "Aghh! Aghh! Aghhhhh! Aghhhhhh!"

We screamed our guts out. I burst into screaming like everyone else. "Aghhhh! Aghhh! Aghhh! Aghhh!"

Pu Phoeun beat the empty barrel hard with a stick, and I heard the footsteps of the wolves running for their lives and bumping into each other.

Minutes after the wolves ran away, one man lit up a torch and everyone got off their hammocks and talked about how scared they were. They were scared and excited, and talked and laughed the whole night. I didn't get off my hammock, because I was still scared.

Face to Face with a Wolf

After lunch, Pu Phoeun assigned me and another person to collect wild rice. I carried a small *thass*, a round metal deep tray the size of a big plate. We went deep into the field, passing tall grasses, in search of wild rice.

We distanced ourselves far apart from each other without realizing it. I was busy picking wild rice, and the man was collecting wild fruit. I continued to walk and look for wild rice. Then I spotted movement out the corner of my eyes. I turned and looked. I saw a wolf and several puppies standing silently over their den. They were watching me.

I was stunned. Motionless. I looked at the wolf eye to eye. I stared wide in a panic. My heart pounded fast, and sweat dripped down my head.

Then my natural instincts kicked in. I shouted and screamed, banged the tray and ran several steps toward the wolf, as if I wanted to kill them all.

The puppies ran for cover into their den. The mother wolf stood firm and looked at me without any fear. I quickly turned and ran. I banged the tray. I ran. I shouted. And I screamed for help.

"Aaaaaaaaaaaaaahhhhh! Aaaaaaaah! Help! Aaaa help me! Help! Ahahahhaha help me!"

I ran and looked over my back to see if the wolf was chasing me. I looked to my left. I looked to my right. I didn't see the wolf chasing me, but I was still scared. I continued to run. I continued to scream and shout and hit the tray until I got to the hut.

Exhausted, I lay flat on the ground under the shade tree near the termite mound. I could barely catch my breath. Minutes later, the man who was collecting rice with me showed up.

"What happened to you?" he asked. "I heard you shouting, like in pain. I thought you got bit by the poisonous snake."

"Where were you? I was scared to death. I shouted for help, but you didn't come to help me."

"Didn't you hear me calling you? I ran after you when I heard you scream."

"No, I didn't hear a thing."

"Maybe you were too frightened. That was the reason you didn't hear anything."

"Yes, maybe."

After we talked about the incident, I thought it was funny. He felt the same way. We talked and laughed off the whole incident. I felt proud of myself for escaping the wolf.

How to Catch Birds with Three Chopsticks

Pu Phoeun was a compassionate man. Instead of having me work on the farm, he taught me how to catch birds for food. One afternoon, while I was sitting under the shade tree in front of the hut, Pu Phoeun approached me and gave me a small bamboo container, the size of my wrist. At first, I didn't know what was in it or why he gave it to me. I thought he wanted to share his food. I looked inside the bamboo and saw a thick white fluid in it.

"What is in it? Can I drink it now?"

He cracked into a small laugh. "Oh, no, this is not for you to drink. These tree saps are for you to catch birds!"

I raised my eyebrows. "How do you catch a bird with tree saps in the bamboo container?"

He cracked into a small laugh again. "You will see. I will teach you how."

He sat near me and crafted long chopsticks. While I watched him crafting the chopsticks, I thought he was stupid for telling me to catch birds with tree sap.

He gave me three chopsticks and told me to place them inside the bamboo container. I did what he told me to do.

"Now, stir the tree sap inside."

I didn't know how to mix them well. He grabbed the bamboo container from me and showed me how he mixed it. He sat on the ground and held the bamboo container with his heels. Then he spun the chopsticks with his palms.

"What kind of tree sap is that?" I asked.

"Three different tree saps: jrai tree, snay, and trach tree sap."

"I know those trees."

He got up and gave me the bamboo container. "I want you to mix it well together until they stick like glue," he said. "The three chopsticks are the trap to catch birds." Then he went to work with the rest of the work crews.

Although he told me it was a bird trap, I didn't believe him. I thought there was no way we could catch birds with just these chopsticks.

About an hour later, Pu Phoeun came back with a live baby mouse. "Marin, follow me. I will show you how to catch birds with three chopsticks."

I followed him into the farm, with curiosity. He found the potential location to place the trap. He cleared a small patch of land and told me to push the chopsticks into the ground.

When I didn't know how, he took one stick from my hand and pushed it into the ground. The tip with the glue was exposed, facing the sky.

I pulled the other two chopsticks and did exactly what he showed me.

He helped me to secure and position the sticks into a triangle shape, like an Indian teepee, framed to prevent each of the sticks from falling. He then tied the live mouse by the neck with a string to the base of the chopsticks and let the bait run around within the center. Then we walked back to the hut.

"I want you to watch the trap from here. Once you see a bird trapped in the sticks, just run to kill it." Then he returned to work.

Although Pu Phoeun showed me how the trap work, I still didn't have a clear picture of how a bird would be trapped into this teepee of three chopsticks with glue on the tips. I was anxious to see how a bird would be trapped.

From where I was, I looked at the farm, the trees, and sky to see if any birds were around. After not long, I saw a bird hovering high in the sky. It circled a few times and dove to catch the mouse.

I didn't see the bird flying back up into the sky. I grabbed a bamboo whipping stick the size of my big toe and ran to kill the bird. When I got to the trap, I saw the bird caught in it, with its wings and feathers stuck to the glue. The bird was trying to escape, but it couldn't. The more it struggled, the more glue stuck to its feathers.

The bird shrieked. When I raised the stick over my head, I could see its black and yellow eyeballs looking at me and the stick in horror. I hit the bird a few times until its screaming went silent.

I was excited. I grabbed the bird and ran to Pu Phoeun. I shouted from the distance, "Pu, I caught the bird!"

"Don't shout! Stop shouting!" he said and looked at me impatiently, afraid of the Khmer Rouge soldiers sneaking up on him. He clenched his teeth and said, "Stop shouting! I don't want the soldiers to hear!" That day, the soldiers were not around. Then he asked, "What kind of a bird is it?

"I don't know…"

"Oh, it is a hawk. Take it back to the hut. Once I finish working, I will cook the bird for dinner."

Since that first catch, my technique of catching birds improved drastically. I could catch almost any bird with the three chopsticks. Sometimes I used crickets and grasshoppers as bait to catch smaller birds. A bird was caught in one of my traps almost daily for a whole season.

One hot afternoon, I went to check a trap and forgot to bring my whipping stick. When I got to the site, I noticed that the chopstick traps were missing. I looked around the area and saw a crow running fast. I ran after the bird and saw two of the chopsticks traps stuck under its wings, one on each side. The bird couldn't open its wings to fly. When I tried to catch it, it resisted. It chased me with rage. I didn't want to kill the bird right way. I wanted to catch it alive to show everyone at the hut. However, every time I approached the bird, it shouted and tried to peck me with its sharp beak.

I chased after the bird a few times, but it didn't give in. We were chasing each other back and forth until my patience ran out. "You think you are tough! Let me show you how tough I am!"

I pointed at the crow as if it knew how to speak back to me. I picked hardened dirt and threw it at the bird furiously until it retreated. The bird ran for its life, with the chopstick trap stuck on each side of its wings, like a horse pulling a chariot without wheels. I threw hardened dirt chunks and hit the bird a few times. Then it collapsed. I killed the bird without any sense of remorse. I took the dead crow to Pu Phoeun to cook and he shared it with everyone.

Chef for the Pigs

It was almost summer. The pumpkins and yucca roots reached their maturity for harvest, and the Khmer Rouge came with their oxcarts to harvest the crop. The majority of them were women ages thirty to fifty. They were amazed at the healthy pumpkins.

There are two types of pumpkins. Some are round. Some are flat. These pumpkins were flat and shaped like a wheel, almost as large as a car tire. The yucca roots weren't as good; they were small and decayed.

After the pumpkins and yucca roots were harvested, the Khmer Rouge separated me from Pu Phoeun's group and integrated me into a group of fifty teenagers. They moved my new group to work in the Provincial City of Pursat. The city was small and surrounded by rice fields. Approximately, five hundred people lived in the city. More than half of them were Khmer Rouge-affiliated.

I lived near the river and the railroad bridge. I could see across the river the train station and a Buddhist temple. West of the railroad bridge was the National Road No. 5 bridge; it was the only paved road in the town. The two bridges ran parallel to each other, about half a kilometer apart.

The Khmer Rouge continued to starve people and force them into hard labor. Every day, I saw long rows of starving people walking along the rice-field levees to work. They continued to build rice-field levees and canals.

I was fortunate. The Khmer Rouge didn't send me into hard labor. Instead, they taught me how to make food to feed the pigs. I was happy with this job. Being the cook for the pigs, I realized that the level of my starvation was much less than for the rest of the people. Also, this job position gave me the opportunity to roam in the field and catch crickets, grasshoppers, and frogs for snacks. I could even eat pig food for sustenance.

One morning when everyone went to work in the fields, a Khmer Rouge woman who worked in the communal kitchen ordered me to pick *pti-tmor*, a type of vinery weed that has thick and tiny leaves. These weeds grew naturally in the field and along the railroad. Each day, I collected two full *bonkees* of *pti-tmor* and brought it to the communal center.

When I cooked, I didn't even wash the pots or clean the weeds. I dumped everything into the pot that set on the ground stove, including roots, dirt, and bugs. I poured lots of water into the pot. Once the water boiled, I put into a cooking pot some amount of *kagn-jonk-an-kor*, the poorest quality rice dust that was only used to feed animals.

When I prepared food for myself, I used a small cooking pot, the size of a soup bowl. I cleaned it well and filled it half full of water. I set it on the ground stove and let it boil. Then I collected the best quality *pti-tmor*, cleaned it thoroughly, and put it into the boiling water. I then poured some *kagn-jonk-ankor* in and stirred well until it turned slimy. I added no garlic, salt, sugar, or fish sauce. The food didn't taste good, but my starvation forced me to cook *pti-tmor* and eat like the pigs.

After countless days of feeding the pigs, I noticed they had grown to an incredible size. They were big and fat. Their cheeks were round and their bellies were almost touching the ground. A funny thought occurred to me. I was eating the same food as the pigs! Why didn't I grow any bigger? That left me wondering about my method of cooking for myself. Maybe I shouldn't clean the weeds!

One afternoon, after I finished feeding the pigs, the son of the Khmer Rouge official came to chitchat with me. His name was Pol. He was about my age, eight years old. He had the same dark-brown complexion and thick black hair, like me. Pol looked much cleaner and stronger than me, though. He wore a black uniform and thick sandals made from car tires.

After we knew each other for a few days, he asked me to play tossing marbles and hopscotch with him. He and I quickly became best friends. Every time he came to play games with me, he brought me food. Sometimes he gave me a bowl of rice. Sometimes he gave me fruit, such as ripe bananas, mangos, and coconuts.

By knowing Pol, I had the opportunity to play and run around like most kids would do. One afternoon, while we were playing hopscotch, we heard the train blowing its horn and approaching the station.

"Let's stop the game!" Pol said with excitement. "Let's go to the train! I want to see how many cabs the train pulls."

Suddenly, we raced to the coming train. When we got there, the train had just approached the railroad bridge. We stood about ten meters from the bridge and felt the vibrations of the train rolling along the railroad track and the bridge. A loud rumbling noise in the air made it hard for us to hear each other speaking.

"Marin! Look at how thick the black smoke comes out of its head! The head has lots of fire!"

"Pol! I'm amazed at the thick metal arms pushing and pulling the train! I have seen the train before, but I have never seen it up close! This train is very strong! It could pull hundreds of cabs!"

"I know! That is why it goes slow!" Pol shouted.

"Did you see the man standing on the side of the train's head and tossing firewood in the stove!" I said.

"Yeah! He puts more firewood in the head of train to make it go faster!"

"Pol! This train moves like a centipede that Vichet and I ate for breakfast! The centipede crawls so fast! It doesn't even need any fire burning in its head!"

"What? You ate a centipede?" Pol questioned me in disbelief.

"Yeah! I ate it because I was hungry! It tastes like burned crab meat! Did you know?" I said with a laugh. "A centipede has no wheels! It has many legs! But it could outrun me!"

We stood and talked until the train went past us. Then we walked back to continue our hopscotch.

Whenever Pol and I heard the sound of the train blowing its horn when approaching or leaving the station, we would stop whatever we were doing and run to watch the train up close. The sound, the black smoke that came out of it head, and the motion of the train made it very exciting.

Pol was generous. He even let me wear his black uniform. When I had his uniform on, I felt proud, strong, and brave. I felt like I had power, like the Khmer Rouge. I felt like I could eat all the food in the communal kitchen. I felt like I didn't need to worry about work. I was worry free and I forgot all my past traumas.

11

Brainwash and Confuse

The Revolution Dance

Every other day, after lunchtime, the Khmer Rouge's daughters came to the wooden, stilt hall to practice singing and dancing to praise Angkar. The hall was about seven meters wide and twelve meters in length. It had only three walls: the back and the sides. This was the place where I slept every night.

Most of the girls who came to practice dancing were in their teens: fifteen to seventeen. There were ten of them. One afternoon, while Pol and I were playing hopscotch, one of the girls called us to practice the revolution dance with them.

"Pol! Why don't you and your friend come dance with us?"

Pol turned around, brushed the dust off his hands, looked at them, and said, "I don't know how to dance."

"Come on, we will teach you two how to dance," the girls said and waved their hands, signaling us to approach them.

Pol gave in and walked toward them. I walked behind him and climbed up several steps into the hall.

One of the girls handed Pol and me a black wooden toy rifle that looked similar to the rifles the Khmer Rouge used. "Here is your rifle," she said. "Put it on your right shoulder and hold it firmly." She guided my hand to hold the rifle stock in front of my right shoulder, with the barrel pointing from my back. She guided my body to stand up straight, with my chest puffed out to look brave and strong.

"Now, you have to march alongside me in a coordinated formation, by following my footsteps," said one of the girls.

At first, I was stiff and shy. My body was tense. I felt sweaty, and I had difficulty dancing in rhythm and formation.

Another girl sat in a kneeling position and pressed the rewind button of the cassette player, searching for the right song. I didn't understand the lyrics of the song. All I cared about was following the movement of the girls in a synchronized formation. At the end of the song we aimed the rifle, pointed it into the air, and shouted, "We! Angkar sons and daughters must kill all the enemies of our mother land!"

I was totally brainwashed by these girls. I had lots of fun rehearsing the Khmer Rouge Revolution Dance. I had fun marching on the stage. I had fun aiming the play rifle into the air and shouting, "Kill the enemies!"

Some performances required carrying a hoe and a *bonkee*, to imitate hard labor in the field. I practiced with Pol several times, and performed twice in front of a small group of Khmer Rouge soldiers.

During the performance on the stage, Pol and I proudly led the girls. Our performance was based on imitating the hardworking canal builders and farm workers. We also imitated killing the enemies in our Motherland.

Who Are Enemies?

About four months after my job of feeding the pigs, a small group of Khmer Rouge workers came to claim the pigs and I overheard them talking with Pol's father.

One of the Khmer Rouges said, "Those pigs are big! They are good enough to be slaughtered to serve Angkar Luer."

That day, the Khmer Rouge captured the pigs from the barn, tied their legs, loaded them onto an oxcart, and transported them to the Khmer Rouge headquarters.

A few days after the pigs were transported out of the barn, a female *mittbong* who worked in the communal kitchen ordered me to collect firewood.

"Where do I find firewood?" I asked her.

"You walk along the railroad bridge to the other side of river. There is plenty of firewood over there."

I did what I was told to do. I walked to the railroad bridge and tried to walk across it. The one-hundred meter railroad bridge looked rusty and dilapidated, and crossing it was horrifying because it had countless gaps. Each gap was a half meter to a meter wide.

I was afraid I would slip into a gap and fall into the milky river and drown. Every gap that I crossed, my body shook, sweat drooped down my forehead and rolled into my eyes. With my arms and legs shaking, I managed to cross the bridge by hopping and creeping slowly, and holding onto the railroad nuts and bolts until I reached the other side.

Once I crossed the bridge, I collected falling dead mango, guava, and wild branches. I piled up the firewood and tied it together with vines. Then I carried the bundle of firewood on my shoulders across the bridge. This was one of the most horrifying experiences I ever had.

Also, while I was crossing the bridge, the wind blew and almost knocked me down through a gap and into the milky river. However, after crossing the railroad bridge several times, I was no longer afraid of it.

As I ventured further, I began to realize that the provincial city was small and quiet. There were no dogs or cats roaming the washed-out clay roads. Nor did I see many people walking.

One afternoon, I approached a Buddhist temple that was full of green vegetation of tangled vines that wrapped around the concrete staircase and guardrails. Around the temple, I heard leaves clattering and birds calling in the trees. I walked slowly on the broken tiles of the courtyard and stepped onto the twisted vines, which snaked around the encased walls, windows, and the main entrance. With the entangled, vine-ridden entrance of the temple, a colossal Buddha statue three meters tall sat silently with its eyes half open and peering out into the dust, debris, and spider webs of the temple hall.

Suddenly, birds flew out of the narrow opening of the temple's window and barely missed my head. Startled, I felt a chilling signal of fear down my spine and I ran away from the temple. I ran to the National Route #5 bridge and sat under a huge ompil tree to catch my breath and cool off.

While sitting, I heard a high-pitched woman's voice echoing, "Hummm, huuummmm, please help me."

It sounded like a woman desperately crying for help. Her shattered voice frightened me and I thought I was being haunted by a ghost. I peered up into the tree, but I didn't see anything, only the small falling crinkled red-orange leaves. I looked to my left and to my right, nothing. I turned my head and looked behind me, but I still didn't see anybody.

Then the sound pierced my ears again. Quickly, I moved to sit on the bridge. Then I saw a skinny lady lying motionless. She was baking in the sun by the mouth of the river, less than fifteen meters from where I was.

She shouted, "Please help me."

The moment I saw her, I had a flashback of my own near-death experience when Sophal had saved my life by splashing water over my body and forcing me to drink. I remembered how Sophal had carried me to his house and his mother had revived me back to life by coining my body.

The skinny lady's shattered voice shouting for help traumatized me. It numbed my head and I couldn't think clearly. I wanted to help her, but I couldn't. I had no home. I had no food. I had no power. If the Khmer Rouge saw me helping her, they would kill us both.

For my own safety, I walked away from the site and left the woman to die in the scorching sun. Empathy and guilt still rides in my heart and soul to this day.

That afternoon, I walked along the railroad track farther away from the train station to find firewood. While I was walking, I noticed an empty village with burned scars. The village looked like a ghost town. All the houses were completely burned and had turned into charcoal and ashes. Only a few wooden house posts stood still on their concrete foundations.

The deserted village was surrounded by mango, coconut, guava, and cashew-nut trees. There were plenty of dried tree branches that I could use for firewood. While I roamed around the village to pick up firewood, I encountered several mass graves, which were filled with scattered human skulls and bones, big and small. My body jolted and sent shockwaves of fear into my spine. My hands lunged to my chest, trying to prevent my soul from escaping. I ran and shouted, "Kamorch! Kamorch! Help! There are many kamorch! Kamorch!"[4]

I ran away and fell many times, but I didn't feel any pain. I ran all the way nonstop to a tree near the railroad bridge about one kilometer away. I stopped and rested under the shade of a tree, trying to catch my breath. My body gushed out sweat.

Alone under the shade of the tree, I began to raise questions that had no answers. Why were there so many dead people in the grave? Were the dead people the enemies of the Khmer Rouge?

When the Khmer Rouge had moved my family from the jungle to settle in another village, I had seen men with their hands tied behind their backs being escorted by the Khmer Rouge soldiers. Were those men enemies of the Khmer Rouge? Had the Khmer Rouge put them in prison or killed them in mass graves? What had they done to be the Khmer Rouge's enemies?

Why did the Khmer Rouge deprive people of food? When my

---

4   Ghost or dead body.

mother and I had killed the injured bird for food, the Khmer Rouge had threatened to kill my whole family. Had the Khmer Rouge considered Mak and me their enemy? When the Khmer Rouge man caught me stealing rice from the warehouse, he had tried to drown me in the water canal. Did he consider me his enemy?

Why was the Khmer Rouge teaching me the dance performance to kill all the enemies of our Motherland? Who were the enemies? Were all the people who worked in hard labor the enemies? Were Pa and Mak the enemies? Was I the Khmer Rouge's enemy, too?

I tried to distract myself from all these traumatizing thoughts by throwing stones onto the railroad tracks and hearing the clank of the rocks hitting the metal. But my worries were constant. I wondered what had happened to all the people who were missing. Had Angkar Luer moved them somewhere else, or killed them in the mass graves I saw?

My hatred of the Khmer Rouge contradicted the love I felt living with the Khmer Rouge. I was well-fed and I felt the Khmer Rouge would not hurt me, because they treated me like one of them.

I was confused. In the back of my mind, I also wanted to have all the Khmer Rouge soldiers killed.

I looked at the sky and prayed, "Tevada, why don't you come down to the earth to create a powerful thunderstorm and lightning to kill all the Khmer Rouge soldiers? Why do you allow the Khmer Rouge to starve and kill people?"

After discovering those mass graves, I was afraid to collect firewood farther away from the train station. I found firewood along the river, instead.

The Buddha Statues

It was a hot summer. I didn't know what month it was, but it was the hottest month of the year. The sky was a sharp, clear blue. There were barely any white clouds moving in the sky. All the fields turned from greenish to brownish. Dirt devils often formed and sucked the dead leaves and dust into the sky. All the rice fields were harvested, and only dead brown rice straws were left. Water in the ponds dried out, leaving only a few lotus plants to survive. Only the Pursat River survived the drought. It was less than half full of water. Some parts of the river were so shallow that it exposed the bottom soil.

As the weather conditions changed, the Khmer Rouge also changed their policies. They destroyed the Buddhist temple and Buddha statues. They beheaded hundreds of Buddha statues, cut off the arms and legs, and threw the bodies into the river. Some Buddha statues were cut in half and left face down at the mouth of the river.

I thought, *Why do the Khmer Rouge soldiers destroy the Buddhist temple and its statues? Are they stupid? Don't they know how to respect Buddha?*

Before the country fell into the hands of the Khmer Rouge, Pa and Mak had dressed me up nicely in a white button-shirt, short navy-blue pants, and black dress shoes, and took me to the Buddhist temple. When we got to temple, we took off our shoes before entering the temple hall. Once inside, we sat in a *bot-jerng* position, with our palms together in front our faces. We made *sompiass* to the monks, nuns, and the Buddha.

The Khmer Rouge now not only had destroyed the Buddhist temples and Buddha statues, they may also have killed many people in my group. After the temple was destroyed, Pol no longer came to play hopscotch with me. I thought perhaps his family had moved or relocated elsewhere. I no longer had a friend with whom I could play hopscotch, dance, or sing.

Within two weeks, the Khmer Rouge moved me again, to live in another place far away from Pursat.

A Rebellious Catfish

One morning on my way to collect firewood along the route No.5 railroad bridge, I saw a group of fifteen Khmer Rouge men on canoes in the river. They deployed a large commercial fishing net and moved toward the bridge. After watching them for several minutes, I walked across the bridge to the other side of the river to collect more firewood. It was noon.

When I returned from collecting the firewood, I saw the Khmer Rouge men quarantining the fish in an entire section of the river. I dropped my bundle of firewood off my shoulder onto the railroad tracks and sat behind a prickly thorn bush next to the bridge. I watched how the men were attempting to haul in the fish with a military jeep, which pulled the net closer and closer.

When the jeep pulled the net closer to the shore, hundreds of fish jumped wildly in and out of the water attempting to escape. A snakehead fish, the size of a man's thigh, jumped high over the fishing net.

"Wow, that is the largest snakehead fish I have ever seen!" said one of the Khmer Rouge. "I can't believe that fish could jump that high!"

"It jumped two meters over the fishing net!" said another.

Once they pulled the net out of the water and onto the sandy shore, I saw that the snakehead fishes were twice as big as my thighs. I had never seen fish that enormous. It amazed me how rich this river was. I wished to eat one of those freshly caught fishes. However, I was mad at the Khmer Rouge for restricting people from catching fish for food and allowing us to starve to death.

The minute the fish were hauled onto the shore, the Khmer Rouge grabbed their axes and sticks and rushed to hit the fishes in the head.

One catfish, the size of a car bumper, managed to escape. It struggled side to side. One of the Khmer Rouge, who appeared to be in his late thirties, attempted to kill the fish. He grabbed the catfish by the tail. The fish squirmed side to side, trying to escape, and its sharp fin penetrated the man's heel and shredded his feet like paper. He screamed. Blood gushed out of his feet and soaked the sand. The catfish squirmed its way back into the river.

I was proud of that catfish. I smiled and laughed inside. My heart was cheering for the fish. I was wishing the person who had been hurt by the catfish was either Mittbong-Mai or Mittbong-Seouth, who had whipped and threatened to kill me in the water canal infested with leeches, or the man who had threatened to drown me for stealing rice.

After seeing the fish inflicting the pain on the Khmer Rouge man, I thought to myself, why didn't the people rise up to take revenge? If I were as big as an adult, I would fight any Khmer Rouge. I would break their arms and legs. I would break them into submission. If I had a rifle, I would kill them, one by one.

I hoped one day that Tevada would descend from Heaven to help the people rebel against the Khmer Rouge. I hoped that one day the people would team up with poisonous snakes, centipedes, and other furious creatures to take revenge against the Khmer Rouge.

After all my death wishes for the Khmer Rouge, I picked up the bundle of firewood and carried it to the communal cafeteria, hoping my wishes for the Khmer Rouge would come true.

My Second Fight with a Khmer Rouge Son

After countless relocations, the Khmer Rouge resettled me to yet another unknown place. The landscape and condition of this village was different from all the places I had stayed. The village had rice fields, a tobacco plantation, and a fruit-tree farm. To the south of village was a jungle, which looked more well-supplied than the other places I had lived.

All the big and small stilt houses were well-built. They were made of wood, and the roofs were made of red tile. The communal cafeteria and living quarters were built from wooden slabs; and the communal center was surrounded by plenty of fruit trees that provided fruit for people to eat and plenty of shade to stay out of the heat. This was very different than the huts and rice fields I was used to staying in.

This village was occupied by hundreds of Khmer Rouge families. Older folks, age fifty and older, worked on the tobacco and fruit-tree plantation. A group of ten men worked as blacksmiths near the communal cafeteria.

Upon my arrival in the village, I didn't have any work to do. So, I watched the blacksmiths pounding metals to make machetes, swords, spears, horseshoes, and agricultural hoes. Sometimes, I observed the women shredding the tobacco leaves to make cigarettes.

A couple of days later, the Khmer Rouge ordered me to work independently, watching chickens, ducks, and swans. One of the Khmer Rouge men walked me to the barn and said, "Marin, this is a poultry barn. Your responsibility is to protect them from being stolen. If you see anyone stealing these chickens or ducks, you must report it to Angkar Luer."

"Yes, mittbong," I responded humbly. "How many chickens?" I asked.

He ignored my question and walked me to the river nearby. "Look into the river. Do you see those swans and ducks? We have four swans and eight ducks." He pointed.

I saw swans floating on the water freely, like they owned the entire river. The fat ducks were swimming and diving near the shore, as if they had no fear.

The Khmer Rouge walked me to the termite mound where the chickens roamed. He did a head count and said, "There are seven females and three roosters."

"Have some of these chickens laid eggs?" I asked.

"No. Not yet. They may lay eggs in the next several days. When they do, I want you to count them." Then he walked back to the communal center.

During the first day, I tried to identify each one of the chickens and ducks, and I made sure they didn't walk out of my sight. After several days of watching them, I began to get bored. The only big task of this job was to free the birds from the barn in the morning and lock them up in the evening. These birds were smart. In the mornings, they roamed the field to feed themselves. In the afternoons, before sunset, they walked back to the barn by themselves.

When the chickens and ducks laid eggs, I stole the eggs from the nests and ate them raw as a snack. I didn't steal the swans' eggs because they didn't lay as many as the chickens and ducks did. The swans only produced a maximum of four eggs in each nest. If I were to steal them, the Khmer Rouge might notice.

After many days of watching the birds, a son of a Khmer Rouge official came to hang around with me. I don't remember his name. He was bigger and slightly taller than me. His round face and thick black hair reminded me of Pol, the Khmer Rouge's son who had shared his food and a love of trains with me. However, Pol was more handsome, and Pol always wore a clean black uniform. This boy looked unclean; his black uniform was faded and old.

He taught me how to play *hurng*, a game that punishes the losing opponent to run from a distance to the base without breathing. It's a typical game of farmer boys who herd cows and play during their free time.

After a few games, I started having conflicts with this boy. When I won, he picked a broken tile off a roof and threw it at me in anger. I dodged the object left and right. I even ran and hid by a coconut tree, but he continued to throw tiles at me. I didn't throw back at him, because I was afraid his dad would kill me.

Then exhausted from running, hiding and not standing up for myself, I lost my temper. I picked up a flat, broken roof tile that he threw at me and quickly threw it back at him. It smashed him in the forehead and blood gushed out of his face. He screamed and shouted for help.

My natural instincts kicked in and I ran for my life. Minutes later, several men from the village chased me with sticks and machetes. They followed me along the oxcart road. While I was running, I turned my head to take a quick look at them. They grabbed whatever they could to throw at me and propelled stones, sticks, and hardened dirt at me. I didn't get hit because I was already far ahead of them. My adrenaline and fear made me run faster and faster.

When I got to the sharp turn of an oxcart road, I ran inside the large bamboo bushes growing along the road. The Khmer Rouge men thought I had run into the jungle on the left and started beating the bushes and trees with sticks.

"Get out now, you stupid boy! Get out of the forest if you want to survive!"

I gasped for air and tried to hold my heartbeat from pounding too hard. I peeked through the bamboo leaves and saw the Khmer Rouge looking frantically for me. I prayed silently for the souls of Pa, Mak and all Tevada to help shield me and to make me invisible.

"How dare you hurt my son! You will see what will happen to you when you get caught!" the boy's father shouted.

After a brief search and more threats to kill me, another man called everyone to go back to the village. "That is enough! Let's go back to see your son! That boy didn't run too far!"

"He will come out of the jungle! We will catch him later!" said an elderly man.

When they walked back, I heard the other man say, "Don't worry, the tiger in that jungle is going to eat him alive!"

After they left, I tried to get out of the bamboo bush, but it was difficult. The bamboo branches were woven tightly, like a web, and stuck out in all directions, up, down, and sideways. Getting out was a slow and painful process. I pushed and pulled individual branches that wrapped my clothes. I crawled under and leaped over the branches to prevent myself from getting cut. When I got out, I had small ragged cuts all over my body. My arms, legs, and back all trickled with blood. And my whole body itched. Despite my injuries, though, I still felt much better than getting caught by the Khmer Rouge, who would torture and kill me instantly.

After I got out of the bamboo forest, I snuck into a fruit-tree farm the size of five soccer fields. The farm consisted of mango, guava, jackfruit, and coconut trees. Several wild trees also grew there. I climbed up on a wild bushy tree to hide and lay down on a tree branch seven meters above the ground.

I scanned every angle to see if anyone was approaching. The distance from the tree to the communal cafeteria was approximately two hundred meters. I tried to look at the area around the cafeteria but I could barely see anyone because the blowing winds moved the small branches and tree leaves, blocking my view. All I could see were small glimpses of the blacksmiths hammering away at their metals.

Eating Tree Ants

While I was scanning the communal cafeteria, hundreds of soldier tree ants began crawling on me and biting me furiously. They bit my legs, my arms, my head, my back, and even my genitals. I was furious at them!

To slow down the tree ants from attacking, I urinated on them, and slowly they retreated. I urinated on the tree branch where the ants had tried to attack, to mark my territory.

Then I kept thinking to myself, *If any tree ants crawl into my territory, they will be eaten.*

Some tree ants violated my territory and I slowly devoured them, one by one. They actually tasted sour, like lemon. I had fun killing and eating them.

While I was waging war with the tree ants, the bell rang signaling dinnertime in the village. The sound of pounding metal from the blacksmiths went silent; they stopped working and went to get their evening meal. I was hungry, but I didn't dare go eat. I was afraid the Khmer Rouge were waiting for me at the communal cafeteria.

The sun was setting and the tree ants continued to invade my space to bite me. I was hurt and frustrated. I thought of killing all of them. I looked up on the tree branches above and saw a few tree ant nests. Each was about the size of a coconut.

I climbed up to the nests and beat the hell out of their nests with a stick. I was completely surprised and said silently to myself, *Oooh woow! No wonder they are so mean. They were protecting their eggs and babies!*

I carefully broke small branches that held to their nests and dropped them to the ground. Then I got off the tree, smacked the nests open with a stick, quickly grabbed their eggs and baby ants, and shoveled them into my mouth. That was my dinner.

I climbed up the tree again and rested on the same branches where I had urinated on the soldier ants. That night I slept like a monkey, face down, limbs hugging tightly onto the ant-free branches.

I was overwhelmed by loneliness and frightened of being killed by the Khmer Rouge. At the same time, I was very proud of myself for being brave enough to stand up to the Khmer Rouge official's son.

This was the second time I had trouble with a Khmer Rouge official's son. When I lived with Vanny, I had punched the high-ranking official's son in the eye. In both incidents, I had run for my life.

Evening turned to night, and I looked at the half moon shining among the stars. I frequently scanned the ground, hoping no one could find me. I was scared of being alone, but not as frightened as being caught by the Khmer Rouge.

I secured myself by sandwiching between several small branches to prevent me from falling to the ground. My desperation led me to constantly pray for help.

"Pa, Mak, and all the deities, please protect me from being caught by the Khmer Rouge. Please don't let the poisonous snake crawl on this tree to bite me while I sleep."

Fighting from the Tree Branches

Night turned into day. I woke up with intense stomach pains demanding food. I sat on the tree branches, figuring out how to survive.

I scanned below and the treetops above, but I only saw a few mango fruits dangling from the branches and clearly out of my reach. The coconut trees also had no small branches to hang from in order to pick the fruit.

Gradually, I hoisted myself from tree branch to tree branch, holding tightly onto overhead branches while my feet slightly stepped onto lower branches to balance myself.

Finally, I got on a guava tree, but it was stripped of fruit, except for its leaves. So, I picked the young green leaves and ate them to fill my hungry stomach. While I was on the treetop, I saw a girl, who resembled the boy I had injured. I wondered, was it his sister? She was about thirteen, had a brown complexion, short hair, and a round face.

I sat motionless and held firmly onto the tree branches, praying for the invisible powers to hide me. She walked closer to one of the mango trees near the guava tree I was on. She lifted her sarong up to her waist and squatted to urinate.

Suddenly, a small piece of branch dropped from my tree and landed on her head. She scratched her head, looked up, and gazed up intently. She stood, clenched her lips, and grit her teeth. Then she threw spastic hand gestures and said many things, but I couldn't hear her. She was a mute. She attempted to climb the tree many times, but she couldn't, because she wasn't strong or clever enough.

Then she saw a bundle of dead bamboos leaning against an adjacent mango tree. She trotted over to the pile of bamboo, picked one up and brought it back. She began to thrust it up and down violently. Although the bamboo appeared well-trimmed, it contained razor-sharp edges.

I was on a tree top and there was nowhere to go. My only option was to defend myself. I stepped on branches and grabbed onto small branches to prevent me from falling off the tree. I kicked and blocked her bamboo thrusts. After many minutes of kicking and blocking, I caught the tip of her bamboo spear with my right hand and tried to pull it away from her. But I couldn't. I had trouble holding onto a tree branch with one hand while stepping on a smaller branch. I was trying not to step too hard on the branch because I didn't want it to break.

She poked me with the bamboo stick. She pulled, twisted, and turned the bamboo until I lost control. The sharp edge of the bamboo cut me left and right on the stomach. Blood oozed everywhere, but I kept myself from crying and screaming in pain.

She ran away frantically in horror. I was mad at her and wanted to kill her.

The Unexpected Reunion

When she ran toward her village, I got off the tree and ran out of the fruit farm and away. I ran from one tree to another, trying to escape.

After I got out of the village, I felt secure that no one would see and catch me. I walked past countless rice fields in the north and ran into the forest. In the forest, I scanned every bush and tree for wild fruits and edible leaves to eat.

Eventually, I lost all sense of direction and time. Then I heard the sound of girls calling each other. "Hey, come over here! There are a lot of *derm-kantraing-ket!*"[5]

I followed the sound to investigate. When I approached closer, I saw teenage girls cutting the plants. I approached them cautiously and asked, "*Bong,*[6] do you know a girl named Vanny? She is my sister."

"Who are you?" the girl with a handful of *derm-kontriang-ket* asked.

"I'm her younger brother. I haven't seen her for a long time. And I really miss her."

"What does she look like?" the girl with the machete asked.

_____

5   A type of bush plant that Cambodians use to make natural compost.
6   I called everyone who was older than me "bong."

"She had straight hair and a light-yellow complexion. She was about your height."

Then another girl, walking out of the bush with a fistful of wild fruit, said, "I knew one girl with that name. But I don't think she is your sister. Her group is cutting bushes over there." She pointed to another direction and group.

I approached several groups and finally found somebody who knew Vanny.

"Vanny! There is someone looking for you! Vanny, your brother is looking for you," one of the girls shouted.

Out of the bushes emerged Vanny, my sister! The moment she caught my eyes, she was frozen and stood still for seconds. She opened her mouth to talk, but no voice was coming out. Then she dropped a bundle of plants over her head and the machete in her hand and hugged me. My excitement jolted me from head to toe. I forgot about my wounds and how starving I was. We hugged each other furiously. We cried and held each other's hands. Minutes seemed like hours as we wiped each other's tears.

"How did you know I was here? And what are you doing here?" she asked.

It was difficult to understand her because large blisters had swelled inside her mouth and she had an abscess on her lower lip. Otherwise, Vanny's physical appearance looked much healthier than when I first saw her at the Toul Somphy village. She looked bigger and taller.

"I missed you, Marin," she said.

"I missed you too, Vanny. I have been looking for you for a long time, but I couldn't find you. There was a lady who told me you were severely ill and stayed in the Toul Somphy Hospital. I walked for days looking for you. Did you stay in the hospital?"

"No, I never stayed in the hospital." She let go of my hands, took a step back and said, "Look at you! You're grown up! You look taller!"

I cracked a smile at her.

After we talked, laughed, and cried for a while, Vanny peered down and noticed my bleeding shirt. "What happened to you?"

"I fell from a tree and got cut in the stomach," I said. I lied to stop her from worrying.

She lifted my shirt and saw the jagged cuts from the bamboo. Immediately, she rushed to her work crew, frantically screaming, "My brother has fallen from a tree and got a cut in the stomach. Do you know how to treat his wound?"

I was amazed at how her friends came up with all sorts of remedies. Some of them picked tiny vines and collected sap to apply on my wound. Others collected crushed, fresh leaves to put over my wound. It seemed like everyone there was genuinely concerned about me. I welcomed their help, although I can't say what treatment really worked.

After my wounds were nursed, the only thing on my mind was food. "I am very hungry, Vanny," I said.

"Be patient, brother. I will take you to see my leader. I will ask her to provide you food." Meanwhile, Vanny picked a few wild fruits for us to eat. It was noon and the sun was high overhead. "Marin, I know you are hurt and hungry," said Vanny. "Would you help me carry a small buddle of *derm-kontriang-ket?* It's not that heavy."

"Yes, I could carry it."

She picked up the bundle and placed it on my shoulders. "When you carry that, I can tell Mittbong-Sareth you are a hard worker, not a useless child. In return, I will ask Mittbong-Sareth to have you stay with me. Do you remember Mittbong-Sareth?" she said.

"No, I don't."

"She was my former group leader who accepted you to stay with me after Mak's death. Do you remember?"

"Oh, yeah, I remember her. She has two dimples on her cheeks," I said.

"You have a very good memory," she responded with a small

laugh as if she was proud of me.

When we arrived at the center, Vanny held tightly onto my hand. We approached Mittbong-Sareth who stood under the shade of the tamarind tree.

"Mittbong, this is my younger brother. Would you please accept him to live here with the group? We were separated for a long time. We just met again. My brother is a great worker. He knows how to work hard to serve Angkar." Vanny spoke firmly.

"Is he the one who stayed with you last time?"

"Yes, mittbong."

"Is he the one who fought with the son of *kanak-dombon?*"[7]

"Ahhmmmm…ahhmmm…ahm," Vanny said hesitantly and pulled me behind her.

Mittbong-Sareth stood with one hand on her waist and another pointed at me. She thought for a few minutes, then said, "If you were a girl, I would let you stay with your sister. But you are a boy. I cannot let you live with my group. But you can come to eat at our communal cafeteria with your sister. I will tell the chef to provide you food. You can come to visit her as often as you like."

"Where can he live?" Vanny said.

"I will take your brother to live over there, with the *Yuk-Vak-Jun,* a male teen group." She pointed to the huts two hundred meters from us.

"Thank you, mittbong."

After thanking her leader, Vanny walked to the other tamarind tree to drop off the *derm-kontriang-ket* plants from off her head. Then she took me to the communal cafeteria for lunch. All the girls were curious as to who I was.

"Is he your brother? Why is he so dark?" said one girl, who sat in front of my sister.

"Did mittbong allow him to eat with us?" another whispered into

---

7   Regional Khmer Rouge official.

Vanny's ear.

The food was about to be served. I sat on the ground in a squatting position with Vanny, among nine other girls. We sat in a small circle, each with a rice plate set in front of us and a bowl of soup in the center.

The communal chefs brought a big pot of rice and a big pot of soup. They scooped the food from the pots and distributed to each group. I was starving and anxious. My stomach growled, and my mouth watered. I could barely wait for my turn to have food on my plate. The minute the communal chef scooped the rice and put it onto my plate, I shoveled it into my mouth.

"Don't eat too fast, Marin. You might choke," Vanny said.

I began to slow down a little bit, and finished everything. Vanny gave me another half portion of rice and scooped a small amount of *somlor-majoo*, a sour soup, onto my plate. I finished the food in a matter of minutes.

After lunch, I helped Vanny chop the *derm-kontriang-ket* into small pieces to make fertilizer. When it was done, everyone roamed onto the field to pick cow manure and bring it to the center. We mixed the chopped *derm-kontrain-ket* with cow dung to make natural compost.

Confusing Homophones

Before sunset, Mittbong-Sareth walked me to meet the man who managed the boy group. The man sat on a black hammock. He turned his head toward us.

When we got closer, he stood and walked toward us. "Who is that boy? Is he your son?" he asked Mittbong-Sareth.

I looked at the man and studied him. The medium-build man had straight black hair and a dark complexion. He was in his late twenties.

"Mittbong-Thoeun, I have a boy for you. Would you please let him stay with your group? He is an orphan child."

"Where did you get him from?" he asked.

"His sister brought him to the center."

Mittbong-Thoeun looked at her and slowly gazed down at me. "At first, I thought he was your son," he said. "What is your name, young comrade?" he said to me.

"My name is Marin"

"How old are you?"

I clenched my face and eyebrows and tried to guess my age. "I don't know. I think I'm about eight years old."

"I don't mind. He could stay in my group," said Mittbong-Thoeun. Then he and Mittbong-Sareth talked about other subjects.

"We haven't received any work order from Angkar Luer yet," said Mittbong-Sareth. "Do you know what are we supposed to do in the next couple weeks?" Then she laughed. "If we don't hear anything from Angkar Luer, maybe we don't have to work."

"That is true. Now, all we need to do is continue to keep the group together. Do you know that Angkar Luer is busy fighting with *yeak-kong*?" said Mittbong-Thoeun.

Cambodians called the communist Vietnamese soldiers "*yeak-kong*" which means Vietcong. However, I was too young to differentiate between the words "yeak-kong" and "yaik-kong." The two words have a similar sound but a completely different meaning. Yaik-kong means "giant monkey" or "king kong." My eight-year-old mind translated the word *yeak-kong* as a giant monkey. I thought, *Why do Angkar Luer soldiers want to fight with giant monkeys?*

After the two mittbongs' brief conversation, Mittbong-Sareth went back to her place and Mittbong-Thoeun walked me to a big communal hut where all the boys stayed.

"We have a new member," he told them. "He is going to stay with all of you."

Most of the boys were in their late teens. They were somewhat loud and rowdy. While they were preparing mosquito nets to sleep, I overheard them talking about Angkar Luer fighting with *yeak-kong*. I didn't ask how the giant monkey would fight with the Khmer Rouge soldiers; however, I had many dreadful wishes for the Khmer Rouge.

Giant monkey, if you capture the Khmer Rouge soldiers, please chew off their heads. Please capture the man who attempted to drown me in the water canal. I want you to kill him by squeezing his neck, throw him into the canal, and let him drown. Please kill all of the boy's relatives who chased after me. Giant monkey, please kill Mittbong-Mai and Mittbong-Seouth who tortured and left me to die in the village. Giant monkey, please punish Mittbong-Vel, who lashed me with three whips and ordered me not to cry. Giant monkey, please don't kill my friend Pol. He is a very nice boy. Whenever he came to play hopscotch with me, he always brought food to share with me. He even allowed me to wear his sandals. Giant monkey, please don't kill Mittbong-Sophal. He saved my life. Without him, I would be dead in the baking sun. He is the one who carried me from the water canal to his home.

I had countless wishes for the giant monkey to kill the Khmer Rouge soldiers. Nevertheless, I soon discovered what *yeak-kong* really means, "Vietcong," the communist soldiers from North Vietnam. When I realized that, I cracked into laughter.

After living in the center for a day, I noticed that the dynamic of this group was completely different from what I had experienced. Mittbong-Thoeun and Mittbong-Sareth didn't force people into hard labor. The workers were more relaxed. They could have conversations with one another. People who came to work late were not punished or threatened to be killed.

Returning to Hostile Ground

Ten days after I found my sister, Angkar Luer moved everybody to another location. At first, I didn't know where the Khmer Rouge would move me.

It was morning. The sun rose just below the treetops.

Mittbong-Thoeun and Mittbong-Sareth ordered everyone to grab their belongings and to stand single file for a body count. After the body count, I saw Mittbong-Sareth ordering the girls to move one row at a time along the foot-trail that ran across the forest. I saw Vanny carrying a *bonkee* in her hand and an improvised bag on her shoulder. After all the girls left, Mittbong-Thoeun began ordering the boys to follow the same path.

Just before noon, we got out of the forest and walked along the rice-field levees toward a village. I began noticing the tobacco plantation, fruit tree farm, and the communal cafeteria building—and realized this was the place I had run away from.

My head jolted. I felt like something had dazed me. My heart began to pound, and sweat started pouring down my head.

I began to get mad at God. *Buddha and Tevada, why did you take me to this village again! Do you want the Khmer Rouge to kill me? About ten days ago, the Khmer Rouge family chased me with sticks and machetes to kill me!*

I clenched my teeth and thought of running away. I put both hands on my buttocks and ran to Mittbong-Thoeun, who walked behind the group. "Pu, I have diarrhea and stomachache. Please let me go to the restroom." I pretended it was an emergency.

"Why do you need to tell me? Just go and do what you need to do," he responded.

I ran across the rice field and hid behind bushes. My fear of being caught and being killed by the Khmer Rouge prevented me from thinking clearly. I thought of living in the forest. On the other hand, I didn't want to be separated from my sister. I loved Vanny and I wanted to be with her. However, I didn't want to get killed by the Khmer Rouge.

Vigilantly, I sat in a kneeling position behind the bush and looked in every direction. I looked through the forest behind me, to see if the Khmer Rouge would sneak up on me. I scanned the tobacco plantation, which was east of the communal cafeteria and the fruit-tree farm on the north. From where I was, I could see Vanny's group walking behind the communal cafeteria into the living quarters next to it.

After hours of looking, I didn't see anyone working in the tobacco farm or in the fruit farm. Even so, my fear of being seen by the Khmer Rouge was at the top of my concerns. I tilted my head up to look at the sun above and prayed to all the deities in Heaven to help me. *Tevada, please use your power to blindfold the Khmer Rouge. Don't let them see me running into the fruit-tree farm. I want to hide there so I can see my sister.*

After the brief prayer, I crept and crawled alongside the rice-field levee into the fruit tree farm. I ran to conceal myself in the same bushy wild tree where I had hidden from the Khmer Rouge and had peed on the tree ants, where I had destroyed their nests and eaten their eggs.

I was back in the tree, and it was late noon now. I hadn't eaten or drunk anything. The horror of being caught and killed by the Khmer Rouge had made me lose my appetite.

I didn't hear blacksmiths or hammering metal. So, I got off the tree and snuck closer to investigate. The blacksmiths' site was abandoned. Trash and charcoals were all over the place. I climbed a jackfruit tree near the site to hide and sat on a sizable branch, hugging onto the tree tightly.

With one hand, I moved some tree leaves to get a better view of the communal cafeteria and living quarters. I didn't see any of the former residents. It seemed like the entire place had been taken over by Mittbong-Sareth's and Mittbong-Thoeun's groups. The boy group was carrying tobacco leaves from the farm and leaving them to dry in the sun near the communal cafeteria. Other boys were piling tobacco leaves into the communal cafeteria. I saw Vanny and her group shredding tobacco leaves.

Inside the communal kitchen, I saw the chefs in Mittbong-Sareth and Mittbong-Thoeun's groups working together, cooking dinner. It was time for supper.

Everyone stopped working then and walked to the communal cafeteria for the evening meal. I continued to sit in the tree, to see if the other Khmer Rouge family, who used to live there, would be coming for supper. But I didn't see anyone. So, I got off the tree.

Cautiously, I approached Mittbong-Thoeun and asked, "Pu, where did the people who live in this village go?"

He looked at me and asked, "Where have you been?"

The lie slipped through my lips. "Pu, after I relieved myself, I had strong stomach pains. I decided to rest under the shade tree until I got better. Now, I got better, but I'm still feeling a little sick."

"I know you must be hungry. Go eat," he said and walked away.

I followed him and asked, "Pu, where did the people who used to live in this village go?"

He turned his head and looked at me. "Angkar Luer moved them to somewhere else. Now, new people are moving into this place."

The moment I heard what he said, every tension in my body flew out. I felt relieved as if my body possessed a new soul. I turned around and looked for Vanny. I saw her sitting with her group having supper. Before I even got to her, she saw me.

"Marin, come over here! Where have you been? I was looking for you all day!"

I didn't answer her questions. I approached her and she pulled me to sit next to her. She inspected my face and body, and asked me again. "Where were you this afternoon? I didn't see you come for lunch. I was concerned about you."

"I didn't feel well," I lied to her. "I took a long rest under the shade tree over there."

"What happened? Are you sick?"

"Yes, I was sick. Now, I'm very hungry."

She grabbed me by the hand. "Let me take you to the communal chefs."

She approached the chefs and said, "Mittbong, my younger brother, Marin, didn't get his food yet. Do you have any food for him? He is hungry," she said in a humble tone.

The chefs looked at us and said, "I thought everybody already got food."

"No, my brother didn't get any food. He was sick. He didn't even have lunch."

The communal chef picked a plate and scooped a small amount of rice on it. Then she scooped a vegetable soup and poured it over the rice. The moment she handed the food plate to me, I engulfed everything on the plate.

The next morning, Mittbong-Thoeun approached me and said, "Marin, follow me. I've got a job for you to do near the river."

Once I heard that, my instinct told me that it must be my old job of watching over the poultries. I was right.

Mittbong-Thoeun ordered me to watch over the chickens and ducks, once again. I was the only boy there. The job suited me well.

When I got to the river, I noticed that more than half a dozen of the chickens and ducks had disappeared, but the two swans still swam on the river.

The Retreat of the Khmer Rouge

Several days after I returned to this village, I heard the sound of bomb explosions rumbling in the distance. The rumbling sounds pierced the jungle nonstop, day and night, for about seven days. I knew the sound of explosion was far, but I didn't know the exact distance.

A few days after the bomb explosions stopped, I watched thousands of Khmer Rouge soldiers marching along the oxcart road. They had rifle magazines strapped around their chests and waists, and rifles slung over their backs. Their faces looked grim as if they were disappointed. They walked as fast as they could to get out of the village.

Behind each battalion were rows of oxen pulling oxcarts filled with artillery, machine guns, cases of ammunition, cooking pots and pans. I prayed to the souls of my parents to prevent these soldiers from pulling their rifles out to shoot me.

I stood by the mouth of river and watched them with hate and fear. But I pretended I had no fear, and I watched them retreat.

The Last Celebration

A few days after the Khmer Rouge soldiers retreated, the Khmer Rouge family members who were living in the village moved out, too. Lower ranking Khmer Rouge like Mittbong-Thoeun and Mittbong-Sareth continued to control us, however. They didn't know that Angkar had lost its grip of power.

Around that time, I saw an airplane flying in the sky over the jungle. Each day, it flew closer and closer to the village. One morning, the airplane flew over the village and dropped thousands of leaflets. I had lots of fun trying to catch the yellow leaflets before they landed on the ground. I couldn't even catch one because the wind kept blowing them away from my hands.

Then I picked up the leaflets off the ground. They were about the size of the money notes Pa and Mak had taken out of the pillow to burn. There were messages written on the leaflets, but I didn't know how to read them. My four days of education under the shade tree were not enough. I was disappointed.

So, I used the leaflets to make paper airplanes. I didn't know how to make them well. When I threw them into the air, they didn't glide. The paper airplanes dropped straight down.

One late afternoon, I saw three Khmer Rouge soldiers meeting with Mittbong-Sareth and Mittbong-Thoeun at the blacksmith site. After the soldiers left, Mittbong-Thoeun called everyone to attention. Everyone stopped what they were doing and paid full attention to him.

"A short while ago, I had a meeting with Angkar Luer! They told me that our enemies, the Vietcong, have been defeated! Our soldiers have chased them out of our country! To celebrate this victory, Angkar Luer has told us to kill our livestock for celebration! Bravo to our victory!" he shouted.

The people shouted repeatedly after Mittbong-Thoeun, "Bravo! Bravo! To our victory!"

After more than three years of food deprivation and starvation, the people were excited to kill the livestock for food. They killed all the chickens, ducks, and pigs, even the swans.

Vanny and her work crews helped the communal chefs prepare the food under shade trees near the mouth of the river. They cooked *jrook-quay* (pig barbecue), tae-quay (duck barbecue curry), and *nom-bagn-jok* (a type of noodle). I stood by Vanny and watched her sorting the soft and tiny long strings of noodles. She organized the noodle strings into small bundles and placed them in a *kagn-ger*, a deep bamboo basket.

After watching her for a while, I became bored and walked to the big tree near the mouth of the river. I entertained myself by throwing dirt into the water. I threw the flat hard dirt to make it skip on the water. When the food was cooked, Vanny brought two bowls of *nom-bagn-jok* soaked with red curry on top and set them on the ground next to me.

"Marin, here is the *nom-bagn-jok*. Don't eat it yet."

I dropped the dirt and watched the hot steam coming out of the food bowls. "Why can't I eat now?"

"Just wait for me. I will be right back with some roasted pork."

Vanny trotted back into the cooking areas. I walked into the river to wash the dirt off my hands. She returned carrying a few pieces of roasted pork and duck wrapped in banana leaves. Then she tore a small piece of banana leaf to make a float the size of her palm. She put a small amount of food on the float and held it in both hands.

"Marin, I really miss Mak, Pa, and Roth. Let's pray and call their souls to have lunch with us. When they died, they didn't have a chance to eat delicious food like this," said Vanny.

"I miss them too, Vanny."

She put her palms together and raised them in front of her chest and said, "Mak, Pa, and Roth. Come have lunch with us. Marin and I have delicious food for all of you in front of the river."

It was very emotional for us. Tears built up in our eyes, and our throats were tense. We got up, walked to the river with the float, placed it on the river and let it drift away. Then Vanny placed her hand on my shoulder, pulled me closer to her, and said, "Marin, let's go eat."

After we finished eating, she walked back to stay with her group. That was the last time I saw her.

The next morning, Angkar Luer ordered everyone to continue to stay in their groups and to move out of the village. That morning, each group packed up whatever leftover food there was and left. I frequently looked back in the distance and saw a few girl groups walking behind mine. It led me to believe that Vanny was in that group.

I continued to walk with Mittbong-Thoeun's group until we passed the forest into a vast rice field. The rice was already harvested, and all that was left in the rice field was dead rice straws.

When I got into the vast rice fields, there were thousands of people walking single file, packed like a huge herd of cows moving in one direction, north. Mittbong-Thoeun led his boy group to join with hundreds of other groups, who walked out of the rice fields into the vast open plain. Nobody knew exactly where we were going. All we knew was to follow each other.

The situation became chaotic. At this point, I believed that the Khmer Rouge had lost their power and were now trying to create fear and confusion in the people. The Khmer Rouge officials who held ranking positions as a cook or a group leader didn't even know what was happening. They, too, just followed orders.

After long hours of walking into the vast open plains, people walking in front shouted, "Move back! There are landmine fields ahead of us! Move back! Move back!"

The people turned back. Everyone was in fear as if they were being chased or stalked by a tiger.

After we walked for a long while, another person in front shouted, "Stop! Stop! You can't walk this way, because *yeak-kong* has laid landmines and deployed their troops ahead of us! *Yeak-kong* will kill everyone!"

It was noon. It was hot and humid. Small dirt devils constantly formed and disappeared in the thin air. Water was hard to find. Sweat came out of every pore on my head and dripped onto my face. My throat was dry. I was extremely exhausted and thirsty. I swallowed my own saliva, trying to prevent my throat from being hurt. Despite all my exhaustion and pain, I continued to follow my group leader.

Then a person shouted, "We are all free! You don't have to be in the group anymore! You can go home and live with your family!"

At that moment, people talked noisily nonstop. Where would they go? Who would they see?

Mittbong-Thoeun called all the boys following him to sit under a shade tree. "Now, it is time for lunch. For those who know where your parents are or know where you live, you can leave the group. If you don't know where to go, just stay with me."

"I have to find my mother," said one boy.

"I have go back to Battambong Province to find my family," said another.

"I don't know where to go. I don't know where my family is," said another boy. "I don't even know if they are dead or alive. Can I stay with the group for a while until know where about my relatives are?"

Several minutes after Mittbong-Thoeun's speech, more than sixty boys left the group to search for their loved ones.

We ate leftover food from yesterday, *nom-bagn-jok* and roasted pork. After we finished eating, many more boys left the group. Now, the group had less than ten boys. My heart began to pound and I thought to myself, *Who am I going to live with? Where should I go? I have no mother. I have no father. Now, my sister Vanny has disappeared. I don't know if I have aunts or uncles.*

Totally lost and confused, I looked at the blue sky and the bright sun and said silently in my heart, *Buddha and Tevada, please raise my parents from the dead so I can live with them.*

That afternoon, I walked out of the group and looked for Vanny. There were thousands of people walking in different directions, trying to find their loved ones. While I searched for my sister, I overheard many people talking about taking revenge.

"That fucking Khmer Rouge killed my father. He tried to escape on the oxcart. I ran after his oxcart and they hacked his head off with a machete."

"I pulled the Khmer Rouge off the oxcart and beat the hell out of him," said another. "I would have killed him if he didn't have children crying."

"I didn't kill the Khmer Rouge who hurt my brother," said another. "I threatened to kill him with a machete. I ordered him to get off the oxcart and I let him walk away barefoot. I took the cows and everything in the oxcarts."

All this talk of chasing and killing the Khmer Rouge overwhelmed me. I thought about slaughtering Mittbong-Mai, Mittbong-Seouth, and the old man who had attempted to drown me. Unfortunately, I could never find them.

According to history books, the Khmer Rouge reigned over Cambodia three years and nine months, from April 1975 until January 1979.

After three years and eight months under the Khmer Rouge reign, the horrors of my own life experience were over. However, surviving without any relatives was just the beginning.

PART IV
After the Khmer Rouge, Vietnamese Invaders

12

Becoming Homeless

My First Adopted Family

I looked for Vanny for a full day, but I couldn't find her. Instead, I found a lady who used to live in the jungle near me. Her name was Thon. I called her "Aunty Thon."

Her husband was the first person I had seen the Khmer Rouge soldiers escort to kill in the jungle. Her son Visoth was the boy who had fought with me over the leftover bones the Khmer Rouge had thrown to the ground.

I approached Thon and asked, "Aunty, have you seen my sister Vanny?"

"No, I didn't see her, son."

"Where is Visoth?"

"Ohh—Ohh, my son! Visoth? He is dead." She wiped her tears with her sarong. "Where are your mother and father?" She then asked.

"Mak…Mak…Pa…Pa…Pa…and Roth are dead." I stuttered statically and fell into tears.

"If you don't have anybody to live with, just live with me, son."

"Yes, thanks, aunty. But once I find my sister, I will go to live with her."

She looked at me and smiled.

Aunty Thon was a widower woman who had survived the Khmer Rouge regime with her two daughters, Chanthy and Channy, and her son, Song. She accepted me to live with her family. Chanthy was the oldest at eighteen. Song was seventeen. Channy was the youngest at twelve.

Aunty Thon sat on the *kontael* and groomed Channy's hair. I sat on the ground, next to them.

"How old are you, Marin?" Aunty Thon asked me.

"I don't know my age."

"If my son Visoth were alive, he would be seven. Maybe you would be one year older than my son. I believe that you are eight years old," she said.

I remembered Visoth well. He had a light-yellow complexion like Roth. When I had fought with him over the bones the soldiers threw away, Aunty Thon had slapped my hands and warned me not to hit her son again.

After we sat and talked for a short while, Chanthy and Song arrived. Chanthy dropped half a sack of rice on the *kontael* near me and said, "There is a lot of rice in the warehouse. People took as much as they could carry. But it was heavy for me. All I could get was half a sack. Those who had oxcarts filled them."

"Mother!" said Song. "I got two cows! There were hundreds of cows in the barns! But I was a little too late in catching them. All the big and healthy cows were gone. Some people got three cows, some people got five cows, others got ten cows. These are the two cows I caught." He proudly stood next to the cows.

Because the Vietnamese soldiers were invading, we decided to flee this province, looking for a safe place. We couldn't go to Aunty's home town, Phnom Penh, the capital city of Cambodia, because of the Vietnamese. So, each day we moved from one deserted village to another.

Along the way, we captured abandoned ducks and chickens. One morning, Chanthy and Song caught many ducks and chickens near the National Road #5. Song wanted to slaughter them and preserve them for food for our long journey. However, his mother stopped him. She pulled him to sit in the shade.

"Don't do it my, son. I don't want you to kill these animals. I'm afraid you will have bad karma in the next life."

"I don't believe in bad karma, or care about the next life," Song said to his mother.

"You are my son. I don't want to see you doing it. I want Marin to slaughter them," she said. Aunty Thon then approached me. "Marin, can you kill all these chickens and ducks?"

I thought for a moment, trying to get the logic of what she had said. She was afraid that her son might have bad karma in the next life. It was okay for me to have bad karma, but it was not okay for her son to have bad karma? Even so, I said, "Yeah…yes, aunty. But how do I kill them?"

"Song, where is the knife? Give Marin the knife and teach him how to kill chickens," she ordered.

Song walked toward me and gave me the knife. He took a few more steps to grab a chicken. He folded its wings backwards and locked them. He stepped on the chicken's feet to prevent it from moving. Then he grabbed the chicken's head, twisted it a little, and pulled some of the feathers from its neck. "Marin, just watch me," he said. "Once you pull a few feathers off the neck, you slit the chicken's throat and let all the blood pour into the bucket."

Song explained to me step by step, but he didn't kill the chicken. He got up and left the chicken on the ground. He gave me the sharp knife and coached me to slaughter the chickens and ducks one at a time. "Are you sure you know how to slit their throats?" he asked me.

"Yes, I am."

Then Aunty Thon interrupted. "Marin, don't kill them yet. Let me say a prayer to them first."

She dipped her fingers into a small container of water and sprinkled the chickens and ducks while saying a prayer. "Buddha and Tevada, please be our witness. Today, we take the lives of these animals for food. We don't want to kill them, but we have to. Please don't let them take revenge in the next life. I wish them to be born as human beings in the next life. We don't want bad karma in the next life."

After she said the prayer, I slit the chickens' and ducks' throats without fear or remorse. That day, I slaughtered twenty chickens and ten ducks.

Chanthy and Song processed the poultry by dipping them into boiling water one at a time for a minute. Then they pulled the poultry out of the water and pulled off the feathers until they were completely naked.

Aunty Thon cut the poultry in half and removed all the intestines. She cleaned the poultry and cut them into small pieces. She marinated them with salt, crushed garlic, and spices to preserve them. Then she dried them in the hot sun.

Every day, we walked from one place to another, searching for a safe place to stay. We followed thirty other families to Battambong City, the second largest city in Cambodia. We tried to walk out of the rice field onto the National Route #5. However, when we found no cars or trucks driving on the road, no people driving motorcycles or riding bicycles, and nobody walking on the road, we grew concerned. The empty road brought fear for everyone's safety.

Several adult males who were escaping with us tried to investigate whether the road was safe to walk on. They felt the road was a trap for the Khmer Rouge or the Vietnamese soldiers.

After hours of investigation, however, we decided to walk on the road in small groups, and nobody walked empty-handed. Some people carried cooking pots and pans. Others carried a *kontael* and a small pack on their heads or shoulders. I held a rope that was tied to the two cows. On the backs of the cows, Song and Chanthy had placed some of our supplies.

We were the first wave of refugees to arrive in Battambong City. It took us two days of walking to get there. When we arrived, the entire city was quiet, a ghost town. All the houses and buildings were empty. No cats or dogs were around. Only small birds were flying in and out of the buildings through broken windows and doors. The land in front of commercial buildings, hotels, schools, and Buddhist temples had completely been taken over by tall wild grasses and vines.

One of the men shouted in a whisper, " Ahh….Ahahh. Be careful! We don't know what is out there. The pathways into these buildings could have landmines. We don't know what is in the buildings. It could be a dead body. It could be bombs. It could be Khmer Rouge soldiers waiting to kill us."

Despite all the fear and nerves, people cautiously walked on each other's footprints to investigate the empty buildings and to see if we could stay in them. We were lucky. There were no landmines or bombs in the area. We got into the building safely, and cleaned out the dirt and dust to stay for a few nights.

Two days later, Vietnamese soldiers arrived. There were about one hundred of them. They came with five big green military trucks. The soldiers were well-equipped with bullet magazines and hand grenades strapped to their bodies. They stood on the backs of trucks, with their rifles drawn, and roamed the city.

They didn't find the Khmer Rouge, but they found many wooden boxes and loaded them onto their trucks. One of them said, "Those boxes could have been weapons." Another said, "They could have been gold or jewelry."

After seeing the Vietnamese soldiers, Aunty Thon and many other families felt unsafe staying in Battambong City. So, we decided to move to Svay Sisophorn, a city near the Thai border. We walked on the road under the scorching sun. The hot temperature melted the thick black tar on the road. For fun, I used a stick to pick the hot softened tar on the road, mold it into a ball shape, and toss it up and down while walking. As we walked further, I smelled hundreds of dead corpses in the rice fields. The rotten smell was so thick and strong that it forced me to pinch my nose and breathe through my mouth.

Finally, we arrived in Svay Sisophon. The city was entirely occupied by refugees. Most of the houses, buildings, and apartments were taken. We took refuge at the foot of the Svay Sisophon Mountain, located about one kilometer from the provincial city. Chanthy and Song built a temporary shelter under mango trees.

That week, the first monsoon arrived. Thick black clouds moved in fast and blocked out the blue sky, wind blew everything in its path. The wind blew tree branches from side to side. Dead leaves and small branches fell and flew, like cotton. The mango tree leaves above our shelter rattled. Thunder and lightning dominated the sky like bomb explosions. An hour later, rain began to pour ferociously. Despite the storm, the thunder and lightning, I enjoyed running around in the rain. It was fun.

After two hours of pouring rain, all of Sisaphon City was full of murky potholes. The soccer field was flooded, ankle deep. The sky turned to clear blue and the bright sun continued to shine to heat up the earth once again.

Two days after staying under mango trees, Chanthy and Song found an unoccupied *ptias la-veng,* a type of apartment unit that we could see through, from two large folding doors in the front straight through to the backdoor. Chanthy and Song rushed everyone. We grabbed our belongings and moved into this apartment at the outskirts of the provincial city. When I got there, I noticed that the apartment was relatively small and narrow. It was about five meters wide and eight meters long. Most of the tenants left their doors open for air ventilation and sunlight.

Homeless

All the food that we brought was about to run out. Concern and frustration about our food shortage began to build in Aunty Thon, and she began limiting food rations to me. Each meal she only gave me a small scoop of rice and a small amount of soup. But she didn't limit the food for her family members. They could eat as much as they wanted. This made me jealous.

After two months of living with Aunty Thon, she became increasingly agitated with me. Whatever I did or said would result in verbal or physical abuse. Sometimes she would hit me in the head with a rice plate. Other times, she knocked me in the head with her fist.

One time during lunch, I asked Aunty Thon for more rice. She knocked me on top of my head with a spoon and said sarcastically through gritted teeth, "Is your mother a magician who could produce rice on the spot for me?"

"N…no…" I stuttered.

"If your mother doesn't produce food for me, why are you asking for more?" She scooped a small amount of rice from a cooking pot, tossed it onto my plate, and hit my head with the spoon.

My head stung but I didn't cry. The pain deep down in my heart was much more painful than the physical one on my head. My heart throbbed and gave me pain in my chest. Tears rolled down my cheeks and dropped onto my rice plate. Despite all of that pain, I continued to eat the food until not one grain of rice was left.

After we finished eating, I walked out of the apartment and herded the two cows. I let them roam onto a grassy field like I usually did. Then I climbed up a tamarind tree to pick its flowers, young fruit, and young leaves to eat as a supplement to my meager rations.

I was tired and depressed, so I took a nap on a big tamarind tree branch. When I woke up, the cows had disappeared! I tried to find them but they were nowhere! My heart pounded. My head jolted. Being scolded and hit by Aunty Thon was imminent. Despite all my fear and frustration, I decided to go home and ask her if she had taken the cows.

"Aunty, did you take the cows?"

"No! I didn't! You watch over the cows, and you don't know where they went?" she said with outrage.

"Well, I....I...I was tired and I took a nap on the tree branches. When I woke up, the cows were gone."

She clenched her teeth and said, "You have to find the cows, now! If you cannot find them, you will be in big trouble!"

Minutes later, the rest of the family went in different directions to look for the cows. I went alone to the foot of the Sisophorn Mountain to look for the cows, for hours, but they were nowhere to be found.

My only hope was for a miracle. I tilted my head up, looked directly at the bright sun above my head, and prayed, "Buddha and Tevada, please help Aunty Thon and her family find the cows. Once they find the cows, I won't have any trouble. Please, please, please. I beg you."

It was late afternoon and the sun was about to set. I went back to the apartment to see if the family had found the cows. I walked slowly and cautiously into the apartment. I didn't know that Aunty Thon was hiding behind the door. Once I got inside, she grabbed my hands, pulled me by the hair, threw me to the ground, and started to whip me furiously with a stick as thick as my big toe.

"You useless motherfucker! I fed you! I took care of you! And you couldn't even take care of the cows! The cows went to eat corn plants at someone's farm. The farmer confiscated them."

"Please! Someone help me! Please! Help me! Help!" I cried and shouted for help. "Please stop hurting me. I am very sorry." I cried and begged her for forgiveness. But she didn't forgive me.

Suddenly, a light-complexioned man who lived next door came to stop her. She cursed and screamed at him. She continued to hit me and kick me. But the man stopped her and grabbed the stick out of her hand.

"You can't live with me anymore!" she shouted at me as if she wanted to kill me. "I can't have a useless person like you living with me! I found the cow. How the hell can you let the cows enter a corn farm and eat corn plants! Do you know how much gold I need to bail the cow out! You stupid motherfucker, get out of my face!"

I ran out of the apartment with pain and madness. My head was boiling with anger at everything. I got mad at Buddha. I got mad at Tevada. I got mad at the cows for eating corn plants. I got mad at the farmer who had captured the cows. I got mad at Aunty Thon. I got mad at everything around me.

I cried with pain and walked up to the mountaintop in an attempt to commit suicide to end my suffering. I stood on the mountain peak in an attempt to jump. The moment I was about to jump off the cliff, I wondered, what would happen if I didn't die instantly? What would happen if I survived the fall with broken arms and legs? How much suffering would I go through if I didn't die?

I looked at the dark clouds and the gray moon above and shouted, "Buddha and Tevada! Why don't you come down on Earth to kill me! Come on, Tevada! Kill me now! I don't want to live!"

After shouting several times, nothing happened to me. There was no Buddha or angels from the sky to kill me. After a short while, my madness cooled off, and a cool breeze blew over my body. I picked up small stones and threw them off the mountain peak to release my anger and frustration.

Now, I was homeless. I had no family. I had no father. I had no mother. And my older sister, Vanny, was nowhere to be found. I had no aunt or uncle to take care of me. I lived in desperation, not knowing whether I would have food to feed myself the next day or where I would sleep tonight. That evening, I didn't get off the mountain. I tried to find wild fruit and edible leaves to eat. But edible leaves and fruits were rare on this mountain, because many people cut the trees to make firewood.

I slept near the small Buddhist shrine on a strange thick concrete structure wall that was elevated two meters off the ground. The agonizing pain from the beating made it difficult to fall asleep. My arms, legs, and back were full of bruise marks.

The night was mildly cold but the concrete slab released heat to keep me warm. I looked at the sparkling stars and bright half-moon, and again asked Buddha and Tevada to come down and take me to live with them. I twisted and turned and prayed for the soul of Mak and Pa to protect me from the snakes, scorpions, and centipedes during my sleep.

In the morning, I got off the mountain and went to the main road below. I walked along the road and politely asked people to adopt me. Many of them said "No" with a sympathetic voice that echoed with guilt and sadness. They told me many reasons why that they couldn't adopt me:

"I have five children. I barely have enough food to feed my children. I'm very sorry. I hope that someone else who is richer than me will adopt you," said one man.

"I am going to the Thai border. My journey is very dangerous. And I don't know when I am going to come back. I would love to adopt you when I come back," said another old man.

"I'm on a journey to look for my relatives, and I don't know when or where my journey will end. I don't have a place to sleep, just like you," said a young man.

The Poor Fisherman and Me

That hot afternoon, there was a man in his late thirties who was carrying a rusted metal bucket and a *somnagn-bonk-trey*, a type of fishing net. He wore old short pants, a torn short-sleeved shirt, and a *kroma* wrapped on his head. He carried the fishing net on his shoulder. In the bucket was a knife, a small ax, and a small cooking pot filled with uncooked rice.

I approached him and said, "Uncle, my name is Marin. Would you please take me to live with you?"

He stopped, took a deep breath, looked at me, and said softly with sympathy, "I feel pity for you, but I can't take you to live with me because I am very poor. I have five children and I barely have enough food to feed them. But you can come fishing with me."

"Yes, uncle, I'm going with you. Let me help you carry the bucket," I said and grabbed it from his hand.

I was happy. My stress and depression began to subside, because I knew I would have food to eat that day. I knew I would not be alone, starving.

I walked with the poor fisherman along the road and away from the mountain, to look for flooded rice fields to catch fish. After a long walk, we decided to get off the road and we walked into the flooded rice field waist deep. We approached the broken bridge of a small canal. Most of the canal was cut off by flood, except the area around the bridge. Everything else around us and beyond was water. The only good portion of the bridge was in the middle. Less than seven meters of concrete still hung onto its frame.

"Marin, I think we need to settle on the bridge," he said and led me to the bridge.

We held onto the guardrail and moved slowly to the middle platform.

"Marin, go find firewood so we can cook food to eat."

"Yes, uncle."

"Do you know how to cook rice?" he asked.

"No, I don't."

"Here is the rice and cooking pot. Go wash the rice two to three times and put some water in it." He instructed me with hand gestures.

I washed the rice as he instructed, filled the pot halfway with water, and gave it to him.

"That is too much water," he said with a soft laugh and poured out some water out of the pot. He then set the pot on stones above the fire.

"Marin, you watch over the rice. When the rice is boiling remove out some fire and let the rice simmer. I'm going fishing."

"Yes, uncle."

He grabbed the fishing net, walked into the water waist deep, and began to look for signs of fish. He stood still for a moment. Then he swung the fishing net into the air. The fishing net spread in a circular form and fell into the water to trap the fish. Afterward, he pulled the fishing net back toward him slowly. In about fifteen minutes of fishing, he got a few small fish. He cooked the fish and served them with the rice.

After we finished eating, the fisherman went into the water again to catch some more fish. I stripped myself naked to wash my only set of clothes: old brown khaki shorts and a brown short-sleeved button shirt. I didn't remember when, where, or how I had gotten this set of clothes. I washed them to remove blood stains and sweat. Then I hung them on the bridge guardrail to dry.

The wind blew my clothes into the water without me noticing, and I couldn't find them. I shouted to the fisherman for help. "Pu! Can you help me find my clothes! I dried them on the guardrail and now they disappeared!"

"When did you lose them?" he shouted.

"I don't know! It must have been a while!"

Without saying anything, he walked against the slow current in the water, waist deep, and tried to find my clothes. He moved his feet side to side, hoping to feel my clothes in the water with his feet. He walked from where he was toward the bridge, but he couldn't find them.

My frustration began to build up, and my heart boiled with anger. I bit my teeth and began to curse at Buddha and Tevada in a whispering voice. "Buddha and Tevada! You must be stupid and blind! That was why you didn't see me suffering! I lost my mak, my dad, my younger brother, and my sister. Then I lost the two cows. And now I lost my only set of clothes."

That night, the poor fisherman didn't go home because he didn't catch enough fish to feed and support his family. He folded his hands, leaned against the guardrail, watching the sunset, and said, "I don't know how much fish I'm going to catch tomorrow. Usually, there aren't much fish during the flood."

That night, I slept naked on the platform of the bridge next to the fisherman. He took off the kroma from his head to cover me and said, "This will protect you from the midnight dew."

"Pu, why weren't there much fish in this water?"

"Because we just received heavy rain and most of the fields are flooded. In the next several weeks, all the fish eggs will be hatching. And there will be plenty of fish in this water."

In the morning, the man continued to fish even harder. Again, he stood waist deep in the water, ready to deploy the fishing net from his shoulder when there was a sign of a fish swimming nearby. Around afternoon, he caught more than a half bucket of fish and decided to go back home. I walked with him, naked. No pants. No shirt.

On the way back home, he tried to trade a few fish for a can of rice.[8] One lady who tried to trade with him saw that I was naked.

"Why is your son naked?" she asked.

"Oh, he... he's not my son. He's an orphan boy I met yesterday on the street. He came with me to fish. When he dried his clothes, the wind blew them away."

The woman walked inside her house, grabbed a t-shirt and yellow shorts. "Here, these are my son's clothes. You can have them," she said to me.

---

8   Cambodians used a can as a standard of measurement to measure rice; whereas, westerners use a cup.

"Thank you." I grabbed the clothes from her and quickly put them on.

"Would you please help adopt him?" the fisherman asked the lady.

"No, I can't, because my husband is not here and I already have a few boys of my own. I would adopt you if you were a girl, because I don't have a daughter," she said to me.

Then she went into her house again and grabbed some food. "You must be hungry. Here is the food." She gave me a plate of rice and two small pieces of fish jerky.

While I was eating, the fisherman said to me, "Marin, I have to go. I wish you luck in finding someone to adopt you." He walked away with sorrow and guilt that he couldn't support me.

When he left, I got emotional. I controlled myself from crying out loud, but I couldn't control my tears from swelling up and dropping to the ground.

Street Survival Techniques

After I finished eating, I gave the lady back the plate, then continued my journey on the streets. I was depressed and thought about how I was going to live my life. Living in a city that was ravaged by war, finding food was much harder than finding bullet shells. Every time I roamed the field to look for grasshoppers and crickets for snacks, I ended up picking bullet shells or a live round of bullets to play with. There were bullets everywhere: on the streets, in the fields, and on the mountain.

Fortunately, around this time, the swap-meet market began to form. People who smuggled goods from the Thai border gathered along the intersection of the main road to display their goods. Within days, the long strip road of the intersection was crowded with buyers and sellers. Men and women sold all sorts of goods, including fabrics, shirts, bras, underwear, pants, bicycle tires, bicycle tubes, and cigarettes. They carried their goods, walking back and forth in the market, and shouted the brand names of their goods, hoping people would buy them.

However, at that time, Cambodia didn't use money to buy goods. Since the country had fallen to the Khmer Rouge, money had no value. So, people in the entire city used rice, silver, gold, and sapphires as mediums of exchange. For example, a small bundle of vegetables could be traded for a can of rice. A kilogram of fish was equivalent to one can of rice. A bicycle was worth 100 kilograms of rice or two sets of gold necklaces.

Despite the difficulty of finding food, my hope for survival began to increase. I took every opportunity to steal food to eat. I felt guilty and ashamed of myself for being a thief. But to survive was the only option I had.

Selling goods along the street was illegal. The Vietnamese soldiers often arrived with sticks and rifles to raid the emerging outdoor swap meets along the street. They arrested the people and confiscated the goods. When Vietnamese soldiers raided the markets, the vendors ran for their lives, grabbing whatever they could. Some people ran to their apartments to hide their goods. Others ran into the bushes.

During the raids, I took every opportunity to seize food. I ran along with the crowd and snatched food from vendors who were carrying baskets of food. Sometimes, I didn't need to steal. When people tried to run away in a chaotic raid, they often dropped food on the ground. Fruits and canned foods were more likely to be dropped during the raid. Instinctively, I would just pick up and run with the food, especially *nom-sorm-ang*, a type of food rolled in banana leaves and grilled on charcoal.

People were desperate to sell their goods to get profit and to support their families. Meanwhile, I was desperate to have food to survive the next day. It didn't matter how many times the Vietnamese soldiers raided the market. People always got back onto the street, selling their goods again within hours after the soldiers left. Sometimes, the soldiers raided and closed the market completely. They raided and stationed themselves along the intersection of the road to ensure that traders would not come back.

Whenever the Vietnamese soldiers closed the market, I became starved, and my desperation forced me to beg people for food. At noon, I walked from one apartment to another to see if people were sitting with their families to eat. Most of the apartments had no electricity. During meal time, they left the front and back doors open for light and to let fresh cool air come in. That gave me the opportunity to see what they were doing.

When I saw them eating, I approached them. I stood outside their open front doors and did a *som-piass*[9] (bow) and politely said, "Aunty, may I have a scoop of rice to eat? I'm an orphan. I don't have a mother. I don't have a father."

They turned their heads, paused, looked at me, and talked to their family members. Most of the time, they felt sympathetic for me and gave me food. But they didn't let me eat with them. They would rather gave me a plate of food and tell me to eat outside by the doorway. Once I finished eating, I gave them back the plate and spoon, *som-piassed* them, said thanks, and walked out of their sight.

One afternoon before dusk, I approached a family of five who were sitting in a small circle on a *kontael* and were eating in harmony. I used the same approach. I stood by the open front door, *som-piassed*, and politely said, "May I please have some food to eat. I'm an orphan. I don't have a mother or a father. I live on the street."

The father, the mother, the two daughters, and a son who was about my age all turned their heads with sorrow on their faces. The father and mother slightly faced each other.

"Just give him a plate of food," said the father.

---

9   A formal Cambodian greeting. You put your palms together, raise your hands to your chest, and bow slightly.

The mother turned sideways to scoop the food in the pot next to her. She put it onto a plate and set it between her and her daughters.

"Come in and eat with us," the father said and waved his hand. "Once you finish eating, you can go back to finding your family."

I was surprised and hesitated to go into the apartment. After begging and living on the streets for about two months, I felt strange and stiff. But the warmth and genuineness I felt in their daughters' and son's tone of voice made me feel at ease.

"Come in and eat with us," said one of the daughters.

"Don't be afraid," the boy echoed. "You can come eat with us."

I slowly walked into the apartment. Everyone moved back slightly to make room for me to sit with them. I sat in front of the designated food plate.

"Don't be afraid," said the mother. "Just eat."

"Where are your *mak and pa?" asked the girls.

"Do you have a brother and sister?" asked the boy.

I heard the questions, but my mouth was too busy chewing. At the same time, I tried to ignore their questions.

Before I even had a chance to answer, the father interrupted and told the children not to ask me questions while I was eating.

"You three are very lucky," said the mother. "You still have Pa and Mak to take care of you."

I didn't even have a moment to look at everyone's faces. My eyes were concentrating on the food and my mouth was busy chewing. I finished the food on my plate, then took a few drinks to settle the food in my system. I got up, *som-piassed*, said thank you to them, and walked out of the apartment.

Evening turned into night. People shut their folding doors and shutters and went to sleep. I roamed along the street, looking for a safe place to sleep. I slept on the ground in front of an apartment, like an unwanted dog or cat. I hoped to wake up the next day, begging for food again.

During the period under the Khmer Rouge, I had known how to catch food. I had caught rice snails, fish, centipedes, snakes, and birds to survive. But living in the provincial city with its thousands of refugees and a large number of Vietnamese soldiers was extremely difficult. All the survival techniques I had used in the rice fields and in the forest didn't work in the city.

The refugees and the Vietnamese soldiers had more sophisticated techniques than I did. The Cambodians deployed fishing nets to catch fish in rivers and ponds. The Vietnamese soldiers threw hand grenades and shot rocket propelled grenades (RPGs) into the rivers, streams, and ponds to catch fish. I couldn't compete with them. I knew how to catch fish in shallow water in the rice field and streams, but not in the deep river.

Many times, I saw Vietnamese soldiers chasing people out of the river. They yelled and shouted in their language, and waved their hands signaling everyone to move out of the river. People young and old, male and female who were bathing and playing in the river rushed to shore. A moment later, the soldiers threw several hand-grenades and shot RPGs into the rivers. The explosion sent splashes high into the air and created shock waves in the water, killing every creature that lived within the proximity. Several minutes after the explosions, fish were floating in the water. The Vietnamese soldiers swam with a floating black tube to collect the dead fish and put it into their baskets.

Even birds were afraid to land in the city, because the soldiers would shoot them for food. Monkeys and dogs were among some of the favorite dishes of the Vietnamese soldiers. One afternoon, a domesticated monkey ran away from home, and its owner chased after it in bare feet along the street. The rebellious monkey climbed up the trees and went all the way to the top. The owner tried to bribe the monkey with a ripened banana and called it to come down, but the rebellious monkey refused.

The Vietnamese soldiers saw that as their opportunity. They

grabbed their rifles and fired several rounds. The monkey got hit and fell down to ground. The Vietnamese soldiers picked it up and walked out of site without any sense of guilt. The monkey's owners were sad and mad at the Vietnamese soldiers. They cursed at the Vietnamese soldiers in the Khmer language in all sorts of ways. I, too, felt sad for the monkey. I loved monkeys, because they were smart, naughty, and full of curiosity. They were fun to play with.

13

Many Homes

My Second Adopted Family

It had been more than two months. I still roamed the streets, the market, the fields, and the mountain, homeless.

One afternoon, I was on the mountain, trying to catch grasshoppers and crickets in the fields near the road for a snack. As I roamed around the field, I saw a buff, light-yellow complexioned man walking alone on the street. He was in his mid-twenties, had a thick medium build, and straight black hair. He walked fast past me.

I ran after him, calling him "*Pu,*" or uncle.[10] He stopped and turned to face me. I greeted him with the *somp-piass* and said, "Would you please take me to live with you? I'm an orphan. I have no one take care of me and give me food."

"What happened to your parents?" he asked.

I told him about the whole situation with my family members.

After he heard my story, he took a deep breath and looked away to hide his emotions. Then he put his hand on my shoulder and said, "Let's walk to my place. I will take you to see my wife. I don't think

---

10   In Cambodian culture, it is polite to address someone who is older than you as "aunt" and "uncle."

my wife would mind having you living with us."

"Thank you, Pu." I tilted my head up to look at him with a smile.

As we walked, Pu Ti talked about everything that came into his mind. "My wife stays home by herself most of time, because I travel a lot to the Thailand border to smuggle goods to sell in Cambodia. It would be good for you to stay with her. Marin, by the way," he added, "before the country fell to the Khmer Rouge, what did you father do?"

"I don't know. Maybe he was a doctor. I'm not sure what he did. But I saw him on several occasions with a white coat and stethoscope hanging on his neck. He diagnosed patients."

"So, how do you know your father is dead?" he asked.

"I don't know, Pu. But I saw two Khmer Rouge soldiers with rifles come to our house. They invited him to work on a canal project far away from home."

We walked and talked until we arrived at the shotgun apartment complex. Surprisingly, Pu Ti lived in the same apartment complex where I had lived with Aunty Thon, the lady who had tortured me and kicked me out for losing her cows. Aunty Thon was no longer there. She had moved.

The apartment door was open. Pu Ti and I entered the long, narrow apartment.

"Sross! Are you home?" Pu Ti called to his wife, as we walked to the kitchen in the back.

"I'm here in the kitchen," responded his wife. "The food will be ready soon."

Moments later, she came out of the kitchen. She stood by the door and talked to her husband. Sross was beautiful. She had a light-tan complexion, an oval face, big oval-shaped eyes, and long straight hair that ran below her waist.

Pu Ti grabbed her hand and approached me. "Sross, this is Marin. I met him on the street near the foot of the mountain."

"Jom-riapsur," I greeted her with the *som-piass*.

Pu Ti stood beside his wife, one hand wrapped around her waist, and said, "Marin is an orphan. I would like to help him and let him stay with us. When I'm not home, you can stay with Marin as your company."

Sross stood silently for a minute. She looked at me with a frown on her face, then she sighed with sympathy. "Do you have any brothers or sisters?" she asked.

"Yes, I have an older sister Vanny, but I have no idea where she is. I miss her a lot."

After a few minutes of chitchatting about my situation, Aunty Sross told us to take a bath first before we ate. Uncle Ti and I walked to the back of the apartment and took a bath to clean the sweat off our bodies. He helped me to wash by applying a lot of soap, and he rubbed my body with a piece of cloth to remove the dirt.

After we finished washing ourselves, we walked back into the apartment. Aunty Sross already had food set on the *kontael*. She served us *toek-kroeung*, a type of vegetable platter dish, and *khortrey*, a sweetened fish soup to be served with rice. The first day that I lived with Pu Ti and Aunty Sross, I felt a sense of caring and loving from them. I felt secure that they would love and take care of me until I grew up.

After two days of living with this family, Uncle Ti left and went to the Thailand border to buy goods. It would take him two days to walk to the border and even longer to come back with a heavy load of goods on him.

When he left, Aunty Sross and I lit three incense sticks and prayed before small Buddha statues on the altar inside the apartment. We prayed for safety and our prosperity.

I had always overheard people talking about the dangers of crossing the border into Thailand. The journey was extremely dangerous. There were landmines buried in shallow ground, waiting for a foot to step on them. There were robbers hiding in the jungle, waiting to prey on their next victims. There were still Khmer Rouge soldiers waiting in the jungle to capture people to work for them by carrying food and war supplies from one fort to another.

On the Thailand side of the border, there were Thai soldiers waiting to capture and torture Cambodian people who walked across their land. Sometimes, the Thai soldiers allowed Cambodians to cross the border to purchase goods; but when the Cambodians came back, the Thai solders arrested them, confiscated all their goods, and accused them of crossing the border illegally. The Thai soldiers were as ruthless as the Khmer Rouge soldiers had been. They captured Cambodians and tortured them. Then they let the Cambodians run back to the Cambodian side. Sometimes, they shot and killed people on the spot.

Cambodian people had no money, but they had valuable assets, such as gold necklaces, gold bracelets, gold earrings, gold rings, blue and red sapphires. So, when they travelled, they hid their jewelry in their belts and flip-flop shoes. They also hid them up their sleeves, in their waist pants, and in the hems of their shirts and pants.

Five days later, Pu Ti came back safely with the goods. He brought me a new yellow t-shirt and shorts. "I will get you some more clothes on the next trip," he said while giving me the clothes.

I *som-piassed* and thanked him. I was excited and put them on right away. This was the first time I could remember having a new set of clothes. I felt great and looked great.

Pu Ti was a generous and considerate man. He also brought a new pair of shoes, new clothes, and jewelry for his wife. He stayed home for several days before travelling back to the Thai border.

On the next trip, Pu Ti was not so fortunate. He was arrested by the Vietnamese soldiers when he was on his way back from Thailand to Cambodia. They confiscated everything he had bought in Thailand, including dozens of sarongs, packs of monosodium glutamate (MSG), and jeans. They also confiscated personal assets, such as his gold necklace, a gold bracelet, and a watch.

I later learned through Aunty Sross that the Vietnamese soldiers had put Pu Ti in prison. When she found out about his arrest, she was restless, depressed, and fell into tears. She stroked her belly gently; she was two months pregnant.

I was lost, confused, and depressed, not knowing where my life would end up. I felt sorry for Pu Ti. I missed him. Why didn't the angels and Buddha help him? I thought.

Within a few days, Aunty Sross made a drastic decision. She moved out of the apartment to search for her relatives and her husband's relatives for help. She went alone, and left me with a widower woman, who lived two units away.

"Marin, you stay here with Aunty Phim. I will come back to get you when the situation gets better," Aunty Sross said with a grim face and tears building up in her eyes.

I could feel her sadness. I could feel her pain. I could also feel her anger and frustration with the Vietnamese soldiers who had arrested her husband.

"When will you come back to get Marin?" Mrs. Phim asked.

"I don't know, maybe three weeks or three months," Aunty Sross said.

When she walked away from me, I felt emptiness in my heart again. I hoped she would come to get me sooner. Now, my frustration toward Buddha and Tevada began to increase. I stood holding the door and said bitterly inside my heart, *Tevada and Buddha, are you blind? Don't you see us suffering? I live with Pu Ti's family for less than one month. Now, the Vietnamese soldiers arrest him. Why don't you come down to earth to help Pu Ti escape from the prison? Why can't you kill all the Vietnamese soldiers?*

My Third Adopted Family

Aunty Phim was a widowed woman. She was a smart, assertive business woman. She traded goods to support six people in her family.

Now, it would be seven, including me. She had two younger sisters. One had a hunched back and was a widow, with two sons named Aka and Da, ages nine and six. Aunty Phim also had a fourteen-year old daughter named Somphors.

Aunty Phim was in her mid-thirties. She had a dark complexion, long straight hair, and was as tall as an average Cambodian woman. She had lots of tiny dark spots on her face, like little birthmarks.

Living with Aunty Phim's family was a blessing for me. I was well-fed and got along with everyone in the family. Every morning, Somphors, Aka and I, carried water from the well to fill up the big jars that sat near the kitchen, which were used to cook, wash clothes, and bathe. Afterwards, we played games such as hopscotch, jump rope, and shooting rubber bands, or *kup-vong*.

One month after I started living with Aunty Phim, three of her male friends convinced her to make a risky journey to the Thailand border with them to smuggle goods. They wanted her to assess a possible route to escape from Cambodia to the refugee camp in Thailand. Smuggling goods from Thailand to Cambodia was highly profitable. At first, she hesitated; but later she gave in and made the journey with them.

After her first trip, she was hooked into the business, because she made a good profit. When she came back from the Thailand border, she only stayed home for a few days, then she made a trip back.

On Aunty Phim's third trip, the man who came with her gave us a puppy.

"Where did you get the cute puppy from?" Somphors asked.

"I caught it in the jungle," he said. "I believe it is a baby wolf."

All the children in the family fell in love with the puppy because it was puffy and cute; its brownish fur made it look like a baby bear.

So, we adopted the baby dog and named him Akki. Somphors, Aka, Adda, and I paid full attention to Akki for months, until he was fully grown. We fed and bathed him and took him to sleep inside the mosquito net with us every night.

After about three weeks, we noticed that Akki had grown taller and lost his cute puffiness. But he was still beautiful and playful. He liked to roll on his back and have us rub his belly.

Adda and I made a round object out of plastic bags to toss around in the apartment for Akki to chase after. He also could recognize his name and we had fun playing with him by having him run after us from one tree to another outside, like playing hide and seek. All the four of us had a great time with Akki.

Sometimes, early in the morning, I took Akki out of the apartment and ran along the dirt road of the apartment. It was my first childhood memories of love and fun.

When Akki was about three months old, the Vietnamese soldiers killed him for food. We didn't see the soldiers kill our dog, but several eyewitnesses said, "The Vietnamese soldiers shot the dog in the neck, and took him to their place." Somphors, Aka, Adda, and I were sad and got mad at the Vietnamese soldiers. We didn't speak the Vietnamese language, so we cursed at them in Khmer.

"You stupid Vietnamese soldiers, you ate our dog! You will go to hell!" Somphors shouted.

Journey to the Refugee Camp

After Aunty Phim completed a few trips of smuggling goods from Thailand to Cambodia, she thought of helping her entire family to escape to the refugee camp in Thailand. Her first plan was to move her family to the Jomrum-Tmey Refugee Camp, which was located inside Cambodia just a few kilometers from the border of Thailand. Then she would proceed to another refugee camp inside Thailand called Khao-I-Dang.

Aunty Phim sent me to Jomrum-Tmey Camp first, to live with her friend. It was early in the morning. The sun was barely meeting the horizon. Aunty Phim woke me up and told me to wash my face to refresh myself.

"Marin, these two men are my friends. They will take you to live with my friend, Vannsina, a woman who lives in the refugee camp."

I briefly looked at the two men, then I turned my head toward Aunty Phim.

"Who is this woman?" I asked.

"Ohh, Vannsina! She is a great business lady. She smuggled goods from Thailand to Cambodia a few times with me. She doesn't have any children. She will take care of you and love you like her own child," she said.

While we were talking, everybody woke up and listened to our conversation. "Are you going to leave now, Marin?" asked Akka.

"Don't worry," said Aunty Phim, "Mr. Sreng over here also knows Vannsina. Just go with him. The rest of the family and I will see you there in a few weeks."

"Let's go, Marin," Pu Sreng said and gently pulled my hand to walk alongside him. "Our journey is long. We have to leave now."

I turned and waved. "Goodbye, aunties! Goodbye, Somphors. Goodbye, Akka. Goodbye, Da! See you in the next few weeks." That was the last time I would ever see them.

I walked barefooted on a big dirt road past many rice fields and stilt houses. After about an hour of walking, we met a man who was walking a buffalo along the road.

"Where are you taking this buffalo?" Pu Sreng asked him.

"I'm taking this buffalo to sell at Kook-Khajoong Camp."

"How much are you going to sell it for?"

"I don't know. It depends on the bargaining," said the buffalo man. Then he asked, "Where are the three of you heading to?"

"We are going to Jomrum-Tmey Camp. But first we have to go to Kook-Khajoong Camp."

"Okay, we are going to the same direction. We should walk together."

After chitchatting, they quickly changed the subject. They talked about a possible safe foot trail to the Kook-Khajoong Refugee Camp.

It was afternoon and the sun shone straight above and was hot on my head. We got off the main dirt road and walked along the foot trail surrounded by tall grasses and bushes.

After hours of walking, I was exhausted and thirsty, and I began to walk slower than my normal pace. Pu Sreng picked me up and had me ride on the back of the buffalo. Not knowing how to ride, I tightly grasped the buffalo's leathery skin to sit upright as best I could. Being dehydrated and exhausted from the long journey, I drifted in and out of sleep, sitting on the moving buffalo. Then before I could react, I abruptly tumbled off the huge animal, and the buffalo crushed the middle toe of my foot and stripped off the nail. My foot was instantly soaked in blood. My heart pounded with such a force that it felt like someone was beating on my chest. As the pain shot to my brain, tears rolled down my cheeks, dropping onto my feet. And there was no first-aid kit to treat my wound.

"Urinate on it!" the buffalo man ordered me. "Boy, just pee on it to clean your wound."

My reaction to his order wasn't instantaneous because I was focused on the pain. Within a few moments, though, I did what he told me to do. I pulled down my pants and urinated on my wounded toe, but this brought even more pain. After cleaning the gash with my own urine, I continued to walk with the others, but limping along.

At a rest area where people sold food and water, we ate rice and grilled chicken thigh, then took a short nap under the shade of a tree.

Then we continued our journey deeper and deeper into the jungle. The man with the buffalo didn't come with us. Instead he said, "Good luck with your journey. Now, I'm on my way to Kook-Khajoong Camp."

The journey to Jomrum-Tmey Refugee Camp was long and extremely dangerous. There were landmines buried in shallow ground, waiting for any foot to step on them. There were robbers hiding in the jungle, waiting for their next victims. There were Khmer Rouge soldiers waiting to capture people for forced labor, which meant carrying food and war supplies from one fort to another. Walking on the wrong trail or even one wrong step would mean losing one's leg, life, or enslavement.

I walked between the two men, following every footstep behind Pu Sreng, while the other man walked ten meters behind me. Our journey was completely silent. We didn't talk, cough, or even sneeze. We concentrated on walking on the small foot trail, believing it to be safe.

From a distance, we saw a part of the forest catch on fire. Thick black smoke curled into the sky. Every so often, I heard bombs and landmine explosions where the fire was. I continued following Pu Sreng's strides.

Around five o'clock in the evening, I heard a few wild dogs howling. The two men stopped, stood still, listened, and asked each other in a low tone, "Is it a two-legged dog or a four-legged dog?" The "two-legged dog" referred to either a band of deceptive robbers or Khmer Rouge soldiers who would make sounds imitating dogs.

"I don't know," said the man behind me. "It sounds like four-legged dogs." The howling stopped, and we continued walking as silently as we could.

Right before sunset, I heard the sound of people talking to each other less than one hundred meters away. Again, the two men stood still and listened, lowering their bodies and cautiously peering through the trees, bushes, and thick giant reeds. We couldn't trust anyone in the jungle. As the voices got closer and closer to our next fork in the trail, it was necessary to test and identify the unknown approaching group.

Pu Sreng yelled, "Who is it?"

"We are good people," a man shouted back.

"We are good people, too. How many people do you have?" Pu Sreng shouted.

"I have two small children and three adults. We are going to the refugee camp," the man replied.

"Do you have any weapons?" Pu Sreng asked.

"I swear. I have no weapons. All we have are the clothes on our backs and some food for the journey."

After a somewhat lengthy probing and shouting match, both men agreed to step forward and meet at the upcoming fork in the trail, which was about fifty meters away. After both sides developed a sense of trust of each other, everyone came out from hiding to introduce themselves. When I saw the woman carrying a child against her chest and another man carrying a small boy on his back, I felt safer meeting them. After quick introductions, we joined and made a larger group. Then we continued our journey in silence along the main foot trail.

Soon, the sunset disappeared from the horizon and left us walking in the dark on an uneven smaller foot trail that sandwiched us between pampas grass, giant feather grass, fountain grass, bushes, and tall trees. The visibility ahead was low. I stayed closely behind Pu Sreng.

I was exhausted. I'd been limping for hours under the scorching sun and into the night. The pain from my wounded foot made it difficult for me to walk. The dust and dirt from the trail mixed with my blood now became solidified onto my wound making it increasingly more difficult for me to travel.

Then Pu Sreng decided to rest under a tree where he used to stay on his previous trips. The woman with the baby broke a small piece of *nom-pank*, a long French baguette, and gave it me. Pu Sreng had brought raw crispy noodles and water, and shared it with everybody.

It was a scary night. Everyone kept whispering to each other. I didn't pay any attention to what was spoken. All I cared about was relaxing and nursing my injury. What scared me the most were the landmine and bomb explosions. I prayed to my parents' spirits and

Tevada to help protect me from all the dangers of this journey.

The bombs and landmine explosions grew much louder as the night progressed. Every ten or twenty minutes, loud booms echoed in the distant forest. Pu Sreng gave me his *kroma* for me to sleep on the ground nearby. Although I was fearful, it didn't take me long to fall into a deep sleep that night.

When I woke up, everyone had disappeared. I was alone in the middle of the jungle. Goose bumps appeared on my arms and legs. I sat. I stood. I looked at my injured swollen toe and saw dried dirt clumped around it. It was painful but I diverted my attention to the possibility of getting out of this jungle alive. I limped around the tree several times in disbelief. I shouted for Pu Sreng and the rest of the people for help.

"Pu….! Where are you! Why did you run away from me? Can you come to get me?"

After ten minutes of shouting without seeing a single soul, I continued my journey along the foot trail. I had no idea how far or how long it would take for me to get to the camp. While I was limping along the foot trail, my mind raced with questions. I could not believe Pu Sreng and the rest of the people had disappeared! Were they robbed last night? Did the Khmer Rouge capture them? Did the Vietnamese soldiers capture and imprison them like they did to Pu Ti? Why didn't they capture me? Didn't they see me sleeping? Why didn't anyone wake me up? I couldn't comprehend the whole situation. I blamed myself for sleeping like a log.

The foot trail curved through the jungle toward a part of the forest that had caught on fire. The fire ignited random landmine and bomb explosions every ten or fifteen minutes. Every time they exploded, my body jolted. When I approached the fire, the explosions were louder and stronger than the ones last night.

I continued to walk along the foot trail through the jungle, potentially risking my life. I put my palms together and pressed them upon my chest and prayed, "God, please have this foot trail turn away from the direction of the endless fires and explosions. I have suffered so much in my life. You must help me." No matter what, I had to stay strong and try to get out of this jungle alive.

To divert my attention from being scared, I extended my palms to catch falling ashes that were descending from the sky. White, black, and gray ashes landed softly on my palms. Some ashes were as big as my thumbs, others were much smaller.

The path moved away from the fires. I was relieved and I thanked all the spirits above. My fear of being alone began to fade away. After a few hours had passed, I saw a Khmer Rouge soldier standing on top of a huge termite mound and leaning his back against a tree. My heart pounded. My gut instincts told me not to show fear, and I continued to walk along the foot trail at the same pace. I pretended I didn't see him.

Then I saw him walking down from the termite mound. He approached me. "Ahh! Little boy! Where are you going?" he asked.

"I'm going to the refugee camp," I said firmly.

"How many people are coming with you?"

"It's just me," I said. My senses told me he didn't believe a thing I had told him.

He looked at me briefly and said, "Are you sure it's just you?"

"Yes, it's just me."

He removed his rifle, held it in front of him and walked in the opposite direction.

I continued to walk with a pounding heart. Every few minutes, I glanced back to see if he was chasing me. But he wasn't. I continued walking away until he disappeared.

It was afternoon. The sun continued its journey to set on the horizon. I was now far away from the fires, and I no longer heard the sound of landmine explosions. Instead, I heard music from somewhere in the distance. I stood still and tried to move my ears to catch the sound of the music and the direction from which it came.

The low summer breeze not only brought me the sound of music, it also sent me sounds of human voices. At that moment, I gained a new energy, which replaced my fear of loneliness in the jungle and I limped faster along the foot trail. When I got out of the jungle, I saw a huge refugee camp before me.

As I approached the camp, I saw a small group of men gathered under the shade trees as if they were waiting for the opportunity to smuggle goods back to their hometowns. Others were waiting for newcomers, like me. When I got into the camp, many people came and asked me many questions.

"How many people came along with you?" they asked.

"I came with three other people, but I had no idea where they are at right now," I said.

"Which route did you take? Did you see soldiers or Khmer Rouge along the way?"

"Yes, I did," I answered.

My Fourth Adopted Family

I walked inside the camp without any sense of direction of where was I going or who I was going to see. Then a strange man approached me and asked, "Are you Marin?"

I looked at him and said, "Yes, I am."

"Where are the rest of the people?"

"I don't know. They are still in the jungle I guess. How do you know my name?"

"Oh, someone told me that you came here to live with another lady in this camp."

I didn't ask any more questions, because I thought that Aunty Phim had set up everything for me already.

"Follow me," he said. "I will take you to the person you are supposed to live with."

I followed him to a dilapidated hut where several women were.

One of them offered me food. While I was eating, they asked me many questions. They asked about my trip to the camp, my family members, how I had survived, and with whom I had lived during the Khmer Rouge regime. The questions went on and on for what seemed like hours. They felt sympathy for me.

Then while I was still eating, the man brought a plump-sized lady into the hut. Compared to most Cambodian women, she was chubby. She sat on the platform and watched me eat. She had a round face, broad cheeks, and long wavy black hair; and she had a dark-brown complexion, just like me.

Then she asked, "Are you Marin, who lives with my friend Phim?"

"Yes, I am."

"My name is Vannsina. I'm Phim's friend. You can call my Aunty Sinna."

"Oh, Aunty Phim told me to live with you. She told me you will take care of me."

Everyone in the hut cracked into laughter.

Then Aunty Vannsina took out a pack of cigarettes from her button-shirt blouse pocket. She pulled a cigarette out, put it in her mouth, and lit it. She puffed away intensely and removed it with her two fingers. Then she leaned against the bamboo post of the hut.

"What did Mrs. Phim tell you about me?" she asked as the smoke swirled out of her mouth and nose.

Softly, I muttered, "Aunty Phim told me that you are a very nice lady. You have no children. And you are a wealthy business woman."

She cracked into a laugh and said lightheartedly, "You are a very smart boy. If my son was alive, he would be about your age."

"Boy, you are very lucky to have Mrs. Vannsina adopt you," boasted another woman who sitting next to her. "She is a very generous lady."

"Vannsina, this boy looks very similar to your son. If you were to tell someone that he is yours, they would believe you," said the lady who had a wrapped *kroma* hung around her neck.

Aunty Vannsina instructed me to go to the local market, located less than fifty meters from the men's hut. She gave me a Thai paper bill to purchase tangerines to eat.

In the crowded market, I found large baskets of all kinds of delicious fruits: golden bananas, jackfruit, watermelon, mangoes, papayas, and longans, an Asian tropical fruit. Finally, I spotted a tangerine seller. I carefully looked in her bag for the one tangerine with the smoothest skin, and I handed over the money. Eagerly, I rushed back to the hut.

Aunty Vannsina helped me to peel off the tangerine's skin, and we shared the juicy fruit. While eating, she asked, "Where is the change?"

"What change?" I replied.

"I just gave you a 20 Baht bill (equivalent to $1.00 USD) to buy the tangerine. This tangerine cost only 5 Baht. You should have 15 Baht for change," she said curtly while lighting up another cigarette.

"I'm sorry, aunty. I didn't know that was a 20 Baht bill. I didn't know. I don't know the Thai currency."

Aunty Vannsina was disappointed with me. She looked at me and asked, "Do you know who the seller was? Do you know who the seller was?"

"Uhm...uhmm... She is a lady...and... and she walked around with the tangerine baskets," I said in a quivering hesitant voice, trying to picture what the seller looked like.

"Whoever that stupid lady is, she should have given you back the change. And you, young man, next time you should be smarter than that."

Knowing this was my first bad impression to Aunty Vannsina, I crouched in the corner of the hut. All I could think was, *How could she get mad at me? I don't know how to read Thai money or Thai numbers! I can barely count to a hundred in Khmer! I barely recognize Cambodian money, the Riel!*

I kept murmuring over and over to myself, "I just got out of the jungle, it doesn't mean I'm stupid. If she explained a little bit about how currency worked, I would have known."

In the distance, Aunty Vannsina just chatted away with her friends, ignoring me. Finally, she took me to her hut, two-hundred meters away. There, she introduced me to Sokheoun, her younger half-sister, who looked completely different from Aunty Vannsina. Sokheoun had a light-yellow complexion, straight long hair, a slim build, and was petite.

"*Jom-riapsur*, aunty," I greeted.

"Who is this boy, *bong*?" Sokheoun asked her sister with a smile.

"Well, he is the child I wanted to adopt. He just arrived in the camp. Here is some money. Go to the market and buy him a set of new clothes."

Sokheoun extended her hand out to grab the money from Aunty Vannsina, and asked, "What kinds of clothes do you want me to get for him?"

"You could buy him shorts and a t-shirt."

Minutes later, Aunty Sokheoun walked out of the hut. Aunty Vannsina also left the hut to visit her friends. While they were gone, I sat on the platform inside the hut and spent time thinking. Were Aunty Vannsina and Sokheoun going to love me and take care of me like my real parents? Were they going to treat me like Pu Ti's family had? Were they going to feed me enough? Would they let me have as much freedom as other children who have parents?

Less than half an hour later, Aunty Sokheoun came back from the market. "Here, Marin," she said while showing me the clothes. "I got you shorts and a yellow t-shirt. I think they fit you perfectly."

I was excited to have a new set of clothes. I grabbed the clothes from her hands. "Thank you. They look nice! Can I put them on now?"

"No, Marin. Don't put them on yet. Your body is dirty. Go wash yourself first." Aunty Sokheoun walked me to the back of the hut and pointed to two rusty water buckets.

"Which water bucket would I use?"

"Use that one." She pointed to a half-full bucket.

"How long have you been living in the camp, Marin?" she asked me.

"I just got here. I just got out of the jungle about an hour ago."

"Take off your old clothes and put them in the bucket over there. I will wash them for you."

I striped myself naked, as I was told. She scooped the water out of the bucket and poured the water over my head and my body. She handed me soap and told me to apply it on my body and wash myself.

After I finished bathing, I put on the new clothes. I felt great. Finally, I had a new family to take care of me again.

14

Being a Refugee

Caught in a War

After less than ten days of living in the Jomroum-Tmey Refugee Camp, war broke out between the Khmer Rouge and the PARA soldiers, which were a new military faction fighting the Vietnamese and the Khmer Rouge occupations in Cambodia. People seemed to know that war was imminent. Many people escaped to the Kao-I-Dang Refugee Camp in Thailand a day before the war even started.

It was morning. The sun was already showering heat over the camp. Aunty Vannsina and Aunty Sokhoeun packed their possessions into bags and we moved out of the camp with thousands of other people.

After walking away from the camp about one kilometer, I heard a grenade launcher exploding. That explosion triggered a furious response of fire from a barrage of rifles and artillery. Bombs exploded in the field and sent thick scarred black smoke into the air. Instinctively, I dropped to ground.

A man next to Aunty Vannsina shouted, "Run! Run! Run to the water well!"

Vannsina dragged my hand and we ran to the water well, where we hid behind a pile of elevated dirt. She pushed my head low to the ground to protect me from getting shot; but for some reason, I didn't feel as fearful as they did. Maybe I was used to the sounds of fighting. Maybe the large crowd of people was more comforting than being alone. Maybe I had become immune to war.

I was kneeling in order to observe the chaotic situation. PARA soldiers were running sporadically in all directions away from us. People jumped feet first into the unknown depths of the water well. An old crippled lady screamed for her son to help her. A mother frantically ran and held onto her *kroma,* which held her crying baby. A man was intensely praying and reading his magical Sanskrit handkerchief, which called all the deities to protect him and his family. I was consumed by all the different actions they took to ensure their survival.

As the battle intensified, bullets hit the ground only three meters away from me. The bullets broke the hardened dirt into small pieces and sent a small amount of dust into the air. Out of curiosity, I crawled out to pick up the bullet heads. Before I even got to the bullets, I got knocked in the head.

"Come back here!" Aunty Vannsina grabbed me by the back of the shirt. "Are you stupid? Aren't you afraid of dying? Stay here!" She stared at me with clenching teeth. Her knuckles stung deep into the back of my head and created an instant bump. My only recourse was to cover my head with both hands, protecting myself from being knocked again. I was upset at her, but there was nothing I could do or say to her to soothe my pain.

After hours of intense shooting and bomb explosions, I saw a helicopter flying from the Thai border. It flew high in the sky as if the pilot crew was observing the fleeing refugees caught in the war.

When the shooting and bombing explosion eased, the helicopter flew lower, just above the treetops. From the ground, I saw a big red plus sign painted under the belly of the helicopter and on the door. People were shouting and waving their hands at the helicopter for help. The helicopter flew past the panicked refugees and landed about one kilometer from where I was. Thousands of refugees got up and hurried to the border of Thailand. Others ran to the landed helicopter. Aunty Vannsina and Aunty Sokheoun grabbed my hands and ran toward the helicopter.

Closer to the landing site, I saw a tall white man with facial hair emerge from the helicopter. He was escorted by two soldiers. Minutes after he got out of the helicopter, he waved his hands in a crisscross flagging pattern and shouted loudly at the rushing refugees. His message was clear: Do not across the Thai border.

Minutes later, a refugee man who appeared to speak the white man's language, approached him. Then that refugee man shouted in Khmer to us: "*Kom-dae-jlong-kat-Prumden-Thai. Maen-laan-mok-dek yerng-tov-jenh-pi-niss.*" In English, it translated to, "Don't walk across the Thai border! There will be vehicles coming to transport us from here."

The message spread from one person to another. From the distance, I could see hundreds of Thai solders aiming their rifles at the refugees. Without the white man's warning, the refugees would have been killed by the Thai soldiers for crossing their border.

Less than half an hour after the helicopter landed, hundreds of commercial trucks were driving toward us. The trucks drove fast along the dried grass landscape, creating a fume of dust rising in the sky, like a sandstorm moving in my direction. The trucks stopped near the area of the helicopter. Then the white man waved his hand, signaling to the refugees to get on the trucks.

Aunty Vannsina and her sister grabbed my hand and we ran toward the trucks. Refugee men helped pushed the women and children onto the trucks, me included. The trucks received a full load of refugees within seconds. Then the truck driver drove us to the Kao-I-Dang Refugee Camp in Thailand, a thirty-minute drive away from the war zone.

When I arrived at the Khao-I-Dang Refugee Camp, people there gave me food and water. Everything was wrapped in small plastic bags. In one bag was a small amount of steamed rice mixed with small pieces of chicken. In another clear plastic bag was water. Amidst the chaotic situation of war, I devoured the food.

That afternoon, the camp commissioner designated an area of vast grasslands and small bushes for fleeing refugees to set up camps. They named the site "Songkat 8," meaning District 8. The refugee authorities provided to the people tools, bamboo posts, and palm leaves that were crafted like giant hair combs so we would be able to build our own shelters.

Within one week, thousands of narrow fifty-meter-long huts were erected. Each hut accommodated as many as fifteen families. There was no electricity in the camp. People used firewood to fuel their cooking. At night, we made improvised lamps from tin cans, fueled by cooking oil, to illuminate our huts.

Khao-I-Dang Refugee Camp, Thailand

Khao-I-Dang Refugee Camp was the largest camp I had seen. It had more than twenty districts stretched along the foot of the Kao-I-Dang Mountain. I lived in Block B of District 8, near the barbed-wire fences of the refugee camp.

Days after we settled in the camp, Aunty Sokheoun got married and moved to live with her husband and in-laws. Aunty Vannsina also had a new relationship, with Mr. Iv Saroeun. I called him Pu Saroeun. He was the tallest and thinnest man in the district, perhaps the tallest and skinniest man in the refugee camp. When he was half naked, his thin frame showed all of his ribcage. His arms were long and slender as if there was no meat attached to his bones.

Pu Saroeun came to live with Aunty Vannsina. He was then elected to be the block captain and he became responsible for food and water rationing to the individual blocks. Two weeks after he became the block captain, he placed me in the orphanage center, hoping that there I would have a better chance to get sponsored by a wealthy country quicker.

The orphanage center was about two hundred meters from where I had lived with Aunty Vannsina. To admit me to the orphanage center, she and Pu Saroeun first took me to the 8th District Headquarters for the interview and documentation process. The headquarters hut was about fifteen meters wide and thirty meters long. Half of the hut had walls and shutters; the other half was open. The district headquarter was crowded with people who needed help writing their documentation. Others needed help searching for their loved ones.

I was in the section where workers were processing paperwork for orphaned children. After I had waited for a short while, a man carrying a carbon white document called, "Marin!" He scanned the room for me.

I was sure he was staff. He had thick, groomed black hair, broad cheeks, and was as tall as the average Cambodian man. He wore a long-sleeved collared-shirt and old jeans.

Aunty Vannsina pushed me slightly, through the crowd, and said, "Marin is here."

The man talked to her briefly about her relationship with me, then told her to go back home. Then he walked me several steps to a long shredded-bamboo bench and interviewed me.

"What is your name?" he asked, writing my answers.

"My name is Marin."

"How old are you?"

"I don't know. I don't know my real age, Pu."

He paused for a minute, trying to guess my age. Then he asked, "Do you remember what year or season you were born?"

"I don't know, Pu. I wish Pa and Mak were here with me so they can tell you my age and where I was born."

"Do you know when you were born?"

"I don't know."

"What is your father's name?"

"His name is Yann."

"What is your mother's name?

"Her name is Yim."

"Do you know how old your parents are?"

"No, I don't. I have no idea how old they were."

"How many brothers and sister do you have?"

"I have one younger brother, named Roth, and an older sister, named Vanny."

"Since when did you separate from your parents?"

That question gave me a flashback of sad memories. My throat and jaws became tense, and my eyes welled with tears. My mouth shivered as I tried to answer the question. "I...I don't know whether my dad is dead or alive. I really miss him. I saw two Khmer Rouge soldiers with rifles hanging behind their shoulders and they invited my dad to build a water canal."

The interviewer took a deep breath and looked at his co-worker who stood next to him. They both turned their heads away. A second later, they looked at me and asked more questions. "How about your mak?"

"My mak died in the hospital. My younger brother Roth died from illness and starvation. My older sister Vanny was separated from me during the Vietnamese invasion. I miss her." I looked down at the ground.

Minutes after completing this interview process, the interviewer got up and walked to another work bench behind him. He spoke to an older man wearing a blue, long-sleeved button-shirt. The man in the blue shirt approached me and tapped me on my back.

"Let's go take a photo picture over there," he said and pointed to the cameraman. He held my hand and walked me to the blackboard. He positioned me in front of the blackboard, facing the camera. The cameraman adjusted his equipment and took my picture.

Then the interviewer approached the cameraman, and said, "Here is Marin's file. Please attach his picture to this document. We will post his information on the bulletin boards in every district. I hope his sister, his aunts, and his pu's can find him through this information."

Minutes after the photographer attached my pictures to the document, the man in the blue shirt said, "Marin, let's go to the orphanage center. I hope that a *barung*[11] family adopts you and sponsors you to their country."

I didn't say a word to the man, because I was still traumatized by the interview questions. I followed him to the orphanage center about three-hundred meters away.

When I got to the center, I felt an immediate dislike toward it. It was surrounded by a bamboo fence. Inside the fence were several huts connected to each other. The center had a red dirt playground and a small landscape. Next to the fence were dead flowers. In the center of the landscape, tiny vinery plants were barely surviving under the hot sun, as if no one cared for them. Seeing this destitute environment, I felt no one would care for me. I felt like they had sent me to live in a prison.

The man introduced me to four female and two male staff. Then he left. The staff lived in the center and coached me to address them as "Mak" or "Pa." It felt a little odd because they weren't my real parents. However, whatever they said, I just said, "Yes."

I was the youngest at the orphanage center. Older boys didn't want to associate with me. They only associated among their own age group. There was no soccer ball or volleyball for me to play. There were no games. After just half a day of staying in the orphanage center, my interest for living in this center dulled and my boredom compelled me to leave.

I snuck out of the orphanage center and went back to live with

---

11   Cambodians called white people "barung"; the term referred to white Europeans.

my adopted family.

"Why are you here?" asked Pu Saroeun and Aunty Vannsina. "Are you supposed to be in the orphanage center?"

"I don't like to live in there. It is boring. I like to live with you, instead."

"Well, I don't know what to say, if you want to live with us that's fine," said Vannsina.

I continued to live with them for several days, and Aunty Vannsina told me to call her Mak and to call Pu Sareoun, Pa. Without hesitation, I started to call them Mak and Pa, like they were my real parents. I felt that by calling them Mak and Pa I would make them love me more.

My adopted father, Pu Saroeun was a nice man and he seemed well-educated. One time, I overheard heard his conversation with my adopted mother. He told her that before the Khmer Rouge had taken over Cambodia, he had a good professional job, working in seaport customs. He had been promoted to become an investigator. During the Khmer Rouge regime, the soldiers had put him in prison and tortured him. The soldiers had water-boarded him and hit him in the chest with their rifles. What he shared with her gave me goose bumps and flashbacks. It reminded me of the emaciated lady who was whipped with the metal rebar. It reminded me of the two prisoners who were killed in front of me. I got sweaty and walked away so I would hear no more.

A few days after I had snuck out of the orphanage center, Pu Sareoun travelled back to Cambodia. I overheard Aunty Vannsina say he had been hired by numbers of Cambodian-French and Cambodian-Americans who lived abroad for assistance in locating their relatives. They would pay him even more if he could help their relatives escape Cambodia to Thailand. For every person that he brought from Cambodia to the Kao-I-Dang Refugee Camp, he would get 20,000 Thai Baht (equivalence of $1,000 U.S.). It was a very lucrative business, but it was extremely dangerous.

Pu Saroeun became an elusive man. Each month, I saw him only a couple of days. He spent most of his time travelling to Cambodia searching for his clients and helping them to escape from Cambodia. He and I seemed to love each other, but we didn't seem to develop a strong bond. Maybe he didn't spend enough time staying with the family.

I had known Pu Saroeun less than three months when his own relatives sponsored him to go to the United States. He went alone, leaving Vannsina and me behind in the refugee camp.

The day he was about to get on the bus and leave the camp for America, both he and Aunty Vannsina put on grim faces. Their eyes turned red. Tears rolled down their cheeks onto shivering lips.

Right before he got on the bus, he put his hand on my head and said, "Just stay with your mother. When I arrive in the United States, I will send you letters and money. I will sponsor you to America." Then he walked in line onto the bus.

At that moment, I felt emotionally connected with him. I felt like I wanted to live with him in America. I walked toward him and waved my hands goodbye, but not a word came out of my mouth.

Weeks after Pu Saroeun left for America, Aunty Vannsina got depressed and began gambling at her friend's home. Every day she walked a few kilometers to the 5th District to gamble. Some nights, she didn't come home to cook for dinner. I ended up eating with Aunty Sokheoun's family.

Life in the refugee camp was simple. Every week, trucks delivered food and water to distribute within the district. The district then distributed the food to the blocks, and the block leaders distributed it to the krom, or group. Finally, the group leaders rationed the food according to each family's size. Each week we received a ration of chicken and vegetables. Some weeks we received small salted sardine fish. Sometimes we received canned fish.

The world organizations gave refugees food and water; they also provided us firewood and fuel for cooking. What refugees didn't have was sugar, MSG, salt, fish sauce, and clothes. So, many Cambodians snuck out of the refugee camp to buy goods from Thai villagers, to sell in the refugee camp.

The Thai authorities didn't allow Cambodians to have a market in the refugee camp or to do any kind of trading. The Thai soldiers drove their military jeeps loaded with soldiers and chased Cambodian people in the market like cats and dogs. One time, I saw the Thai soldiers catch a Cambodian man during a market raid, and several Thai soldiers beat him with a stick. They kicked and punched him in the face until he fell unconscious. The soldier then dragged him and put him onto the back of the pickup truck. The Thai soldiers were brutal toward the Cambodian refugees. Sometimes, they even killed the refugees. Despite all these prohibitions, the Cambodians would still gather together at these swap meet-like events to exchange goods.

At night, the refugee camp presented different difficulties for us. Robbers equipped with rifles and grenade launchers robbed the refugees. They snatched off every gold chain nugget that Cambodians possessed. They beat up people and took gold earrings, necklaces and bracelets, from men, women, and children.

In the Khao-I-Dang Refugee Camp, big megaphones were installed on the top of the wooden posts along the streets. The megaphones were the form of communication from the refugee authority to the people. They delivered voice information to the refugees as well as musical entertainment, including announcing the direction where the robbers were going.

"People, be careful. I have received information that robbers have moved to the 5th District," said the radio announcer. Half an hour later, he said, "People, please be careful. Now, robbers are moving to the 8th District."

My district! I clenched my body tight in my sleep and covered myself with a blanket, hiding in the corner of the combed reed wall. It wasn't the robbers that scared me. It was the announcement of where the robbers were and the chaos that followed.

With this announcement, the adult males prepared sticks, machetes, and axes to fight back the robbers. Many of us didn't have flashlights, so our men used homemade lamps fueled by cooking oil, which could barely illuminate five meters ahead.

Suddenly, Bang! Bang! Sounds of shooting loud and very close to my hut! It echoed through the dark. I shook. Although that night was warm, I felt chills and my teeth rattled.

Approximately, fifteen minutes after the shooting, people shouted, "Help! I got robbed! The robber is in my hut! Help! Help!"

Suddenly, people in the same hut complex shouted, "Catch him! Don't let him escape! Catch him. Kill him!"

Moments later, another shouting echoed. "We caught the robber hiding in our mosquito net!"

Once I heard that, I removed my blanket and got out of the hut. I controlled myself from quivering and walked out to see the caught robber. I squeezed into the surrounding crowd to see the man up close.

I saw his brown complexion. He was wearing only a *kroma* around his waist, and he was sitting by the corner of the wall, begging for his life. His head was bruised and his palm was bleeding. He held onto his bleeding palm and said, "I'm not the robber. I'm the victim of the robbers. Six Thai soldiers with M-16s came to my hut and robbed me. They pointed the rifle to my head and spoke to me in Thai, telling me not to scream. They snatched off the gold necklace from my neck and bracelet from my arm. They kicked and punched me. I freed myself by jumping through the shutter. Then they shot me and hit my palm. They were looking for me. That was the reason I ran and hid in here. Please believe me. Please don't kill me. Please take me to the hospital."

One of the ladies standing in the crowd was enraged. She

shouted, "Those mother-fucking Thai soldiers are as ruthless as the Khmer Rouge! They would kill all of us! When I got caught outside of the camp, the Thai soldiers robbed me of all my jewelry and hit me with the rifle. Now, they just came inside the camp and robbed us! I have had many bad experiences with them. Without the international community to protect us, all of us would be killed, like animals."

I didn't see the lady very clearly, because the light from the improvised lamps didn't reach far enough. But people were at ease. Several people helped the wounded man to the district and saw to it that he was transported to the hospital for treatment.

15

The Gods Must Be Blind

Kamput Refugee Camp, Thailand

After I had lived in the Kao-I-Dang Refugee Camp for about six months, the camp authorities closed several districts, including District No. 8. I didn't know why.

In the evening, I helped my adopted mother Vannsina wash pots, pans, dishes, a chopping knife, spoons, and pack them in a box. We didn't have many things to pack.

It was morning. The sun had barely risen. I woke up and prepared to leave the camp. Aunty Vannsina packed her clothes, blanket, and mosquito net in her large homemade green plastic handbag.

"Marin, you carry this box," she said and put the box on my head.

"Yes, Mak."

"Is it heavy?" she asked.

"No, not really, Mak. I can carry it."

Then we walked out of the combed palm leaves compound to the camp headquarters where the buses came to pick us up.

The headquarters was crowded with people waiting for the buses and to see off their loved ones.

After a short wait, I saw a long row of buses in the distance driving toward the camp. Thick dust fumes swirled into the sky like dirt devils following one another. Less than ten minutes later, our bus finally arrived. The camp authorities didn't waste any time. They checked our refugee documents, moved us to the designated bus number, loaded us up on a bus, and transported us to the Kamput Refugee Camp, located farther inside Thailand.

It was almost noon. After a few hours of riding roads of varied conditions—some paved, some dirt—I had finally arrived. The bus driver made a sharp turn onto the dirt road and entered the camp. He continued to drive slowly, then he stopped. A few Khmer women workers walked up into the bus and distributed warm steamed rice and chicken packed into a clear plastic bag, one for each family.

The food distributors got off the bus, and the bus driver continued to drive slowly up the hill. He stopped along the road near a large open field. A few minutes later, a Cambodian worker walked onto the bus with a sheet of papers on a clipboard and he began a head count. His eyes and hands moved as he counted everyone on the bus.

"Everyone who is riding on this bus must live in the *Sonkat-Domrey*, Block No.2. It is right across the street." He pointed. *Sonkat Domrey* means "elephant district."

Once I heard the name of the district, my thoughts traveled back to the first time I had seen an elephant. Before Cambodia fell to the Khmer Rouge, I had seen a huge elephant walking on the road in front of my house. The owner of the elephant had commanded it to suck water out of the bucket, with its large elongated nostril, and to spray the water into the air. I had been amazed at the elephant's intelligence and capabilities.

I loved the name "Domrey District." It captivated the depths of my imagination. I thought that a long row of elephants would walk into the district along the dirt roads, and spray water into the air to cool us off in the hot summer heat. I got off the bus with everyone else, food bag in my hands. The bus driver opened a bus hatch to let people unload their belongings.

"Hold onto my rice bag, Marin," said Aunty Vannsina. "I will go get our belongings out of the bus."

"Yes, Mak. I'm waiting for you over there." I pointed to the shoulder of the road.

She squeezed herself into the crowd to get our belongings. Moments later, she squeezed herself back through the crowd with the bag and put it on the ground in front of me.

"Watch the bag. I'm going back to get the box."

"Yes, Mak."

I stood barefoot, guarding the bag. My heels felt the burning heat from the uneven edges of the gravel on the road. My feet couldn't endure it, so I moved to stand on some weeds. Then my stomach began groaning, demanding food. And I was thirsty. I couldn't wait to eat.

After I had waited a short while, my adopted mother came back with the box. "Marin, you carry the box. I will carry the bag and rice."

She took the rice from my hands and put it in her bag, and she placed the box on my head for me to carry. I carried the box and walked behind her across the street, and in a freshly dug open-air sewage system.

When we got to our block, everyone appeared to be confused about where they would live. All six apartments had rectangular shapes that were sustained by only three walls: one in the back, two on the side. It looked like a warehouse. All the apartments sat on concrete posts on different ground levels, slightly less than one-and-a-half meters off the ground, like a stilt house. Some people put their belongings on the ground and waited for further instructions.

My adopted mother leaned her bag on the concrete near a rectangular open-air water tank. "Marin, put that box over there against by the wall near my stuff," she said to me and walked out of the site to acquire more information as to which apartment we would live in.

"Yes, Mak."

A few minutes later, she came back with a cigarette in her mouth. "Mak, do you know which apartment we will live in?" I asked.

She grabbed the bag and removed the cigarette from her mouth. "Marin, let's move our belongings and put it in that apartment." She pointed toward the apartment near the sewage we had just walked past. I picked up the box, carried it in front of my stomach, and followed her to the very end of the apartment. I walked up several wooden steps, and put the box against the wall next to her bag.

She didn't waste any time. She cut the box open and removed plates and spoons. Then she removed the rice from the plastic bag we had been given and placed the rice on our plates. I devoured it.

While I was eating, the camp organizers walked from one apartment to another and said out loud, "You need to appoint a block leader in order to receive rice and other food supplies."

Within minutes, adult males and females gathered in one of the apartments and the block leader was appointed.

At noon, trucks full of various supplies entered the camp and unloaded on the dusty field in the Angkor Wat District. There were firewood-rubber plant branches, whole bamboo, green tarps, and clay stoves. Other trucks delivered rice, cooking oil, canned food, frozen chickens, and fresh vegetables to distribute to each district. The block leader called each head of the household to get their family's rations.

Once people got their supplies, they tried to estimate how much space they needed for their families. People made their own front walls with bamboo and a blue tarp that the camp authorities provided. They made cubicles out of the tarp for their families to settle.

My First Time Seeing Movies

Later, I learned that Kamput Camp had more than ten districts. I didn't know all the names of the districts, but I knew ten of them well. The camp authority named each district after Cambodian provinces in Cambodia, such as Battambong, Siem Reap, Krojest, Steung Treng, Preah Vihear, and Kompong Cham. Some districts were named *Hong* and *Neak Kareach*, a mythological bird and snake. One of the districts was named after a famous Buddhist temple, Angkor Wat.

Large portions of the camp sat on a hill. This camp was much nicer and cleaner than Kao-I-Dang. All the buildings looked exactly the same, with gray walls and roof tiles. The apartments sat on concrete posts. In each block, there were six apartments facing each other. At the corner of each block there were two restrooms. At the center of each block there were two rectangular concrete open-air water tanks that stored water for drinking, cooking, and bathing. The building had a wooden slab floor and three walls. The walls were made out of hard composite materials and twice as thick as cardboard boxes; the roof was made out of the same materials. There were no living rooms, bedrooms, or restrooms inside the apartments. Each apartment was approximately seven meters wide and thirty meters long, and accommodated between five and eight families.

One week after I had settled into the Kamput Camp, the camp authority set up a big movie screen on the dusty soccer field in the Angkor Wat district. That night, two movies were shown. A man sitting down translated Thai and said the first movie was called *The Drunken Master,* a 1978 Hong Kong martial arts/action/comedy film. I didn't understand the movie, because it was dubbed in Thai. Although I didn't understand what they were talking about, I was captivated by the martial-arts moves; I wanted to learn how to fight like they did. I was also fascinated with the array of lights that projected to the big movie screen and displayed the images, characters, actions, and sound. It was my first time watching a movie, and it was amazing!

After *The Drunken Master* ended, *The Jesus Film* began to play. This 1979 motion picture depicting the life of Jesus Christ was dubbed in Khmer. In the movie, Jesus helped the blind to see and the crippled to walk by his gentle miracle touch.

At that moment, I believed that Jesus, the long brown-haired God, would help get me out of the refugee camp.

How Thai Soldiers Treated Refugees

The Kamput Camp seemed peaceful. In reality, the Thai soldiers were every bit as vicious as the Khmer Rouge. All refugees were required to wear identification cards, and the Thai soldiers patrolled the refugee camp and chased after people who didn't wear their refugee IDs.

The Thai soldiers abused their powers. A Cambodian couldn't directly look them in the eyes. If we looked at them, they would threaten to hurt us. The Thai soldiers felt they could do whatever they wanted. They beat up kids and raped young girls. Sometimes, they just beat people for no apparent reason. They weren't much different from the Khmer Rouge soldiers. Without the world organization's protection, the Thai soldiers would have killed all us. They chased me a couple times, but I never got caught.

One of the Thai military guards was famous for his brutal actions. Cambodians named him *Ar-Ngok,* based on his distinct walk of rocking back and forth. Ar-Ngok was one of the tallest Thai soldiers in the camp. He was in his late thirties and walked with his head drooping slightly forward. His posture was like that of a stern, cold, drunken man. He always had a rattan stick in his hand, and he beat and kicked men, pregnant women, and children, for no apparent reason. I saw him a few times walking along the road, but I distanced myself to avoid being whipped by him.

One afternoon, the Cambodians were having a soccer tournament. I stood alongside the road and watched the game along with hundreds of other spectators, mostly teenage and adult males. I squeezed through the crowd to the front for a better view of the game. I watched the players running back and forth chasing after the ball and passing it from one player to another. Once the players moved the ball closer to the goalie, the crowd cheered with excitement. They yelled and shouted, "Shoot! Shoot! Shoot!"

While I was enjoying watching the soccer game, I saw people running for their lives to escape the Thai soldiers' beatings, chasing people who weren't wearing their IDs.

As the crowd moved, a soldier spotted me for not having my ID hanging on my chest. He approached me with a rattan stick. My heart pounded and my adrenaline rushed. I ran, squeezing through the crowd. He chased me along the road. I ran and jumped over the open-air sewage into my block. I barely jumped over the sewage, almost falling down into it.

The soldier continued to chase after me. I zigzagged through the neighborhood, hiding at the back of an apartment for a few minutes, then running back to the cheerful crowd at the soccer game. I was scared and exhausted. Sweat dripped down from my head to my chest. I was very lucky I didn't get caught.

Feeding a Gambling Habit

Life in the refugee camp was pretty boring, because there weren't many things for people to do. My adopted mother Vannsina began to make food to sell along the street. She borrowed *tbal-ken*, a manual rice grinder made from a large piece of stone, to grind soaked rice. She would use the soaked rice to make *jek-jian*, deep fried banana, *nom-bagn-jok*, and *nom-kroach*, for me to sell along the streets. Each day, we made a profit of about 20 Thai Baht, which I thought was pretty good.

As time passed, she began playing cards for money with her acquaintances and friends at the Kompung Cham District. Her gambling habit forced her to sell the jewelry she had earned by smuggling goods from Thailand to Cambodia. She sold her gold earrings, gold necklaces, gold and sapphires rings, and gold bracelets. She gambled at her friend's apartment day and night, until she ran out of money.

When she came home, she got depressed and hot-tempered.

I didn't fear just the Thai military guards. I also feared the brutality of my adopted mother, who had become a compulsive gambler. Any tiny mistake would result in her cursing, pinching and twisting my ears, slapping my face, knocking me in the head with her knuckles or with objects, and whipping me with a stick.

Abusive Adoptive Mother

Late one morning, I was playing a rubber-band game on the street with friends along the road near the open-air sewage and my apartment. We drew a square in the dirt and placed five small rubber bands in it. We used larger rubber bands to shoot the smaller rubber bands out of the square.

While I was playing the game, my adopted mother Vannsina came back from gambling. I pretended I didn't see her, and I suddenly couldn't concentrate on the game. My heart was pounding fast, but I continued to act normal. She walked past me and turned to the apartment.

She looked tired, as if she hadn't had enough sleep. Her hair was messy, her face was oily, and her lips were dry.

She didn't go into the apartment. Instead, she sat on the steps and smoked a cigarette. Then she shouted at me, "Marin, go get the soap and sarong for me. I need to take a bath."

"Yes, Mak! Let me finish my game first. I'm about to finish the game right now."

I was feeling rebellious and pissed-off at her, but I didn't let her know. I mumbled to myself, "She has two legs like me. Why can't she get those things by herself?"

Minutes later, she shouted again. "Marin! Come right now before I go there to beat you up!"

"Hey, guys, I'm not playing anymore," I said to my friends. "Let me have my share of the rubber bands." I grabbed the rubber bands, counted them, and stuffed them into my pocket. Then I ran to the apartment.

When I walked up the stairs, Aunty Vannsina got up and knocked me on the top of my head. It was painful and my eyes welled with tears.

"Next time when I call you, you must come right away! Don't ever shout back at me to wait!"

I was enraged. If she were young like me, or was not my adopted mother, I would have punched her in the face.

I got her a sarong, a container with soap, a toothbrush, and toothpaste.

"Look at the sun!" she said hysterically, grabbing the items from my hands. "Do you know what time it is now! And yet you haven't even cooked rice for lunch!"

Cooking rice was my sole responsibility. She had taught me how to cook very well and I was great at it. I went down the stairs, chopped firewood, and made a fire. Then I scooped rice, put it into a cooking pot, washed the rice, poured in the right amount of water, and placed the pot on the clay stove to cook.

Aunty Vannsina returned from taking her bath and went upstairs to rest for half an hour. Then she got up and cooked food to serve with the rice. I was still mad at her for hitting me on the head.

She sat next to me by the clay stove, to prepare the food. She set the *kontael* on the ground, to protect the food from getting dirty, and placed a cutting board on it. Then she cut squash and chicken into small pieces.

"Marin, go get me the cooking ingredients."

"Yes, Mak."

Quickly, I ran upstairs to grab the basket that contained the cooking ingredients. In it were sugar and salt, which were wrapped in a thin and clear plastic bag, a bottle of fish sauces, garlic, and various roots.

I carried the basket in front of me and ran. As I ran toward Vannsina, I fell and everything in the basket scattered. The fish sauce bottle broke, and the sugar bag split and spilled on the ground in front of my adopted mother.

"You mother-son-of-a-useless-fucker. Are you fucking blind?" she scolded me.

While I was on the ground, she removed a stick of red-hot fire-wood from the fire to hit me. I didn't move fast enough. The fire landed on my calf and burned me, and the sensation registered throughout my spine.

I ran for my life in pain, and furious. Minutes after I got away from her, I looked at my burned feet. A large burning blister had already built up on my calf.

In the heat of the moment, I wanted to run away and out of the refugee camp. When I got to the camp's exit, several Thai soldiers were standing along the road and I was afraid they would beat me.

So, I walked to the back of the chicken farm that was built at the mouth of the shallow valley. The valley was a trash-dump site. The chicken farm was built on concrete and fenced in with chained-link wires. As I approached, the chickens panicked and stomped in an attempt to escape from their tiny cages. They were screaming and shouting. They quickly released their eggs and flapped their wings in a panic.

I continued to walk behind the chicken farm toward a big tree about two hundred meters away at the mouth of the valley. I sat in the shade of the tree and tried to soothe my burning calf. The skin had swelled and fluid had developed inside the bumps and was ready to pop at any time. I picked *kontriang-ket*, fresh young leaves, and smashed them together to apply on my wound to cool it off. Then I lay on the ground on my back, with my hands huddled on my chest.

I was alone, sad, and depressed. Countless questions and thoughts scrambled in my head. *Jesus, why can't you hear my prayer? When are you going to help me? How long will you let people abuse me? Jesus, what can I do for you in order for you to help me?*

On the other hand, I questioned myself, maybe Jesus didn't know me? Maybe Jesus didn't know what I looked like or where I lived? Or maybe I didn't say my name when I prayed? Or maybe when I prayed, I didn't sit in the kneeling position correctly?

My mind wandered to the movie scene where Jesus had kneeled down before a rock and prayed. So while lying on my back, I twisted and turned, looking for a sizable rock in the area. I didn't see one. All I saw were dead tree stumps.

I got up, walked to the biggest tree stump, kneeled before it, with both hands on my chest, and said a prayer.

"Dear Jesus. My name is Marin. I wanted to say a prayer before the rock like you did, but there is no rock around here. Therefore, I have kneeled down before this tree stump to let it represent a rock. I believe that my sitting position for praying to you is correct. Please open your eyes to see me praying to you. Please open your ears to hear my prayers. I'm in the Kamput Refugee Camp, sitting by the mouth of the shallow valley near the chicken farm, and facing the trash dump site. Dear Jesus, I ask you to dig Mak and Pa out of the grave and use your power to make them come back to life. I want to live with my Mak and Pa like many other children do. My real Mak and Pak loved me. They wouldn't hurt me like my adopted mother does. Amen."

After I said the prayer, I walked back to the shade tree, lay on the ground, closed my eyes, and waited for God's miracle to work. Once in a while, I opened my eyes, hoping to see my parents standing next to me. But my hopes and wishes never came true.

After long hours of daydreaming about God's miracle, I became exhausted and hungry and my survival instincts began to kick in. I walked to the back of the chicken farm to steal eggs to eat. Stealing chicken eggs from their chained-link cage was very challenging. I tried to insert my hand through the fence, but my hand wouldn't fit. I tried to rip the wires apart, but I didn't have enough strength. I scanned the ground and looked for suitable objects to make a securing device. Finally, I found a short and rusted metal string. I made a scoop with the metal and connected it to a twig the size of my finger. After many attempts of scooping and adjusting the device, I finally got an egg.

I cracked the tip of the egg open, removed the broken shells, stirred with a tiny twig, and poured the liquid down my throat. It tasted a bit salty and very slimy. The egg didn't satisfy my hunger. I was still hungry. So, I roamed around the camp begging for food to eat.

I ran away from this home with Vannsina many times. Each time was several days. I would move from one district to another, begging for food. I would sleep on the ground under different apartments, like an unwanted dog or cat.

I asked different people to adopt me, but no one could accept me. They were afraid of complications in their official documents. The majority of the refugees had submitted applications seeking sponsorship around the world. Most of them had applied to the United States, France, Canada, Germany, Australia, New Zealand, Japan, and many other countries in Europe. Any complication with their documents could delay their chances of getting out of Thailand, which would put their families in jeopardy.

Enrolling Myself in School

After countless days living in the camp, I heard people talking about a school opening for the children. It would be at the Neak-Kariach District, located at the far end of the camp. I was excited and wanted to attend the school.

After I finished selling *jek-ang*, a grilled banana, for my adopted mother one afternoon, I walked to the school to enroll.

The Neak-Kariach School had three buildings. Each building had two floors, and there were five classrooms on each floor.

The school also had a sizable playground, which was crowded with students playing hopscotch, jump rope, shooting rubber bands, tossing coins into a hole, and playing marbles.

"Can you tell me where I can enroll for the class?" I asked one of the boys.

"I don't know. You can ask my teacher. She is sitting in the classroom over there." He pointed.

I walked into the classroom and approached the teacher, excited; at the same time, apprehensive. Should I call her aunt or teacher? I wondered.

The long-haired lady in her mid-twenties was sitting at her desk in front of the classroom, reading a book. She had a light-yellow complexion and was a bit taller than my adopted mother Vannsina.

I put my palms together, below my chin, and bowed in respect. "Hello, aunty, teacher. My name is Marin. I want to attend school."

She put her book down, turned toward me, and said, "Did you come to take the exam last week?"

"No, I didn't."

"Last week, there were examinations that tested students' reading and writing capabilities. The test gave us teachers a better understanding of the grade level to place the students."

While she was talking, I noticed the vowels on the blackboard, which I had learned during the time of Khmer Rouge.

"Have you ever been in school before, Marin?"

"No, Yes. Yes, I was in school during the Khmer Rouge."

"You were in school during the Khmer Rouge?" she questioned.

"Yes, I was. I studied under a shade tree. I learned how to read and write the vowels like the ones on your blackboard. And I learned to count from one to twenty. I attended class one hour a day right after lunch."

"For how long did you attend class?"

"Uhhm...maybe five times, I guess."

While she was talking to me, I heard the whistle blowing, signaling the students to get back to class. They stopped their activities and rushed into the classroom toward their desks. They were as noisy as a flock of birds.

Then the teacher called for attention. "Attention, everyone! I want all of you to practice writing the vowels on the blackboard. For those who don't have a notebook, just write on the small blackboard on your desk. I will be out a few minutes, and I will be right back. Do you understand?"

"Yes, teacher," the students responded.

"Follow me, Marin. I will take you to another class."

I walked behind her to the second floor of another building. She knocked on the open door of the classroom.

"Excuse me, sir," she asked, "does your class have room for another student?"

A handsome male teacher, who was writing on the blackboard, stopped writing and turned to her. He was in his late twenties. He had a light-yellow complexion, thick straight black hair, and a long nose. He walked to her at the door.

"Sorry for interrupting," she said. "I have a student here. I believe he is appropriate to enroll in your class, because he knows how to read and write the vowels."

"Yes, I have a few seats available in the back of the classroom." He pointed to the seats by the window and said to me, "Go to sit over there. I will see you after class for enrollment."

The two teachers had a brief conversation. Then they went back to work.

"All right, everyone," the teacher said to my class. "Yesterday, we learned how to identify the alphabet. Today, I want you to write in your notebook the thirty-three letters that I have on the blackboard."

He sat behind his desk, and the students copied each of the letters on the blackboard. I didn't have a notebook to write them down, but I could identify a few letters I had learned during the Khmer Rouge regime. The teacher officially added my name to his class and, a week later, he provided me a notebook, pencil, and eraser.

I had great respect for my teacher. This was where I learned basic spelling, reading, and writing. Most importantly, I learned how to write my name. I learned that there are twenty-four hours in a day, seven days in week, four weeks in a month, and twelve months in a year. This was when I learned that the year was 1980.

I attended school for less than two months, then I stopped—because my adopted mother Vannsina wanted me to spend more time helping her to sell food.

I sold all kinds of food: *poud-ang,* grilled marinated corn; *jek-jian,* deep-fried marinated banana; *jek-ang,* a grill marinated banana; *nom-sorm-ang,* a grilled ripe banana rolled with marinated sticky rice; *nom-kompong,* a deep-fried marinated flour and green beans; *nom-akour,* a sweetened cup cake with sesame and coconuts; *nom-kroach,* deep-fried round stuffing of mashed green beans; *nom-bagn-jok,* a Cambodian noodle.

While I was selling food, I tried to find ways to get away from my adopted mother. I wanted to find an orphanage center, but I couldn't find one. Committing suicide was always at the top of my mind. Every time she beat me, I ran away and tried to find strings or rope to hang myself. The strings I found were either too short or not strong enough to do the job.

Committing suicide by hanging was the only way I could think of to end my life quickly, without experiencing long hours of pain and suffering. So, I went back home. But only when I was starving and couldn't beg for enough food to eat.

Getting out of the refugee camp was not an option, either. The Thai guard would torture or kill me if I were caught. In addition, I didn't speak the Thai language.

So, I didn't have any other choice except to go back home to receive more beatings.

Every time, I saw my adopted mother come home from gambling, I felt like I was seeing a ferocious tiger who wanted to eat me alive. I felt like I was trapped in a cage.

I was always nervous and I would shake, because I didn't know what to expect from her.

Sometimes, I slept in the corner of the cubicle, pretending to be sick, hoping she wouldn't beat me. But I was wrong. She punished me even more. She whipped my heels so that I wouldn't be able to run.

People on the block came to help me, but she cursed at them not to interfere with her family matters.

The Soggy Biscuits

Seven months had passed and the rainy season was almost over. My adopted mother no longer made food for me to sell. She negotiated with the bakers who lived in the next apartment, for me to sell their breads instead.

I was excited about the new business. A huge amount of stress and depression was lifted out of my chest. It would mean I did less physical work, and I wouldn't need to grind soaked rice on the *tbal-ken* anymore.

"Mak, how much profit do we get per bread?" I asked my adopted mother.

She pulled out a cigarette from her blouse pocket, put it in her mouth and said, "Every twelve breads you sell, you will profit with 2 Thai Baht. If you can sell one hundred or more breads per day, you will get a profit of about 20 Thai Baht. Do you think you can sell more than one hundred breads a day?" She looked at me, then lit up her cigarette.

"I don't know, Mak. I think I can sell fifty breads a day."

A few days later, I went to meet the bakers under their apartment to get the freshly baked breads to sell. Every day, I walked from one apartment to another, from block to block, and from one district to another, shouting the food's name to alert people that I was present in the area. People who were interested in my food called me to their apartment, bargained the price, and bought from me.

Early one morning, when the sun was still asleep in the horizon, I woke up, washed my face to refresh myself, and walked to the baker's apartment to get *nom-pank*, a French biscuit. That morning, it was windy and cold. I walked under the low stilt apartment with my knees bent to prevent my head from hitting the wooden beams overhead.

The two bakers had made a big dome stove from clay under their stilt apartment. They sat on the ground, with their heads almost touching the wooden beam, while they made bread on their metal trays by squeezing, rolling, and cutting the wetted powder. While they were baking their breads, they were always on the lookout for Thai solders, afraid that the soldiers would punish them for building a stove and baking bread.

"How much bread do you need today, Marin?" asked one of the bakers.

"I believe I cannot sell as many as yesterday. Fifty breads will be enough," I said.

The baker removed the tray full of freshly baked bread from the fire and waited a few minutes until it was cool enough to touch.

Each bread was about six inches long and the size of my forearm. The baker counted out fifty breads and set them in the medium-sized *kagn-ger*, a deep weaving basket. Then he placed a thick white cloth over them to keep them looking fresh and warm. On average, I sold fifty breads per day, and made 10-15 Thai Baht.

I walked from one district to another to sell them. "*Nom-pank, nom-pank. nom-pank kdav-sroy* (bread, bread, fresh and crispy bread)," I shouted to advertise the fresh bread.

As I walked along the road, I got caught in a heavy rain and ran to seek shelter. But I couldn't run fast enough and I got soaked. The breads were also soaked.

The rain was long and strong. By late afternoon, when it finally stopped, I went home in my wet clothes, afraid of getting whipped by my adopted mother because I had sold less than fifteen *nom-pank*.

She was sitting by the staircase with her back to the wall, smoking a cigarette. As I approached, she asked, "How many *nom-pank* did you sell today, son?"

"Mak, I couldn't sell much because I was caught in the rain."

I continued to walk upstairs, believing she understood. I put the basket near the wall, two meters away from her. She moved over to inspect the breads. "Why are the *nom-pank* wet and rotten?"

"Mak, I told you, I was caught in—"

Before I could even finish my sentence, she grabbed the back of my hair and pulled me to look at the bread. "How the fuck am I going to return this bread to the baker? *Ar-kaun-mi-somphirng!* (You motherfucker son-of-a-whore.) You are fucking useless. You can't even shield the bread from the rain."

My heart pounded fast and my head boiled. Sweat came out of every pore on my face. Furiously, I removed her hand from the back of my head and shouted at her, with shivering lips, "I told you! I was caught in the heavy rain!" At that moment, I would have stabbed her if I'd had a knife.

She clenched her teeth and shouted, "How dare you scream at me! You mother fucking son of a whore! You will not get away with this. I will beat the fuck out of you."

She slapped me in the face, grabbed my hair again and pulled me down along the staircase to find a stick to beat me. I grabbed her hand, tried to remove her fingers, and snatched her hand off to free myself. I jumped off the stairs and ran for my life.

I was in pain and depressed. The boiling madness in me wanted to commit suicide. I looked for rope to hang myself. I scanned for a rope on the ground, on the street, in the bushes. But all I could find was a short pink string and a small dead vine. Neither was long enough or strong enough to do the job.

I continued to hate myself, as much as I hated God for not helping me to find a strong rope to commit suicide.

I promised myself I would not go back home. I sat by a huge green water reservoir that provided water to all the refugees in the camp. The reservoir stood on the hill near the barbed wire fence of the camp. As I sat thinking of a safe way out, I heard the sounds of a girl screaming in the bushes outside of the camp.

"Ahah, ahahah, ahahahah."

With curiosity, I scanned through the tall grasses and bushes, and I saw several Thai soldiers' profiles from the shoulder up. They were shouting in their language. There were sounds of a girl screaming and shouting for help. Then the shouting went silent. I walked away.

The next day, I heard rumors about a sixteen-year-old girl getting raped by a group of Thai soldiers. She was hospitalized down the hill inside the camp.

That night, I snuck into the hospital and saw her sleeping on the bed, surrounded by her loved ones. I was curious. I had heard about the situation, and I matched the location with the description and time.

She was sleeping on the hospital bed, with her eyes closed. Her face was swollen, with lots of bruises. I felt shock and sympathy for her. At the same time, I felt anger. I wanted to grow up as big as these Thai military men so I could fight them. I walked out of the hospital ward, shivering and talking to myself.

My frustration made me communicate with the gods more and more. "Buddha and Jesus, if you are not interested in helping me and the rest of the suffering children, I beg both of you to give me the power so that I can help myself and millions of other innocent children who are in desperate need like me."

As I walked out of the hospital ward, I saw a huge poster on the wall that had mountains with green pine trees, a river with a boat by a shore, a home with cars, and a boy playing in front of his house. Next to the exit was another poster with boys and girls playing in front of the house.

"Wow, that is how people in America live?" I was amazed at the beauty, the richness, and the freedom of America.

I prayed to Jesus and Buddha to write my name on an application and submit it to America. I prayed to Jesus, Buddha, Tevada, angels, and the souls of my parents to help me get out of the refugee camp in Thailand.

As I wandered outside of the hospital, next to the Care Center, I saw a white lady leaving the hospital. "*Mieng, yor-knom-tov-nov-jai-mouy-porng?*" I asked her from a distance, in Khmer. This translates to "Aunty, please take me to live with you?"

She looked at me and smiled, waved at me and said, "bye-bye," and continued walking. I had hoped she could understand what I said.

I had seen white people several times. One time, I saw them come to the camp with their families. I saw a boy and a girl about my age, walking with their parents. They looked nice, clean, and very happy. I wished I could be happy like them. When I saw white people working in the refugee camp, I thought they were angels. They looked beautiful, gentle, and generous.

Buddha and Jesus Must Be Blind

I promised myself not to go back home. I would rather be homeless. After living with my adopted mother Vannsina for two years, I'd had enough. Living her was like living in hell.

One night, I found a new place to sleep, the outside hallways of the school building. During the day, I begged for food. Sometimes, I ate at Vannsina's sister's house, Aunty Sokheoun. She and her family knew about my situation, but they couldn't help me. They could only provide me food. They offered me to stay at their place, but I refused because I was afraid my adopted mother would catch me and take me back to live with her. Moreover, I didn't want any tension between them. I would eat, then leave right away.

Early one morning around six o'clock, I had my ID card on and I was walking down the hill along the main dirt road, minding my own business. I walked past the military guard whose nickname was Ar-Ngok, the infamous abuser. The majority of the people were aware of his brutality. Ar-Ngok was thirty-five years old, wore a military uniform, and had a handgun strapped to his waist. He usually held a rattan stick. He was the most brutal of the Thai military guards in the refugee camp.

For my own safety, I distanced myself as I walked past him. At that moment, he snuck up from behind me and whipped me hard with the rattan stick. I felt like my lower-back bones crack. I jumped, held onto my wound, and ran for my life. I cried and cursed at him in Khmer, "Ar-juy-maray! Konduy mae vea! (You're a motherfucker. Your mother's pussy!)" I wanted to kill him. If I'd had a gun, I would have shot him in the head.

My madness raged all the way to the heavens. I grit my teeth and thought to myself, *Buddha and Jesus, why don't you snatch the stick from this motherfucker's hand! Why didn't you block the stick! Why don't you kill this fucking soldier! Buddha and Jesus, you two must be blind. That is the reason you never send angels to help me! Why you didn't see the Thai soldier whipping me. Why you didn't see me being whipped by my adopted mother. You two must blind. That is why you didn't see the Khmer Rouge starving me and torturing me. Buddha and Jesus, you two are fucking stupid! You didn't open your eyes to see me suffering. I hate you! I will never respect you or pray for you again.*

I cried in frustration. I looked at the thin gray clouds spreading across the horizon and the blue sky above, and stared at the gray moon in daylight. I spread my arms out and said, "Buddha and Jesus, if you don't help me, why don't you kill me now! I don't want to live. I beg you to kill me now! And let me be reborn in another race!"

My demands weren't answered by the gods.

I began to calm down, but I continued to hate myself for being Cambodian. As a Cambodian, all I had seen and experienced was suffering, torture, and killings.

I demanded that God kill me so I could be reborn into the white race, like the French or the Americans.

Seeing My Own Picture

It was noon, and I was roaming the camp in sadness. I walked into a well-built small shack to cool off. This shack served as a post office. Half of it was surrounded with shredded bamboo walls and only a roof to protect bulletin boards from the rain and hot sun.

That day, no one was working. Maybe it was Sunday. Maybe it was a holiday. The door was closed and the windows were shut. I scanned the place and saw more than fifteen black-and-white pictures posted on the bulletin board.

As I looked at those pictures, I saw my own photo glued onto a white piece of paper that contained information about me. I was thrilled. In the picture, my hair was bushy, thick, and messy. The picture had been taken by the orphanage staff in the Kao-I-Dang Refugee Camp. I wanted to take the picture, but I couldn't because it was locked behind glass.

With curiosity, I read the information about me and tried to find out what it said. I read slowly, attempting to make sense of what was written.

On the letterhead, written in bold, was "Search for family members." This was followed by a paragraph that said, "My name is Marin Yann. My father's name is Yann. My mother's name is Yim. I have two siblings: Roth Yann, my younger brother, and Vanny Yann, my older sister. If anyone sees this information and is believed to be the relative of Marin Yann, please contact.........us."

At first I was excited to see my picture but, after reading the message, I felt sad and hopeless again. My eyes welled with tears, and my jaw felt tense.

I walked out of the shack to find a sizable stone to break the glass of the bulletin board to get my picture. I found a stone the size of my fist and ran back inside to break the glass. But when I got there, two men had entered and were reading what was posted on the bulletin board. Then before they left, another person came. Then another person came. People came just to read information on the bulletin board to find their loved ones. Or they just wanted to find out if they had any mail from their relatives.

I sat and leaned back against the wooden post of the bulletin board and called to the souls of my parents. *Dear Pa and Mak, can you tell Vanny, or aunties, or pu's who know me, to see my picture? Please tell them to come to this post office and read the information on the bulletin board. Tell them to come and save me from my adopted mother's abuse.*

After a long wait, I cooled off and was no longer interested in breaking the glass to get my picture. My rationality began to kick in and I said to myself, *If I were to take this picture out, how would my sister, Vanny, and my other relatives find me?*

I left and dropped the stone as I walked along the dirt road to the hospital hall. The hall had no wall; only a roof, wooden posts, and a concrete floor. It was like a larger gazebo. On the floor were benches. I lay down on one of the benches and looked at the bright sun. *Gods, please open your eyes and look at me. I don't want to die. I want to live. And I will continue to live.*

After talking to the gods, I fell asleep. When I woke up, I snuck into the hospital restroom to take a bath to refresh myself. Then I walked across the street to the Care Center and begged for food. That night, I found a place to sleep in the Angkor Wat District, which was located in the center of the camp. The district had a school, library, theater, and soccer field. I walked up to the second floor of one of the school buildings and tried to open the doors and windows to sleep inside a classroom, but all the doors and windows were locked. Then I looked for a suitable walkway, where I lay down.

The night was a bit cold, so I lay sideways like a puppy, curling my arms and legs to keep myself warm. I positioned my back against the wall and my face toward the guardrails and the three-quarter moon. I watched as the murky white moon moved slowly from the east. Once in a while, the thin clouds blocked the moonlight.

Suddenly, the Thai authorities turned off the lights at their head-quarters and left all the apartments in the camp illuminated by the moonlight. I realized it was ten o'clock.

I had a difficult time falling asleep because the geckos' calls to each other echoed throughout the school facility. There were also many depressing thoughts lingering in my head.

I looked at brightest star and prayed, "Buddha, Jesus, Tevada, Mak and Pa, please don't let the Thai soldiers come to this building. As you know, the Thai soldiers are very cruel. If they see me sleeping here, they will torture me. Please help me. Please block them from coming to this school."

My anger toward the gods subsided. I turned my head to look at the moon and said softly to the gods, "Gods, no matter what happens to me, I will not commit suicide. I will survive until I become a man. Whoever has attempted to hurt me, I will fight back to defend my life."

As the moon moved higher over the camp, I began to have a few other thoughts. *Gods, do you know what?! I survived the leeches and snake bites. I survived the fruit poisoning. I survived starvation and the Khmer Rouge beatings. I survived the most dangerous journey through the jungle from Cambodia to the Thailand border, without stepping on a landmine. I survived the hail of bullets when the war broke out in the Jumrum-Tmey-Refugee Camp.*

After telling the gods the long list of my survivals, I thought, maybe the gods had helped to shield me from the bullets and bomb explosions when the war broke out along the Thai and Cambodia border?

Gods, did you really protect me from all of that? If you did protect me, please continue to guard my life until I become an adult. I promise you that I will become a strong man and I will do good deeds to help other people who are stuck in similar crises like me. Gods, please send someone to help me. I promise you that I will never curse at you again. Please! Please help me!

The moon continued to rise slowly over the refugee camp. The thin clouds were no longer blocking the moonlight. The bright moon and the sparkling stars provided me just enough light to see my surroundings. I could see the guardrails of the walkway. I could see the staircase of another school structure. Behind that school was the Angkor Wat Theater. I could see its distinct roof with its huge pointy crown that represented Cambodian architecture. I could also see the soccer field and the post office with the bulletin board that contained my picture.

The geckos fell silent, and I fell asleep like a dead log.

16

Finally, the Gods Help Me

My Fifth Adopted Family

After several weeks of begging and roaming around the camp, in early 1981, Jesus, Buddha, Tevada, and the angels finally began to see my suffering and sent someone to help me. Her name was Chhon, with an odd last name "Um." Aunty Chhon was about twenty-five years old, with a light-yellow complexion, an oval face, and straight long black hair.

"What is your name?" she asked me in a sympathetic tone.

"My name is Marin."

"Do you know your father and mother's names?"

I didn't answer her right away. I looked down at the ground and watched my big toe flicking the soil. Finally, I said, "Yes, I remember their names. My mother's name is Yim, and my father's name is Yann."

"Do you remember what your parents looked like?" she asked.

"Hhhhmmm... My father had a dark complexion, like me. My mother had a light-yellow complexion like you."

Then Aunty Chhon drew her own conclusion: that she was my distant aunty, and she wanted me to live with her. Whatever her claim, I didn't really care as long as she provided me food, loved me, and didn't abuse me. It took me several weeks to trust her.

Aunty Chhon was the only person to survive in her family. She was a few months pregnant and divorced. She had her own situation with her husband, but she treated me well and loved me. She cooked and washed my clothes. She registered me in the official documents as her nephew.

Less than two months later, the Kamput Refugee Camp was closed. The camp authorities loaded me back onto the bus and transported me back to the Khao-I-Dang Refugee Camp, to District No.5.

Aunty Chhon and I settled in the camp and she sent me to school. After just a few months of studying, I improved my reading and writing skills. And I learned mathematics; how to add, subtract, multiply, and divide numbers.

First Emigration Interview: Creating My Own Beginning

After living in the camp for about six months, in 1982 Aunty Chhon delivered a baby boy named Chanvirak. A few months after he was born, her husband Mr. Chhim Sarin came back to Aunty. Then he submitted many applications—for all four of us—to Japan, Australia, and America, requesting sponsorship.

Several months after the applications were submitted, our family was selected for our first interview at Khao-I-Dang. I was energized and anxious to get out of the refugee camp. At school, I told all my friends and classmates that I would go to America.

But at home, Aunty Chhon and her husband were worried about the complications of our family situation. They said we had to adjust our documents to make them believable. Otherwise, we would fail the interview and have to stay in the refugee camp for the rest of our lives, all of us.

We had to change our family name, they said. My last name was changed from Yann to Um. I became Marin Um. Chanvirak's last name was changed from Um to Chhim, the last name of his father. The husband's name Sarin Chhim was not changed.

The day of the interview, we walked five kilometers in the hot scorching sun to the District No.2 headquarters. The entire office structure was built from bamboo. The external walls and internal walls were uneven, with small gaps, and were made of shredded bamboo. The benches were also made from shredded bamboo. There was no wooden floor or concrete floor inside, only red gravel dirt. The roofs were made from weaved reeds.

There were at least fifty families sitting on some shredded-bamboo benches, which were laid out in rows, waiting to be called for their interviews. We were the last family to be called. After a long wait, a Cambodian man with thick, black straight hair came out of the office. He held a folder and asked, "Are you the Sarin Chhim family?"

"Yes, I am," said Pu Sarin. "Yes, we are the last family here."

"I'm Vuthy. I'm the interpreter."

The three of us got up and greeted him by saying *"Jom-riapsur."*

Mr. Vuthy walked us to a small office to see the interviewer.

Aunty Chhon carried her son on her waist and walked behind her husband. She said to the interpreter, "I'm very nervous. I don't know what kinds of questions the interviewer is going to ask."

Mr. Vuthy turned and said, "Don't worry too much. During the first interview, they are not going to ask many questions. They just want to help you prepare a solid document for the next interview."

As I entered the office, I saw a big white man with short golden facial hair, sitting behind an old wooden desk. He got up, put his palms together, and said with a thick English accent, *"Jom-riapsur. Soum-unkuy. Ka-ngom-chamous-David."*[12] He opened a brown folder on the desk in front of him and began to ask questions in English. Mr. Vuthy, sitting at the other end of the desk, translated.

"How many people in your family?"

---

12   He said, "Hello. Sit down. My name is David."

"We have four people," said Pu Sarin.

"Is this man your husband?" asked David to Aunty Chhon.

"Yes, he is my husband," she said.

"How many children do you have?" asked David.

"We have one child," said Pu Sarin.

"How is Marin related to your family?" asked David.

"He is my younger brother," Aunty Chhon lied. David looked at her and at me, then asked another question.

"How old is your younger brother Marin?"

Instead of answering David directly, Aunty Chhon asked me, "How old are you, Marin? Do you remember your age?"

I paused. "Uhmm... I don't know. I don't remember when I was born."

David didn't pursue the question. Instead, he looked at Pu Sarin and Chhon asked them many more questions. He wrote their responses on his paper.

After about fifteen minutes of interviewing, David looked at his wristwatch and said, "I want your family to go outside and discuss among yourselves Marin's date of birth and place of birth. Once we come back from the break, I will interview you again."

We stepped out of the office. David and the interpreter also walked out.

Pu Sarin and Aunty Chhon began asking me, "How old are you, Marin? Did your mak or your dad ever tell you your date of birth or and where you were born?"

"I believe they did. I just can't remember."

"Are you eleven, twelve, or thirteen years old?" Pu Sarin asked me.

He ran his fingers through my messy thick black hair, and Aunty Chhon inspected my head and the back of my ears. They came to a conclusion.

"Marin," said Pu Sarin, "if someone asks your birthdate, just say you were born on the fifth, the month of June, and 1970. All you need to remember is 05-06-70. This date makes it easier for all of us to remember. Now, you are officially twelve years old."

Then David came to interview. "Do you know his birthday?" he asked.

"Yes," Aunty said, "he was born on the day of the fifth, the month of June 1970. He was born in Battombong Province," she added.

David then asked us to fill out a few documents and sign them.

Second Emigration Interview: Pretending I Don't Have a Past

Four months after the first interview, our name was posted for the second interview. This interview was held outside the refugee camp, and the interview center was an hour ride away. The camp authorities transported us on a bus, along the dirt and paved roads farther inside Thailand.

Pu Sarin and Aunty Chhon tried to remember everything they had answered during the first interview so our answers were consistent. There were hundreds of families waiting to be called for an interview. Some people were sitting on the ground. Others were sitting on benches under a shade tree. We stood.

After long hours of waiting, our name was finally called. I followed Aunty and Pu to the designated room. When I entered the room, I saw a fat white man in his fifties, sitting behind his desk. A Cambodian interpreter sat at one end of the desk.

The interviewer asked me many questions about my relationships with my fake sister, Chhon. I was a great liar.

"Is Chhon your sister?" he asked

"Yes, she is my sister. We were the only two people who survived in the Khmer Rouge regime," I said with confidence.

"How many steps do you have?" the interviewer asked.

"I don't know. I never count," I responded.

"Does your house have stairs?" the man asked. "Do you have any pets in your home?"

"I don't know. I was too young to remember," I said.

Whatever he asked, I said, "I don't know. I don't remember."

Third Emigration Interview: We Pass

Several months after the second interview, my family got selected to go to the United States of America. Our family name was posted on the bulletin board. I was excited! I thought, *My dream of going to America is coming true!*

But my journey still had a long way to go. In order to go to the United States, we had to go through a rigorous medical examination and a background check. In addition, the camp authorities moved us to various different refugee camps closer to Thai Capital City, Bangkok.

For each camp that we would stay in, we needed to pass thorough background checks and medical examinations. If we couldn't pass these, we would be delayed or denied. Anyone in the family who'd had a disease, such as tuberculosis (TB), would have to stay in the refugee camp until they were treated and completely healed.

It was October 1983. The Camp authority transported my family from the Khao-I-Dang Refugee Camp to the Chhun Borie Camp. We were required to stay there three to four weeks for medical checkups and the documentation process.

During our third week in this camp, our family names were posted on the bulletin board for a medical examination. The night before the checkup, I prayed to Buddha and Jesus for help. *Gods, please don't let any diseases come into our bodies. Please let us be healthy and strong, so that we pass the medical exams and go to America.*

Midmorning, my family walked to the medical center. The doctor examined my eyes, ears, nose, mouth, and knee reflex. Then they gave me a medical shot in the right forearm to test for tuberculosis.

My family all passed the background checks and medical

examinations. I felt relieved. I felt light, like I was walking on air. I thought, *America must be the cleanest and most beautiful country in the world. No wonder people with illnesses cannot go to America. That is why white people who work in the camp look happy and healthy.*

Three days later, we were ordered to walk from the Chhun Borie Camp to the Transit Refugee Camp, which was across the freeway less than half a kilometer distance. Thai police officers controlled both sides of the oncoming car traffic and ordered refugees to walk orderly in two long rows. Approximately eighty families were walking to the other side.

After we had stayed in the Transit Refugee Camp for three days, the bus came and loaded us to go to the Bangkok International Airport. It was November 1983. When I got off the bus and walked inside the airport, I was overwhelmed by the facility and its technology. The glass doors automatically opened and closed. Out of curiosity, I wondered why the door opened and closed by itself. I walked in and out several times, and looked around to see if there was a worker pressing a button to open and close it. But I didn't see anyone.

After I walked past the door, I saw a set of long black automatic stairs moving people up and down. I was anxious to get on it, but I restrained myself from running because I was afraid that Aunt Chhon and Pu Sarin would scold me. I was overwhelmed by the large and beautiful airport building. The huge halls and large glass windows impressed me. It was my first time entering a building full of technology.

After a long wait in the big hall of the airport, two Thai workers came and walked us to the automatic staircase I had seen. I was excited, but I had a little challenge with coordination when I set foot on the moving stairs. I did notice that I wasn't the only person who had a problem getting on. Most of the refugees did, including Aunty Chhon.

The workers took us to the designated gate and told us to wait until our family name was called. Half an hour later, we lined up and walked onto a huge airplane. A lady flight attendant took me to my designated seat, located in the middle row.

This was the first time I had been on an airplane. I couldn't stay still. I was curious about how this giant machine could fly. I constantly moved my head left to right, trying to understand the complexity of objects in the airplane. Buttons on the seat. A headset. I held the headset and tried to figure out what to do with it.

When the airplane accelerated and took off, I was nervous and hoped the airplane wouldn't fall out of the sky and crash into the ocean. About fifteen minutes after the airplane took off, the vibration and noise decreased drastically.

My excitement continued to build. I smiled and laughed inside. I said to myself, *From now on, I'm safe from the Thai soldiers' brutality. I'm safe from my abusive adopted mother. I'm safe from the murderous Khmer Rouge.*

I thought back on my past journey. I cracked a smile. I couldn't believe I had come this far. I had walked barefoot from Cambodia. I had ridden on a buffalo's back. I had run to escape a hail of bullets, to ride on a big truck to the Kao-I-Dang Refugee Camp. Now, I was on an airplane, flying across the ocean.

"I'm very proud of myself," I said out loud.

17

I Dream of America

Halfway to America: Refugee Camp in the Philippines

After three hours of smooth riding in the airplane, we arrived in Manila, the capital city of the Philippines. With all the other refugees, we left the airport and got onto the designated bus. Along the small road, which snaked through valleys and mountains to the refugee camp in Morong, Battaan, I didn't see many cars. Once in a while, I would see a colorful Jeepney, a Filipino jeep-like vehicle, driving in the opposite direction. As we drove further, countless green rice fields stretched from the road to the foot of the mountain; on the other side of road were pockets of sugarcane farms.

The camp was located on a huge foothill in the east of the valley. Our apartment, in District 4, looked similar to the apartment I had lived in with Pu Ti and Aunty Phim in Cambodia. The apartment was small, with two floors. The ground floor was made of concrete; the second floor of wood slabs. The walls were thin plywood.

This was the best refugee camp I had stayed in. There was no barbed-wire fence surrounding the camp, and no military guards patrolled. The Filipino people were very nice and friendly. They always greeted us, in English, with their thick accents.

"My priend, how ar-re you doing?" They didn't look down on Cambodian people as the Thais did.

This camp was structured and organized. Our first week in the camp, which I learned was called the PRPC, for Philippine Refugee Processing Center, the district leader called all the adults to a meeting. All adult refugees were required to work part-time and to attend school part-time. They didn't get paid for work, but school was free.

People with the ability to speak English could hold a work position as a teacher's aide or as an interpreter. Pu Sarin spoke some English, so he worked as a teacher's aide. Aunty Chhon wasn't required to work, because she took care of her son, Virak. She also was again a few months pregnant.

People who had limited English skills worked doing manual labor to ensure the cleanliness of the camp. They cut grass, trimmed plants, watered the gardens, picked up trash, and prevented the open-air sewage system from clogging.

Two months after we were in the camp, Pu Sarin enrolled me in school to study English. I was thrilled. I had always wanted to learn English to communicate with white people.

The first day of class I was timid, because I didn't know what to expect. When I walked into the class, my teacher Ms. Concepcion was facing the blackboard and erasing what was on it. Several students were sitting scattered throughout the classroom.

I walked fast and sat in the middle row near the window. As I sat, more students came in. The classroom was full, with approximately twenty-five students. More than half of them were bigger and taller than me.

Ms. Concepcion was the most beautiful Filipino teacher I had ever seen. She was in her late twenties and had a light-tan complexion. She had an oval face, big oval-shaped eyes, thin curved black eyelashes, and full red lips. She was slimmer and taller than most of the Cambodian women in the camp. Her legs and arms were well-proportioned. When she walked, her straight long black hair stretched down, touching her curved buttocks.

After the students got situated in the classroom, Ms. Concepcion began to talk. She said many things, but I couldn't understand her. Then she began to ask each student in the front row, "What is your name?"

I understood the question clearly, because I had learned some English from Pu Sarin. For example, I had learned from him: How are you? What is your name? Where are you going? Where are you from?

The first week of class, the teacher taught us how to read and identify A, B, C, D. Once we thoroughly understood the alphabet, she taught us basic words to identify body parts, such as head, hair, nose, mouth, arms, legs. Then we learned different words, such as book, pencil, home, school, beach, mountain, and river, to develop a sentence. I loved learning English. It would be great to communicate with the white man in that language.

After three months of learning English, I realized it was a very difficult language. The English grammar had many rules and changes in tense that I could not comprehend, which drove me crazy.

Why couldn't English grammar be easy like the Khmer language? I thought. For example, when I said, "I go to the beach," it was correct. However, when I said, "I go to the school," it was not correct. It was right to say, "I go to school," but it was incorrect to say "I go to home." The rules of the English language frustrated me. I hated it as much as I loved to learn it.

Each month, the camp authority provided kerosene for cooking fuel. They also provided many other things, including toothpaste, toothbrushes, soap, cooking oil, fish, eggs, frozen chickens, pork, and vegetables. Sometimes, they provided canned foods.

Every day, a few Filipino men and women walked from one block to another to trade with the refugees. They called out their trade with thick accents in English and Khmer. When they spoke, they mixed the languages together. It sounded funny, and I couldn't hold myself from laughing or repeating after them.

Most of the time I heard, "My priend. My priend, Knom-Tign, Colgate, Sugares, Caress Soap, Tirk-Trey, Ma-hob ka-pong." Translated to English, they were saying, "My friend. My friend, I buy Colgate, sugar, Caress soap, fish sauces, and canned food."

People who had extra soap, toothpaste, or canned food would sell to the traders for Filipino pesos. It was a great trade off. Cambodians needed the money to buy snacks, ice cream, clothes, and shoes. The Filipinos bought from Cambodians at low prices and sold outside of the camp to make a profit and support their families.

My family was poor. About once a month, I went to the mountain to collect firewood to use for cooking. Aunty Chhon also reserved kerosene for sale. Very few families used firewood for cooking.

People who lived in this refugee camp could travel to any place inside the country as long as they had the money and the will. The Vietnamese refugees, however, were limited in traveling because they had a bad history of stealing villagers' cows. The villagers hated the Vietnamese refugees. For Cambodians, it was the opposite. We could go to any place as long as we had money to travel.

One afternoon, I went to collect firewood on the mountain. Three villagers with machetes approached and asked us in English, with thick Pilipino accents, "Hay, ar-re you Vietnamese? Where ar-re you going?"

A man who was with me said to them, "We are Cambodian. We are going to collect firewood."

They allowed us to go on our way. Whenever I again went to collect firewood on the mountain, the villager men with machetes often asked me if I was Vietnamese.

The majority of Cambodian refugees were broke. We survived on the food distributed inside the camp. Some people received money from their friends and loved ones in America, Canada, France, Japan, or Australia. Others received $10 or $20 from refugee friends who had already arrived in the USA. Some people received as much as $100 per month. Cambodian refugees were very generous. When they left the camp to America, France, or Canada, they promised friends and loved ones they would send some money.

In the summer, the majority of refugees went to the beautiful sandy beach about ten kilometers away. Those who had money rode on a *tuk-tuk*, a three-wheeled motor taxi. I didn't have any money, so I simply walked, under the scorching sun.

People who couldn't afford the trip to the beach could walk down the hill to a stream, which was about three kilometers from the camp. Sometimes, I went to the stream with friends to play in the cool, crystal-clear water. I had lots of fun swimming against the currents and floating along with it.

After we had lived six months in this camp, Aunt Chhon and Pu Sarin were afraid that we wouldn't be selected to the United States. Most people stayed in the camp less than six months.

"Can you go to the main office and ask them about our case?" Aunty Chhon asked Pu Sarin during lunch one day.

"Who should I ask?" he responded.

"Just ask whoever works in the office." She raised her voice. At that moment, a simple conversation became an altercation.

He gazed at her and said, "The problem is that I don't know where the office is."

"You could ask your Filipino friends. You have some Filipino friends who work in the camp. They would be able help you," said Aunty Chhon.

"The headquarters office is in Manila, and I don't know how I'm going to get there," Pu Sarin responded in frustration and walked out of the apartment.

Eventually, three days after the altercation, Pu Sarin spoke to his Filipino friends about our situation. They agreed to take him to the capital city, Manila, and to help my Pu find the refugee headquarters office. They even helped to pay for his trip, his food, and a place to stay for three days.

"When are you going?" asked Aunty Chhon.

"My friends will be leaving tomorrow morning, around nine o'clock," he said.

That morning, Aunty Chhon collected all her savings and gave it to him. "Here is a bag of clothes and the money. I hope you have a chance to speak people who handle our cases."

Pu Sarin looked at his wife in a compassionate way. Then he grabbed the bag and the money from her and said, "It is time for me to go. I will be back in a few days."

Pu Sarin returned four days later. He had bought himself a new set of clothes, a blouse for his wife, and a used YASHICA camera.

While he played with the camera, Aunty Chhon stood next to him and asked, "What did the worker say about our case?"

"A lady who worked there didn't tell me much. She said there must be some complication in the file, that maybe our sponsor didn't provide enough documents. Or maybe because my wife is pregnant," he said.

Aunty Chhon sighed and walked to the kitchen. Seconds later she asked, "Where did you get that camera?"

"I bought it in the city."

"What for? That is a waste!" she said bluntly from the kitchen.

"No. I will not waste money. I know what I am doing. I will have a photograph business and take people's pictures for money." He walked out of the apartment with the camera in his hand.

Every weekend, Pu Sarin went to the beach or to the stream to take pictures of people. He talked to people to see if they were interested in having pictures for souvenirs. Each picture cost between twelve to fifteen pesos, depending on quality. Each month, he took over a hundred pictures. He made good money.

Two months after Pu Sarin opened his photography business, Aunty Chhon bore another child, a daughter. They named her Chhim Rottana. We called her Rottana for short.

My Journey to America

In November 1984, my family was finally selected to go to the United States. My excitement had built up. My exhilaration made me feel weightless. I felt light. The souls of my parents came to cheer me on and lift me up from the ground. I felt like I could walk on water and float in the air.

The week before we left the refugee camp, Pu Sarin sold the YASHICA camera. He bought himself a wristwatch and a new set of clothes for his wife to wear to America. He bought me a pair of new tennis shoes and new set of clothes.

It was my first time owning a pair of tennis shoes. I was thrilled. I took the shoes out of the box and examined them. The light-brown nylon tennis shoes matched the color of my collared button-shirt. The shoes had thick composite rubber soles and beautiful laces that criss-crossed from one eyelet to another. I loved the shoes. I ran my fingers over them a few minutes before I tried them on. Then I put them on and walked a few steps.

"How does it feel, Marin?" Pu Sarin asked.

"I feel great! I love them. They are a bit tight, a bit small for me. I can feel my toes pushing back."

"I bought them in Manila. I cannot go back and change them. It is too far. Just wear them. I hope the fabric of the shoes will expand if you wear them long enough."

"Thank you for the shoes, Pu. I will wear them," I said and put the shoes back in the box.

A day before we left, we threw a small farewell party. Aunty Chhon and her friends cooked *nom-bagn-jok* to serve with red curry and French bread. Pu Sarin invited his friends and neighbors for the party. The neighbor brought a cassette player to play music. We played Cambodian music almost every song. We played slow songs and soft rock songs. Sometimes, we switched to play a few foreign songs, including Santana. Although I didn't understand the lyrics, the beautiful and rich sounds of the guitar enticed me to move my head and arms as if playing an air guitar. Another song we played was "If You Go to San Francisco." Although I didn't understand what it meant, I sang along just for fun.

Everyone appeared to be happy. We sang songs and chatted like never before. I couldn't restrain myself from smiling and laughing. Then I gave my friends my rubber bands and marbles I'd used in the games with them.

Once the party was over, Pu Sarin and Aunty Chhon packed two small boxes of our family possessions: pots and pans, knives, spoons, cutting boards, a small amount of raw rice, lemon grass, mints, and children's clothes. Pu Sarin secured the boxes by tying them with a series of ropes, like a fishing net. We didn't have a suitcase. Cardboard boxes were the only means of packing our possessions.

At seven o'clock the next morning, the sun was bright, the sky was clear blue. We woke up, washed ourselves, and put on our new clothes. I took the shoes out of the box and put them on. With new clothes and new shoes on, I felt bright and proud of myself. I felt taller, stronger, and smarter. Even the tight shoes didn't bother me.

The Heaven of My Dreams

At 7:30 a.m., we said goodbye to all our friends and neighbors. At 8:00 a.m., we walked to the district center and waited for the bus to pick us up and take us to the Manila International Airport.

Pu Sarin carried a white plastic bag. It was the most important bag we had. In it were our visas, airplane tickets, medical records, and family history records. Aunty Chhon carried the new baby Rottana. I walked and held Virak's hand. Our friends and neighbors carried our two boxes. They wanted to see us off at the bus.

Our departure was an emotional moment for everyone—but not me. I had no emotional attachment to anyone in Cambodia except the family I had already lost. I just wanted to get on the bus and go to America.

While we were waiting for the bus, I looked at the time on Sarin's watch. It showed 8:15 a.m. At 8:30 a.m., the buses arrived and the staff began to call each family to stand by their designated bus. At 9:00 a.m., the staff began to do a head count of each family and ordered us to walk onto the bus.

At 10:00 a.m., the bus drove us out of the camp and to the airport. At about 12:30, we arrived at the airport area, where a group of Filipino employees ordered us to follow them to the cafeteria facility for lunch.

During that short walk, a sharp pain began emanating from my toes. The undersized shoes were compressing my toes together, making them sore. I clenched my toes and limped. Despite the pain, I continued to wear my new shoes. They were the only pair I had.

Around 3:00 p.m., we got onto an airplane. Half an hour later, the plane took off. When I was on the airplane, I thought about my sister Vanny and wished she was sitting next to me. I prayed that she would be selected to come to America, or another rich country such as Japan, Germany, France, Canada, Australia, or New Zealand. I missed her and loved her.

At first, it was a smooth flight. It gave me the opportunity to think about what I wanted to do and where I would be living. The list of things I wanted to do in America was long. These dreams were reflected in what I had seen in the posters hanging on the walls of the hospital at the Kamput Refugee Camp. I imagined living in a beautiful house by a lake with a beautiful view overlooking sailboats. I imagined having thick winter clothes and gloves to play in snow and make a snowman with all my white friends. I wanted to practice speaking

English to them. I wanted to have a bicycle to ride around with all my white friends.

I was naïve. I didn't know that America had many different nationalities. I thought America was just white people with long noses. Blacks, Hispanics, American-Indians, and Asians didn't come into my dreams.

The long, smooth flight made me fall asleep, like the rest of the people. Then there was turbulence, and the flight attendants informed us to put on our seatbelts. The airplane shook, and it felt like I was riding on an oxcart in the sky. Sometimes, the airplane felt pushed down to the ground, then pushed back up to the sky. I gripped my pillow and blanket tightly.

Buddha, Jesus, and Tevada, please protect this airplane from crashing. I don't want to die. Let me go to America safely. Please help stop the wind, the storm and the rain, so that this airplane flies smoother and safer.

On November 27, 1984, I finally came to the United States of America. I had no idea what part of America I was in, because I was in the airport terminal and waiting for the connecting flight.

"Pu, where are we in America?"

His hand reached inside the white plastic bag and retrieved the airplane ticket. He examined the ticket and said, "We are in Los Angeles International Airport. We are waiting for a connecting flight to our final destination, Salt Lake City, Utah."

"How long are we going to wait here?" I asked.

"Maybe about three hours."

While we were waiting for the connecting flight, I wanted to explore what was in the airport. But I couldn't because I felt sick and I had jetlag. The terminal in the airport was huge, and I was afraid I might get lost. My body was worn out, so I fell asleep on a bench. Plus, I could barely walk from one point to another, because my feet hurt from wearing the undersized shoes.

After my long nap, Pu Sarin woke me up. When I first got up, I thought I was dreaming. *What is this place?* I thought. *Why am I in this huge structure?*

I tried to orient myself, and then I realized I was still in the airport. Pu Sarin grabbed the document and said, "Let's go to the connecting flight terminal. We are going to Utah."

While we were walking to the connecting flight, I saw two fat black ladies wearing blue-collared shirts and black pants. They were standing by a cart. One of them held a radio to her face and was talking through it. At that moment, I began to question, *Does America have black people? I thought America has only white people?*

At our connecting flight, the attendants greeted us and walked us to our designated seats in the middle row. Then I had a rebellious thought, *Why don't they let me sit by a window? I want to see America from the air. I want to see what it looks like.*

Minutes later, beautiful white flight attendants gave us each a thick winter jacket with zipped hoodies. We put on our jackets, and I felt snug and warm.

"How many hours before we get to Utah?" I asked Pu Sarin.

"Maybe three hours," he said.

"Why does it take so long to get there?" I asked.

"America is big. It may look small on the map. In reality, it is gigantic," he said.

While I was on the airplane to Salt Lake City, I was fully alert. When we landed that evening, I walked to the exit gate with hundreds of other white passengers. I couldn't wait to set foot in America.

Then I heard, "Sarin, over here."

Our sponsor was waiting with a sign written in Khmer and English that said, "Welcome Sarin's Family."

The sponsor and his two Cambodian companions greeted us Cambodian style, by putting their palms together, raised to their chests. They slightly bowed and said, *"Jom-riapsur."*

I greeted them with respect in the same gesture.

Mr. Luke was our main sponsor. He was an Australian-American who had lived in Cambodia. Mr. Keo was our host sponsor. He was a former refugee who had come to the U.S. in 1981.

Mr. Luke and Mr. Keo walked us out of the airport to their cars. The moment the automatic door of the airport opened, I felt the freezing air touching my face. I saw white snow falling from the sky, as if Buddha, Jesus, and Tevada were welcoming me to Heaven.

Epilogue

After living in the West Valley, Utah for about four months with my adopted family, we moved to San Diego, California, to live with their long-lost extended family. Then Pu Sarin moved us to Boston, Massachusetts, where he could better support us with a higher-paying job as an asbestos remover.

After I graduated high school, I left my adopted family to pursue my own goals. In 1991, I moved to Long Beach, California with friends. There, I attended Long Beach Community College and worked part-time as a teacher's aide and community liaison for the City of Long Beach. A job with the United Cambodian Community (UCC) allowed me to help prevent youth from joining street gangs and to avoid other risky behaviors. Next, I became a job developer at UCC to help Cambodian refugees get jobs. For me, this was a perfect fit.

In December 2000, I went back to my native country Cambodia for the first time. My dream was to find my sister, Vanny. My other dream was to see one of the 7th Wonders of the World, Angkor Wat.

My flight from Los Angeles to Bangkok, Thailand, took me more than twenty hours on an airplane; then an additional two hours of connecting flights from Bangkok to Phnom Penh, Cambodia. I had a seat by the window so I could see my country from above.

The airplane flew low when approaching the landing, and the clear view of the vast brownish rice fields made me nervous and depressed. It triggered horrific memories of starvation, torture, and persecution. My body began to shake, the muscles in my legs began pulling, and sweat on my forehead rolled down my face, followed by tears.

When the airplane come to a complete stop, I got up and shook my legs and arms to relieve the tension and emotion. Then I slapped myself on the cheeks and shouted inside my heart, *Marin, you are the survivor! You must be tough and strong. Just enjoy your vacation.*

Outside the airport, I took a taxi to the hotel in the capital city, Phnom Penh. Along the way, we drove over countless potholes in the road. Dirt, dust, and debris dominated the streets and sidewalks. Very few roads were paved, and there were no traffic lights. Plus, countless electrical wires crisscrossed one another disorderly from electrical pole to pole. Most of the buildings were old and had gaping holes, wounds from the war.

To my surprise, the city was crowded with people and full of activity. People were walking, running, smiling, and laughing—as if they had left all the pain and suffering behind. They road motorcycles and cyclos[13] from one place to another, carrying their goods.

When I arrived at the hotel, children were playing jump rope on the sidewalk and a boy was being chased by a puppy. It reminded me of my childhood living with Sophors, Akka and Da, and our baby wolf, Akki.

Soon after putting my luggage in the hotel room, I went to the town of Ta Khmao in search of Vanny. The town was unrecognizable. Countless new stilt houses had been built along the road, and all the tall trees had been cut down. The Buddhist temple was completely destroyed.

---

13   Cyclo is a tricycle-rickshaws transportation that has the passenger compartment up front and the driver in the rear.

Without any picture of my parents, and no memories of extended family like aunts, uncles, or cousins, finding my sister was challenging. I walked from house to house, talking to people. I approached them and said, "My name is Marin. I used to live in this town. My father's name is Yann. My mother's name is Yim. Do you know any women named Vanny?" None of the people with whom I spoke knew my family or my sister.

After three days of exhausting myself looking for Vanny, and I still had no lead, I gave up the search and went to Angkor Wat to explore my history and culture. The moment I entered the Angkor Wat complex, I felt inspired. The beauty and the massive size of the monument galvanized my soul. At that moment, I again felt very proud to be Cambodian.

After five days of exploring the Angkor Wat complex, I visited the Angkor Hospital for Children (AHC) in the provincial city of Siam Reap. I knew of this hospital through Mr. Kenro Izu, a Japanese-American photographer. Mr. Izu is the founder of Friends Without A Border, a nonprofit organization, and he raised money from various generous donors to build the pediatric hospital in Cambodia. After the hospital structures were completed, he continued to raise money to help treat ailing Cambodian children free of charge.

Mr. Izu's work inspired me also to help needy and sick children in Cambodia. So, in January 2001, I quit my job and went to volunteer in Cambodia, where I developed a Capacity Building and Health Education Program (CBHEP) with the hospital administrator, Mr. Long Sedtha. The goal of this program is health education, prevention, and treatment. Today, the CBHEP is growing tremendously. Since its inception in 2001, we have trained more than 200,000 villagers.

In addition to building CBHEP, I have expedited medical supplies and equipment from overseas. Plus, I have managed to get medical operations at no cost for children with cardiovascular disease, in Malaysia, Singapore, and the United States.

Helping the poor and needy children in Cambodia has helped to ease the trauma of my own experiences. My childhood was full of neglect, abuse, and torture. I made a promise to God, Tevada, and Buddha that I would help the neediest children. I felt that God, Tevada, and Buddha helped me to survive much of the chaotic situations of my early childhood.

About the Author

I don't know my exact date of birth. I guess I am now forty-one. I was barely five when the Khmer Rouge invaded Cambodia and put my family into forced labor and impoverished living conditions. My younger brother died of illness at our first relocation. My older sister was forced to live in a girl's work camp. My father and mother died by the time I was six, and I was on my own.

After nine years of fighting to survive, first through the Khmer Rouge genocide 1975-1979, then the invasion by the Vietnamese, I escaped Cambodia to Thailand. There, I lived in five refugee camps: the Jomroum-Tmey Refugee Camp, Khoa-I-Dang Camp, Kamput Camp, Transit Camp, and Chhun Borie Camp. Finally, in 1984, from the Philippines Refugee Processing Center, I emigrated to America with my fifth adoptive family.

After a few months in Utah, we moved to San Diego, California to live with my adoptive uncle's long-lost extended family. Then we moved to Boston, Massachusetts, where he got a better job. After high school, I moved with friends back to Long Beach, California, where there is a large Cambodian-American community. I attended Long Beach Community College and worked part-time as a teacher's aide and community liaison for the City of Long Beach. A job with the

United Cambodian Community allowed me to help prevent youth from joining street gangs. I also became a job developer to help Cambodian refugees get jobs.

In December 2000, I went back to my native country for the first time. After three days of exhausting myself looking for my sister, and I still had no lead, I gave up the search and visited the Angkor Hospital for Children in the provincial city of Siam Reap. Mr. Kenro Izu is the founder of Friends Without A Border, a nonprofit organization that built the pediatric hospital.

Inspired by Mr. Izu's work to help the needy and sick children in Cambodia, in January 2001, I quit my community-service job and went back to Cambodia to volunteer at the Angkor Hospital for Children. There, I developed a Capacity Building and Health Education Program with Mr. Long Sedtha, which provides health education, prevention, and treatment. We have trained more than 200,000 villagers. In addition, I expedite medical supplies and equipment, plus medical operations at no cost for children with cardiovascular disease.

While in Cambodia, I attended the Royal University of Law and Economics to learn Cambodian laws and the process of Khmer Rouge Tribunal laws. In 2005, I graduated with a Bachelor of Criminal Law. In 2006, I returned to California and got a job as a community organizer and advocate at the Asian American Drug Abuse Program, helping with substance-abuse prevention and gambling addiction. I also attended California State University at Dominguez Hills part-time and was awarded a Master of Public Administration in 2011.

Currently, I am studying post-traumatic stress disorder among Cambodians. I serve on the Board of Directors for Building Your Future Today, a nonprofit organization in Cambodia that helps poor orphaned children. I also continue to volunteer to raise funds for Friends Without A Border to support the Angkor Hospital For Children. Helping the poor and needy children in Cambodia has helped to ease the trauma of my own experiences and has become my purpose in life.

Khmer Vocabulary
and Phrases

ar-juy-maray: motherfucker

"Ar-juy-maray! Konduy mae vea!": "You motherfucker! Your mother's pussy!"

Angkar or *Angkar Luer: Angkar* means organization or institution. *Luer* means over the top or above. The Khmer Rouge refers to *Angkar Luer* as the highest communist organization or the top Khmer Rouge official.

bach-trey: a fishing technique that involves draining water out of the pond with buckets

bonkee: a woven rattan basket used to carry dirt

bot-jerng: a sitting position, with one thigh over the other

chaan-srak: a cylinder container with two sets of ears

derm-kontriang-ket: a type of bushy plant used to make natural compost

domloung-tian: a type of wild yam that look similar to a candlestick

dork-somnab: a job that required pulling paddy rice for replanting

hurng: a type of game that punishes the loser to run from a distance to the base without breathing *jek-ang:* grilled marinated banana

jek-jian: deep-fried marinated banana

job-kap: a square blade agricultural hoe

jom-riapsur: a formal way to say hello

jrook-quay: pig barbecue

kagn-ger: a deep bamboo basket

kagn-jonk-ankor: the poorest quality rice dust, only used to feed animals

Kang-Jalat: a mobilized group of young adult ages fifteen to twenty-five

Kang-Komara: a group of boys ages eight to twelve

Kang-Komarey: a female children's group

kaun-ar-neaytun: The word *kaun* means son or daughter. The word *neaytun* means merchant. The Khmer Rouge combined the two words, to mean the son of an aristocrat or the son of a capitalist, a derogatory term.

khor-trey: a sweetened fish soup

kmang: enemies

kmorch: dead body or ghost

kondiev: a curve-shaped blade device used for harvesting rice

kontael: a Cambodian floor mat

kor-saang: a form of punishment through a verbal warning, or death

kors-kajol: a form of treatment that involves coining on the skin surface to stimulate blood and body temperature

krom: group

kroma: a typical Cambodian scarf

mitt: means comrade

mittbong: an older comrade (Cambodians address someone who is older as bong)

mo-mung: a type of flying insect

nom-akour: sweetened cupcake with sesame and coconuts

nom-bagn-jok: Cambodian noodles

nom-kompong: a deep-fried marinated flour and green beans

nom-kroach: deep-fried, round stuffing mashed green beans

nom-pank: a French biscuit or bread from a baker

nom-sorm-ang: a type of food rolled in banana leaves and grilled on charcoal

poud-ang: grilled marinated corn

pous-channa-morm: a type of king snake

prohok: fermented fish

ptaih la-veng: a type of apartment unit you can see through from the front to the back

pti-tmor: a type of vinery weed with thick tiny leaves

pu: uncle (In Cambodian culture, calling someone who is ten years older than you "pu" is a form of respecting age status.)

puk: another term for father, or dad

raik: a Cambodian checkers game

skoe-dei: a ground drum; or an improvised musical drum instrument using a combination of thass, strings, and sticks

somlor-majoo: a sour soup

somnagn-bonk-trey: a type of fishing net

som-piass: a formal Cambodian greeting that involves putting the palms together, raising the hands to the chest, and bowing slightly

tae-quay: duck barbecue curry

tbal-ken: a manual rice grinder made from a large piece of stone to grind soaked rice

Tevada: an angel who dwells in Heaven

thass: a large round metal food tray

toek-kroeung: a type of vegetable flatter

"tuk-kor-men-jomnegn, dogjegn-kor-men-kart": To keep you has no benefit. To take you out is no loss.

Finally, I would like to leave you with three personal principles derived from my experiences.

- ☯ The universe is full of great and beautiful things. People should embrace those things to create harmony rather than war, killing, and starvation.

- ☯ If every powerful man is a great role model for the children, the children not only appreciate him but want to become like him.

- ☯ You feel great when you help a child who is in great need. You feel even better if you help to save a child's life.